The Scenes We Made

The Scenes We Made

AN ORAL HISTORY OF EXPERIMENTAL THEATRE IN MUMBAI

Editor: Shanta Gokhale

Project Sponsor: Sahitya Rangabhoomi Pratishthan

Project Directors: Ashok Kulkarni, Sunil Shanbag

Project Assistant: Irawati Karnik

Supported by: Vinod and Saryu Doshi Foundation;

Mr Chakor Doshi, Walchandnagar Industries Limited;

Dr K. H. Gharda, Gharda Chemicals

SPEAKING TIGER

SPEAKING TIGER BOOKS LLP
125A, Ground Floor, Shahpur Jat,
Near Asiad Village, New Delhi 110049

First published in hardcover by Speaking Tiger Books in 2016
This paperback edition first published in 2023

ISBN: 978-93-85288-96-8
e-ISBN: 978-93-85288-98-2

10 9 8 7 6 5 4 3 2 1

Typeset in Adobe Garamond Pro by SURYA, New Delhi
Printed at Chaman Enterprises, New Delhi

CONTENTS

Introduction

My encounter with Bombay theatre began in 1958, although theatre was by no means uppermost in my mind when I moved to the city. I had visited Bombay as a schoolboy on holidays, but then I was twenty and had come to the city with the serious intention of staying there for at least two years. I had graduated with mathematics from Karnataka University and although I loved pure mathematics, I had come to Bombay to register as a student in the Department of Statistics, for in those days that subject seemed to promise the best prospects for a good, solid job. It was barely ten years since the country had become independent and the air was buzzing with what the Five-Year Plans would do for the economy. P. C. Mahalanobis at the Indian Statistical Institute in Calcutta was being hailed as one of the leading shapers of independent India and I wanted to be in the team with him. The specialization promised employment, a safe niche in the anticipated economic miracle, and I continued to cling on to the discipline, refusing to accept the aversion I soon developed for it, with disastrous consequences for my academic career.

Fortunately for me and my friend Ashok Kulkarni, who had come at the same time from Belgaum to join the Department of Economics, our departments were housed in the beautiful Rajabai Tower in the heart of Fort area. Ashok was as passionate about theatre as I was, and together we haunted every show, every spectacle, every performance, including junior-level boxing matches patronized by Parsi and Anglo-Indian youth, after, and often during, our class hours.

Bombay was alive with Marathi and Gujarati commercial theatre activity, and among all the plays we saw, I remember vividly Pu La Deshpande's delightful *Tujhe Ahe Tujapashi* (To Each His Own), which for its humour, its open structure, social satire and tongue-in-cheek nostalgia for medieval values, was admired as being at the forefront of innovative theatre in Marathi. The Gujarati theatre was obsessed with adaptations of Western thrillers like *Dial M for Murder*, and I much preferred Adi Marzban's Parsi Gujarati farces for their frenetic energy, although much of the verbal wit inevitably escaped me. Then there were visiting groups like Prithvi Theatres in whose elaborate melodramatic set pieces, the veteran Prithviraj Kapoor impressed one with his passionate *Deewar* (Wall) and embarrassed one with his sentimental *Paisa* (Money).

The Cold War was at its peak and the desperate efforts of the US and the USSR to impress the Third World with their cultural richness meant that we were free beneficiaries of some of the most precious cultural artefacts ceaselessly showered at our feet. With visiting orchestras, ballets, dance performances and exhibitions like the *Family of Man*, a whole new sensuous world was being offered to us, altering almost every one of our received notions about the arts. I remember Satyadev Dubey recounting how his entire understanding of choreography was altered by a single visit to Martha Graham's rehearsals, organized by Ebrahim Alkazi for the members of the Theatre Unit.

The net result of this reckless indulgence in the theatre world was that I found myself totally unprepared for my MA examination at the end of my term and left Bombay without a degree. Fortunately, during these two years, I had won the Rhodes Scholarship to Oxford which helped me persuade my parents that my failure to complete my studies was a deliberate strategy to keep my academic records shining.

But from everything I had consumed so indiscriminately during those two years, one person's work had already begun to place my understanding of theatre in a different perspective and shape my own expectations about it. Ebrahim Alkazi had studied theatre at the RADA (The Royal Academy of Dramatic Art) but had refused offers from the London theatre establishment after his graduation and returned to Bombay to start his own Theatre Unit. The reigning figure of Indian drama in those days was, of course, George Bernard Shaw, who was admired for his mastery of handing out incisive social criticism while keeping the audiences chortling over his witticisms. But he had been so widely—and I fear shallowly—imitated by regional playwrights, that his realism had begun to seem stale and wearisome.

Alkazi took one across the Channel to reveal an unknown and breathtakingly different world of theatre, by staging Jean Anouilh's *Antigone* and *Eurydice*, Henrik Ibsen's *Hedda Gabler* and August Strindberg's *Miss Julie*. Not much involvement with social concerns here. This was the existential world with its tragic vision, its intense analysis of human responsibility and the angst it generated. Alkazi evoked a dark and brooding sense of the human condition, presented with an expert weaving of sound, movement and light. It was beyond my wildest dreams. His productions were finely sculpted. In his team of actors were two young women, Alaknanda Samarth and Kusum Behl, whose quivering stage presence in my first play, *Yayati*, which I wrote during the four weeks before I set sail for the UK, is still clearly visible to me.

I completed my studies at Oxford in 1963 and returned to Bombay for what was my second sojourn in the city. This was surely one of the most depressing periods in the history of modern India. It was sixteen years since India had become independent, but the air was heavy with apprehension and gloom. None of the vitality and optimism one would have expected of a newly independent nation was in evidence. After crowing over the liberation of Goa, our army had been thoroughly humiliated by China. The economy was in shambles and sustained by doses of PL 480 kindly doled out by the US. Kashmir, Hungary and the Suez had shown that our proud claim to being the leader of the Third World could be barely distinguished from sheer bombast. The intellectual scene of the country was paralyzed by the nightmare of the brain drain—all those capable of contributing to the building of the nation seemed intent on fleeing it. I was, of course, in no position to point fingers since I too had left for Britain with the firm intention of never coming back. The general atmosphere in India invested the thought of returning home with anxiety; but two developments, both well beyond my control, had given my life an unexpected turn.

Yayati had been published while I was still in the UK. It had been welcomed most enthusiastically by Kannada critics. But the crowning acknowledgement seemed to come with a slashing review of the play by the senior Kannada playwright, Adya Rangacharya, published in *Prajavani*, the largest circulated paper in the language. I was decimated by Adya's comments; but his wrath threw a new light on my situation. I began to wonder if I could ever hope to get such intense attention from anyone, let alone a major playwright, if I were to live in England and write in English. Kannada beckoned me—to receive a pat on the back, to be administered a slap.

The second, and certainly a more decisive factor, was that, even before I had appeared for my Schools (exams), I was offered an editorial post by the Oxford University Press (OUP), so that I was 'coming home to a job'. Those words had a comforting feel of their own in those insecure days, which is difficult to recapture. Working with a British publishing firm would also mean I would continue to be in touch with the literature and the culture of that country, and the doors would still be open, should I feel the need to scoot to the West.

Fortunately, OUP posted me for training in Bombay which was still bursting with theatrical energy. But there was one major change in the theatre world I had known before. Alkazi had moved to Delhi as the Director of the National School of Drama, where he had to initiate a hunt for new Indian plays since there simply weren't enough available in Hindi. His place at the helm of the Theatre Unit had been taken over by his angry disciple, Satyadev Dubey, who had his own notions about the theatre he wanted to create. At our very first meeting, Dubey berated me for writing in English, blushed with embarrassment when I explained that *Yayati* was written, not in English, but in Kannada, apologized and immediately went on to declare that he would produce it if I could provide a Hindi translation. After many frustrating years, he managed to stage the play for the Indian National Theatre in Hindi, with Amrish Puri, Sunila Pradhan, Sulabha Deshpande, Asha Dandavate and himself in the cast. The production was received warmly by the critics and established Dubey's standing as a director. But, in the words of Pradhan, 'Dubey, being Dubey, fought with the INT', and the play closed down after thirteen shows.

Dubey still operated from the Bhulabhai Desai Memorial Institute which was known to me only as an open-air auditorium used by Alkazi for his performances during my previous sojourn in Bombay. But now with Dubey as my mentor, I discovered the many dimensions of the place, and was delighted to find myself moving about with musicians, sculptors and painters whom, until then, I had only known by reputation. Dubey was fond of Chekov's farces and wrote some short plays himself; but his greatest achievement of the period was the discovery of Dharamvir Bharati's *Andha Yug* (Blind Age). With no theatre background, Bharati had written it as a radio play; but Dubey had not only proved that it worked powerfully on stage, but had also sent the script to Alkazi in Delhi, thus bringing it to national attention.

This time I was in Bombay for less than six months, and had a full-time job to handle. So, apart from a vibrant production of Anouilh's *Becket*, directed by John Smithard for the Oxford and Cambridge Society in which Gerson Da Cunha was electric as King Henry—Peter O'Toole's performance in the film which came out some years later seemed mannered to me in comparison—I have few memories connected with theatre during this period.

In order to not give an unfair picture of Dubey, who was far too committed emotionally to theatre to remain an anti-English fanatic, let me jump the story and mention that in later years he went on to direct some magnificent productions in English, particularly of Shaw's plays, featuring Naseeruddin Shah.

In Madras, I worked with OUP for seven years. I knew no Tamil. But those seven years were saved from aridity by two factors. Madras had an English-language drama group called the Madras Players, whose members, though amateurs, had high aspirations about the kind of theatre they wanted to do. Involved with them, I received my first hands-on experience of working for a production from the inside, since one acted, directed, prompted, designed sets and helped tie up the lights. Also, one worked on plays by Tennessee Williams, Arthur Miller, Luigi Pirandello and Anton Chekov, exposing oneself to, and hopefully imbibing, their breathtaking craft. In Madras I had the leisure to complete my second play, *Tughlaq*, and start on my third one, *Hayavadana*.

The other important event in my life in Madras was the entry into my office one day of a man called B. V. Karanth. Karanth was typical of the new breed of trained theatre workers launched in the country by the National School of Drama (NSD) under Alkazi. He had translated Adya Rangacharya's *Kelu Janamejaya* (Listen Janamejaya) into Hindi as *Suno Janamejaya* for the NSD and followed it up by translating my *Tughlaq*. *Tughlaq*, which was staged by Om Shivpuri in 1966, became an instant success, and turned me into a celebrity of sorts, at least among Indian theatre circles.

Since the head office of the OUP was located in Bombay, my contacts with Bombay theatre continued. While during my earlier stays in the city, I was an eager fan, hungrily and enviously watching from the wings, I was now an insider, someone who counted among my friends not only Dubey, but also Arvind and Sulabha Deshpande of the Rangayan group, Vijay Tendulkar the playwright whom they had virtually created and nurtured, as well as Dr Shreeram Lagoo. Dubey had staged *Yayati* in 1967. In 1970, Alyque Padamsee had directed *Tughlaq* for the Theatre Group in an opulent production starring Kabir Bedi. Later that year the NCPA had presented the same play in a Marathi production directed by Arvind Deshpande where the magnificent set, unfortunately, swallowed up the actors.

Dubey and Arvind had managed to turn the Bombay stage into a microcosm of the national theatre scene. I remember that one night in Walchand Terrace, I went to sleep on one of the many mattresses spread out by Dubey on the floor for anyone who cared to spend the night there, arguing furiously with Tendulkar. When I woke up the following morning, Tendulkar had disappeared, but fast asleep on my other side was Badal Sircar who had arrived during the night unannounced. One met every playwright including, of course, the younger writers like C. T. Khanolkar, Mahesh Elkunchwar and Achyut Vaze, at these places; and despite the inevitable jealousies and rivalries, we found ourselves bound in a common enterprise. Ideas and influences flowed and fertilized. Relationships blossomed. Amol Palekar came there pursuing his girlfriend Chitra Murdeshwar and Dubey converted him into an actor. Deepa and Dr Lagoo met there during the rehearsals of the Marathi *Aadhe Adhure* (Incomplete, a Hindi Play by Mohan Rakesh). I remember this play for another curious reason. One day while he was casting for it, an incredulous Dubey, who hailed from conservative Bilaspur, exclaimed to me, 'Dr Karyekar has just asked me if it would be possible to give a role to his wife. Where else but in Maharashtra would you come across a request like that?' And sure enough, Jyotsna Karyekar went on to give a striking performance as the woman in the production.

The playwrights whose work Dubey and Arvind took up, came from different languages and very diverse backgrounds. Only Tendulkar had a large commercial theatre tradition to fall back or draw upon. Although he may have rejected them as models, he owed a lot to the legacy of Mo Ga Ranganekar and P. K. Atre. Mohan Rakesh and Dharamvir Bharati were simply self-made; they had no Hindi theatre from which they took off. Sircar was a confirmed experimenter whom a very prosperous Bengali commercial theatre had rejected. Chandrasekhar Kambar came from a genuine folk performance tradition which was remote from the Kannada urban culture. In his essay that follows this introduction, G. P. Deshpande clubs Kambar and me together as hothouse plants nursed in Delhi.

He is wrong. Kambar's was an authentic bayalata tradition with roots in Kannada soil; it is just that Karanth created an unexpected urban audience for him. G.P.D's criticism would, however, be valid in the case of my plays, since the form of every one of my plays was arrived at after much struggle, and *Yayati*, *Tughlaq* and *Hayavadana*, all found recognition after being premiered in Bombay and Delhi. And then there was that rarity, an Indian playwright in English, Partap Sharma, whose play, *A Touch of Brightness*, directed by Alyque Padamsee for the Indian National Theatre, was invited to the first Commonwealth Arts Festival in London in 1965, was banned by the Maharashtra censor board and became a *cause célèbre* when the young advocate Soli Sorabjee got the ban thrown out by the courts after a battle lasting seven years. But all of us were at home in Walchand Terrace. Wherever we came from, for the first time after the demise of Sanskrit theatre, what otherwise would be considered impossible, was taking shape here, an authentic Indian theatre.

In 1968, Mohan Rakesh and I were in Calcutta watching a popular Bengali musical which had been strongly recommended to us. We started giggling soon after the play began and continued to suppress our giggles throughout the performance. At one point, Rakesh turned to me and said, 'Do you know why we are laughing? We are laughing because we know the future of Indian theatre is in our hands.' That summed up our confidence in our destiny. And I would be remiss if I did not mention that we were in Calcutta at the invitation of Shyamanand Jalan and Pratibha Agarwal of the Anamika Kala Sangam, and that my trip was paid for by Suresh Awasthi, the enthusiastic Secretary of the Sangeet Natak Akademi. Every one was chipping in.

This extraordinary sense of bonding between us playwrights and theatre directors can be witnessed in the fact that Agarwal translated Sircar's plays in Hindi and made them accessible nationally; Priya Adarkar put Tendulkar on the all-India map by translating *Shantata! Court Chalu Ahe* into English as *Silence! The Court Is in Session*; Tendulkar translated *Tughlaq* and *Aadhe Adhure* into Marathi; I translated *Ebong Indrajit* (And Indrajit) into English (and later Elkunchwar's plays into Kannada), Prema Karanth translated *Ashee Paakhare Yeti* (Birds Come and Go) into Kannada. Inevitably, influences crisscrossed.

Let me trace just one of these flows of influence to prove how fruitful the result has been. From the day we met in 1965, Karanth and I, both of whom came from areas where the Yakshagana was still alive and flourishing, had been discussing how the elements of dance, drama, mime and movement from our traditional forms could be utilized on the modern stage. We were in no sense unique in our obsession since even in national seminars organized by the Sangeet Natak Akademi or the Anamika Kala Sangam, this was a central problem constantly debated. One had heard of Sheila Bhatia's Punjabi and Urdu operas like *Heer Ranjha* and Rasiklal Parekh's *Mena Gurjari*, still remembered for Dina Pathak's performance. But those performances were essentially seen as cultural revivals; and since in those days the north was another country, there was no way to judge.

We were not interested in reviving forms on the brink of extinction. We were not even interested in working with artists from the traditional forms. Could one, we kept asking, write a contemporary play, sensitive to modern concerns, using the conventions of medieval theatre, such as masks, mime, monologues and songs, without becoming regressive in content?

Then in Calcutta, during the visit already referred to, I saw the Shouvanik production of Sircar's *Ebong Indrajit*, which Sircar dismissed as a distortion of his intentions. This did not worry me, nor did the fact that the play seemed strongly influenced by Ionesco. I was bowled over by the production, which used a great deal of improvisation and mime, practically illustrating to me how to break away, in concrete terms, from realistic conventions of scenic division of the plot, characterization and choreography. I virtually reproduced the Shouvanik production in Madras in an English translation of my own for the Madras Players. This hands-on experience of directing the play, suddenly crystallized into a new idea one day when I was telling Karanth the story of Thomas Mann's novella, *The Transposed Heads*, which draws, for its narrative, on the *Kathasaritsagara*. After summarizing the tale for him, I casually mentioned that it could make a very interesting film, when Karanth burst out, 'No, no, it will make an excellent play, and I know you will write it immediately.' I knew he was right. Within a month I had written *Hayavadana* (1969), and soon thereafter, Rajinder Paul published an English translation of it in his theatre journal, *Enact*, which gave it a wide circulation.

The play was produced by Dubey in Bombay one day before Karanth staged it for Dishantar in Delhi in 1972. Tendulkar saw Dubey's production, told me he loved it and that it had given him an idea of how to use the folk form in a modern play. So *Ghashiram Kotwal* was written in 1972. In Delhi, Habib Tanvir, who had read the play in *Enact*, told me it had reminded him of Lorca, but he disliked competing with Karanth for the rights. So he created *Charandas Chor* in 1974. Of course, neither Tendulkar nor Tanvir ever acknowledged the source of their inspiration. Karanth saw Jabbar Patel's production of *Ghashiram Kotwal* in Pune (1975) while visiting me, was thrilled by the use of the moving human curtain and reproduced the device in toto in his production of G. B. Joshi's *Sattavara Neralu* (Shadows of the Dead), which proved a runaway hit. In fact, Karanth owed not just the choreography but the seminal use of religious music as a background for human corruption to Bhaskar Chandavarkar's compositions for *Ghashiram Kotwal*. Needless to say Karanth too refused to acknowledge the inspiration. But the flow of ideas had by then created a rich native tradition of musical theatre on the contemporary stage in India. It later provided the base for B. Jayashree in creating *Lakshapathi Rajana Kathe* (The Story of King Lakshapati) for Spandana, and has more recently been freshly mined in the Shakespearean adaptations of Atul Kumar and Sunil Shanbag.

Those years in Bombay and Pune seethed with theatrical energy, discussion, innovation and rivalry. A major event was the dissolution of Rangayan after the return to India of its founder, Vijaya Mehta, which led Arvind and Sulabha Deshpande to start a new group, Awishkar, and Vijaya to do some productions for East Berlin, including an unforgettable *Caucasian Chalk Circle* in Marathi (*Ajab Nyay Vartulacha*) with Bhakti Barve. The Progressive Dramatic Association of Pune splintered over Jabbar Patel's *Ghashiram Kotwal*, and when the production was revived under a new banner, the first show was staged in the film auditorium of the Film and Television Institute, opening to many of the students a vigorous world of performance they were only dimly aware of outside their gates.

An inspired achievement of this era is the building of the Prithvi Theatre by Jennifer Kapoor, unique also in that the funds for the enterprise were supplied by her actor-husband Shashi Kapoor from his private earnings. Jennifer transformed what was once a warehouse for the old Prithvi Theatres into a lovely black-box auditorium where every brick was laid with care and love under her supervision. When she was building it, everyone asked, 'Who will come to faraway Juhu to see a play?' Today this corner of Mumbai is in such demand by theatre groups that it is hard to get a booking. The success of the theatre and the immense activity it has generated, have received a heart-warming tribute in Arundhati Nag's Ranga Shankara in Bengaluru.

What makes performing at Prithvi Theatre with its limited space such a moving experience is the fact that Jennifer showed an acute awareness of what a theatre needs—not merely a stage or storage space or rehearsal rooms, but a space where people could come together, argue and exchange ideas. That kind of space is scarce in any city. Prithvi welcomed the young to come and hang out, not necessarily do anything but just sit around and chat and argue. Bhulabhai Desai Memorial Institute, which had attracted all forms of art to itself and provided them space in the sixties, had now been replaced by a residential tower. In 1980, the National Centre for the Performing Arts (NCPA) had the potential to step into its place and use its enormous facilities to meet the needs of the local theatre. But the Tata Auditorium which rose there, with its wide corridors, sweeping staircases and marble balconies seemed designed rather to mock the deprivations of Marathi and Gujarati theatre groups. Even today only the anglicized patronize the NCPA. The middle class cringes at its opulence.

It was fascinating to see how the Marathi, Hindi and Gujarati aficionados of theatre came forward to accommodate this need of theatre workers for a little private space. I remember so many little gestures, so many responses to unreasonable demands, so many warm and welcoming invitations. Early on, it was in the living room of Kumud Mehta that one met to discuss the current state of theatre with Khanolkar and other younger playwrights. Mehta, the legend went, had travelled incognito to an International Communist Conference in China against government orders; but she was now a motherly presence at the NCPA. The spacious drawing room of Saryu and Vinod Doshi's Neela House on Peddar Road was often the scene of arguments too heated and loud for that elegant space. The living room of Sunila Pradhan's house in Juhu-Andheri became Dubey's adopted residence. In later years we all used the living room of Nira and Shyam Benegal's flat on Pedder Road, by no means vast or spacious but warm and welcoming, as a multipurpose discussion centre. And someone needs to write a research paper on Rani Burra's flat on the fourth floor of Ganga Vihar, majestically overlooking the Marine Drive, which has served for decades as a caravanserai for many from the theatre and new cinema: Bhaskar Chandavarkar, Mohan Agashe, Kulbhushan Kharbanda, Sai Paranjpye, Om Puri, Anand Patwardhan. One can go on.

This age came to an abrupt end the day colour television was introduced in 1982 on a national scale, and the middle-class audiences started locking themselves up in their living rooms every evening. It was like lights being switched off in a theatre before the doors close. For a while it looked as though not just theatre but even the cheaper and universally more popular films would shut shop. Fortunately, there is no substitute for the delight (rasa) generated when an audience is watching an actor perform live; and so theatre has made a comeback. Young actors, directors and producers are active again and I have been fortunate enough to have a play of mine, *Uney Purey Shahar Ek*, (*Benda Kaalu on Toast* in Kannada and *Boiled Beans on Toast* in English) produced by a person of Mohit Takalkar's gifts with a brilliant set of actors, who have often set aside their more lucrative television and film commitments to be on stage for the play. It's a good time to hope that we shall soon see the Bombay and Pune of those days again, when to be doing theatre was indeed 'very heaven'. And this book hopes to celebrate those few years.

Girish Karnad

Preface
Experimental Theatre: What Was That?

It is generally held that the sixties and seventies were decades of experimentation in theatre worldwide. It is also held that this surge of experimentation was impelled by the historical-political-social circumstances that obtained at the time. I came into theatre in the seventies when the Chhabildas School in Mumbai had offered its auditorium to Awishkar—the newly established theatre group—to rehearse and perform its plays. Awishkar then invited other groups also to perform there and so Chhabildas became a meeting place for young people who wished to do a theatre that was different from the dominant theatre of the times. Whether there is anything to the theory of the impulse for experimentation having come from socio-political forces is debatable. But it would appear that having an affordable space to rehearse and perform was a basic need for this kind of theatre to happen. In the following discussion, I shall not comment on what happened in theatre when spaces like the Bhulabhai Desai Memorial Institute and the Walchand Terrace space offered similar facilities to theatre practitioners. I shall confine myself to where my participation in theatre as a playwright began—the Chhabildas School Hall in Mumbai—and to Marathi theatre, in particular.

The first question that presents itself to me is this: was Chhabildas indeed the centre for experimental plays in the seventies and eighties? Because finally, Vijay Tendulkar's *Ghashiram Kotwal,* undoubtedly experimental in every sense of the word, could never have been performed at Chhabildas. Many of the statements made by directors, actors and designers in the last section of this oral history will bear me out. The desire to do a different kind of theatre, which is what most so-called experimental work might reasonably have claimed for itself, came out of the stagnation of themes, performance styles and production design that had come about in the mainstream theatre. The urge to do theatre was strong and yet theatre was dead. So this was a time of interesting tension.

Another circumstance that gave shape to the desire to do a different kind of theatre was that there was an entire generation present then which understood and could use language as literature, as dramatic dialogue and as pure experimentation. This generation related to society and politics through language. Its natural cultural expression was Marathi. Naturally, it had the capacity to fulfill its urge to play with art also through Marathi. Perhaps not consciously, but unconsciously, a class of leaders had emerged in the theatre world which was fully in command of its linguistic and cultural roots.

Such a generation that spoke from and to its roots didn't exist elsewhere, not in Bengal and not in Karnataka where Girish Karnad and Chandrasekhar Kambar wrote Bharatiya plays. Their work took them directly to Delhi. Therefore you didn't see their work impacting the theatre that was being done in Bangalore or Mysore.

Although this class of people with a command over their linguistic and cultural roots is vastly reduced today, it still exists, along with the same urge to do a different kind of theatre. The spurt that we have seen in theatre activity in Pune in recent years bears witness to this. The difference between the two generations is that the earlier generation was aware of the sociological reality, whereas the present generation isn't. Then culture and society went together. Today it is just culture. Ours was a localized modernity—pure and simple. We now have modernity—pure and simple.

But a different kind of theatre is not necessarily experimental theatre. There was certainly a movement away from the mainstream kind of theatre, but it wasn't a radical movement. It claimed a space between the purely commercial theatre and what we might rightly call experimental theatre. I was once asked during a seminar in Delhi whether I would claim *Uddhwasta Dharmashala* (A Charity Inn Devastated) was an experimental play. My answer was, experimentation is not just a bunch of people doing physical theatre. There is intellectual experimentation too. Should this form of experimentation, at the least, not be examined and discussed? Whether my play would be judged as experimental or not is beside the point. It is the idea of experiment that needs to be expanded.

It must be admitted, however, that nobody did the new kind of theatre with any awareness of what and why. Also there was very little critical writing that urged upon playwrights the importance of rigour of thought and expression with society as an essential context. It was this lack of rigour that made it possible for those who spoke so volubly about experimental theatre to slip into the mainstream later without any internal disturbance. It also meant that the subversive charge of truly experimental plays like Satish Alekar's *Mahanirvan* (The Dread Departure) or Tendulkar's *Ghashiram Kotwal* was never really understood by critics. The way both plays made use of songs and music overturned the traditional use of music in theatre for ever.

The lack of rigour and commitment to a social context also made it possible for a theatre group to produce Brecht and then do Ionesco. This was because Marathi adaptations of Brecht had nothing to do with the politics of his work. *Teen Paishacha Tamasha*, Pu La Deshpande's adaptation of *Threepenny Opera*, is amusing if you see it as Pu La's play. But there's no Brecht in it. So it was no surprise that people who did Brecht in this fashion, did Ionesco later. These productions could not be called experimental by a long chalk.

G. P. Deshpande

Editor's Preface

We thought of putting together a history of experimental theatre in Mumbai between 1960 and 1990, for two reasons: one, the work that was done in those three decades had become history but had not been recorded; two, until the mid-eighties at least, Mumbai was the crucible of theatre into which plays from Delhi, Kolkata and Bangalore flowed. In that sense, it was a national movement. Here scripts were being translated into English, Hindi and Marathi from Bengali, Kannada and Hindi, leading to a cross-pollination of ideas, concerns and practices in the important centres of theatre. English translations of significant plays from various Indian languages were being published in *Enact*, the theatre magazine that Rajinder Paul published from his press in Delhi, using its downtime for this unproductive but culturally hugely important publication. These English translations in turn became the intermediate medium for translation of the plays into other languages.

Although the early surge of new plays receded to some degree after the mid-eighties, this part of the story too needed to be told, because it pointed to how theatre, more than the other performing arts like music and dance, was critically affected by changing socio-economic conditions and consequent problems of infrastructure.

It seemed to us that the best way of mapping this entire three-decade trajectory was through the three spaces which had allowed what one might call fringe theatre to burgeon in the city. The most significant theatre visionaries of the time had worked and performed in these spaces, allowing young practitioners to train on the job. With their loss, something vital changed in the kind of theatre that could be done in the city. The Bhulabhai Desai Memorial Institute was lost when it was sold to a developer; the Walchand Terrace space was lost when the family, which had generously made it available to theatre, claimed it back for their own use; and the Chhabildas School Hall was lost when lucrative interests overrode the management's desire to encourage a non-profit making cultural activity like theatre.

Any claim we might make that the theatre that emerged from these spaces was experimental is likely to be challenged from all sides. G. P. Deshpande does so in his essay 'Experimental Theatre: What Was That?' Members belonging to theatre groups which rehearsed and performed in these spaces also did so. If we define experimental as 'the new', which stands in conscious opposition to 'the old', then the theatre that happened in these three spaces was experimental. However, if we define it as theatre that is underpinned by an eloquently articulated theory, then this theatre was not experimental. In a sense, it could not have been either, given the differently inspired groups that came together, driven entirely by an individualistic urge to realize the new ideas and forms of theatre that gripped them. Having the freedom to give free rein to these ideas was in fact the compelling factor in the upsurge of new theatre that we witnessed.

Doing an oral history is dangerous because it can easily slip into rambling anecdotage. To avoid this, we briefed our interviewers—a team of young, enthusiastic journalists—to concentrate on three lines of questioning which would give the interviewees a framework, not too rigid and yet not too flexible, for their memories. We wished them to describe the physical features of the three spaces, to help our readers imagine them. We wanted them to talk about the people who practised in these spaces and the significant plays they themselves had done or seen done. Finally, we wanted them to address the question of experimentation. Did they, while doing their plays, believe they were doing something experimental? And if they did, in what way did they think they were experimental. We believe we were able to confirm at least one thing through the interviews—the availability and quality of each theatre space contributed vitally to the practice and growth of theatre in Mumbai.

Many of the artists and performers we interviewed for this oral history are elderly. It was sad that Satyadev Dubey, G. P. Deshpande and Prafulla Dahanukar passed away a short time after being interviewed for this book. Sad as it was, it also confirmed how right we were in attempting to put together this project now, before it was too late.

PART ONE

Bhulabhai Desai Memorial Institute

Photo credit: Vinesh Gandhi

Bhulabhai Desai Road where the Bhulabhai Desai Memorial Institute once stood.

Bhulabhai Desai was a lawyer, freedom fighter and Congressman who was born in Gujarat but practised in Mumbai. After his death on May 6, 1946, his daughter-in-law Madhuriben Desai, an art historian and author of several books on ancient culture, put his immense wealth to use by converting one of the two buildings that stood on his property into the Bhulabhai Desai Memorial Institute.

The institute stood on Warden Road in south Mumbai. The road was later renamed after Bhulabhai Desai. It was a sprawling ground-plus-one bungalow with a big garden where sculptures and ceramic works were kept. Studio space was given to artists like Gaitonde, Nalini Malani, Nasreen Mohamedi, Ambalal, Tyeb Mehta and M. F. Husain at Re 1 a month. Ebrahim Alkazi ran his Theatre Unit from an office here, Vijaya Mehta and Satyadev Dubey rehearsed their plays here and Ravi Shankar established his music school, Kinnara, here in 1962.

The Institute was a magical place, Vijaya Mehta, doyenne of the new wave Marathi theatre in Mumbai, has said in her autobiography *Zimma* (Clapping Game). Her laboratory theatre Rangayan began working there in the sixties. Reminiscing about rehearsing with a bunch of school children for Vijay Tendulkar's play *Kawalyanchi Shala* (School for Crows) on the Bhulabhai Institute lawn, she says, 'The children used to dance to Kiran Shantaram and Shashank Lalchand's rock band. Every other activity on the premises used to stop during these rehearsals. Everybody, including Ravi Shankar, would gather to watch the fun. Naturally, the children and the musicians used to be chuffed no end.'

The sixties, the decade during which the Bhulabhai Desai Memorial Institute became a hub for art, was also a time when Mumbai buzzed with other cultural activities. Anandam film society held regular screenings of Indian and foreign films and also published a journal, *Montage.* Bharatiya Vidya Bhavan held annual inter-collegiate drama competitions to encourage young theatre enthusiasts to think seriously about theatre. *Bhuvan Shome* (dir. Mrinal Sen), *Sara Akash* (The Whole Sky, dir. Basu Chatterjee) and *Uski Roti* (His Daily Bread, dir. Mani Kaul), all products of this time, pioneered the new Indian cinema. This was also the decade in which fiction moved from the sentimental and romantic to the dark and realistic and the Little Magazine movement for new and protest poetry came into full force. The Bhulabhai Desai Memorial Institute was a unique participant in this age of the new and experimental in art, theatre, music, cinema and poetry. Its closure was the end of a major part of Mumbai's vibrant cultural life. When Vijaya Mehta returned to the city after a sojourn abroad, she went to meet Solibhai. This is how she records the visit in her autobiography: 'I was deeply saddened. Gone were the swaying palm trees, Gandhiji's prayer room and the sea-facing terrace. A ten-storey building called Akashganga was coming up in their place. The first three floors of the building were ready. A room with a terrace attached had been set aside for Rangayan on the first floor. The second floor was occupied by the office, a library and a small theatre of the National Centre for the Performing Arts, which had been founded recently by Mr Jamshed Bhabha. Little Theatre, located on the NCPA complex at Nariman Point, is its exact replica.'

The Anchor: Soli Batliwala

Soli Batliwala, a friend of Bhulabhai's son Dhirubhai, was the manager-trustee of the Bhulabhai Desai Memorial Institute. Madhuriben had full faith in his dedication to the arts and his ability to run an institution for which no previous model existed. Batliwala, or Solimama as some of the beneficiaries of the space fondly called him, shouldered this enormous responsibility with outstanding success, turning the institute into a buzzing centre of Mumbai's dynamic art scene.

In the stories that follow, it will be obvious that not all artists who worked in the Institute regarded him favourably. It would appear from the observations made by some of them that there was a certain amount of autocracy, even wilfulness, in his style of running the Institute. With no other recorded account of his life and work available, we know Soli Batliwala only through the memories of the few who knew him and have survived to tell the tale. Memories of any single event differ so widely that one wonders if it is the same event that is being described. This will be seen in Prafulla Dahanukar's and Akbar Padamsee's versions of the same story.

Gerson da Cunha

Soli Batliwala was, in many ways, the power below and behind the Bhulabhai. It was because of Soli that the place ran at all. Everything like the income-expenditure business, the dealings with the staff or with the authorities, was handled by Soli. I don't think Madhuri would have been at all interested in that aspect of it. He was also a very close adviser of Madhuri's. So he was an important influence on a lot of policy decisions. I think a lot of the success of the Bhulabhai Desai Memorial Institute and what it was able to achieve came from Soli's nudging in that direction.

Prafulla Dahanukar

Solibhai helped a sculptor called Raman to go to Norway where he became a big artist. Raman worked as a peon in the Institute. He used to do wood sculptures. When Solibhai became secretary of the Jehangir Art Gallery in 1961, he helped Raman get an exhibition there. He also introduced him to the consul of Norway. They gave him a scholarship to study there. He went away and stayed on. When he came back, he divorced his wife. Solibhai helped him in that also. Solibhai was a bachelor. He died about twenty years ago.

Akbar Padamsee

There was a film-maker called Bal Chhabda. He was very rich. He wanted to start an art gallery. So Batliwala gave him a whole hall in the Institute. He spent a lot of money and put in the appropriate lighting and everything. It was a beautiful place. Then one morning, when Bal Chhabda came in, there were dancers dancing in the gallery. He said, 'You can't dance here. It's an art gallery.' So Batliwala said to Chhabda, 'There is nobody there. Why can't they dance?' Chhabda said, 'But an art gallery is an art gallery. Some viewer may walk in. In that case, how do you switch off the dance?' But the next day, the same thing happened. So Chhabda got annoyed and came early one morning with his servant and broke all the lights he himself had installed. Then he tore up all the screens. There was rubble everywhere. When Batliwala came, he was shocked. He asked if goondas had broken in and done this. He was told, 'Sahab hi aye the. Bal Chhabda sahab. Unhone sab tod diya' (Bal Chhabda sahib came. He broke everything). When Batliwala asked him about it he said, 'I can't have people dancing in my art gallery. I have torn down whatever I had put up. I haven't damaged anything of yours.' So Batliwala said fine, leave, and then began to use the space for other purposes. But we were very upset.

One day when Gaitonde came to the Institute, he found his studio open, a whole lot of American tourists inside and Batliwala taking out Gaitonde's paintings and showing them. So Gaitonde said, 'This is my studio, why are you here? I don't want you to touch my paintings. They are my paintings. I don't want to show them. Why are you showing them?' To which Batliwala said, 'Look, this is an institute. Here if someone asks, we show paintings. And you are in my institute so you can't tell me what to do.' So the next day, Gaitonde brought a lock and put it on his door. When Batliwala saw this, he said, 'I will not remove his lock.' He removed the hinges of the door instead, and continued to bring people in. Gaitonde had no other place to go to so he suffered this. But he stopped keeping his paintings there. What was a wonderful thing slowly disintegrated this way because of the ego of one man—Batliwala. After so many years, these few incidents remain imprinted on my mind.

When Jehangir Art Gallery opened, he took up a space there too. He wanted to spread outside the Bhulabhai Institute. He wanted to become the main patron of the art world.

But he destroyed the Institute. We used to go there because all the artists were there but we did not like Batliwala or what he was doing. And when we complained to Madhuri Desai, she just said, 'He's running the Institute. What can I do? I can't interfere.'

There was a boy from a tribal area called Raman Patel. He had come in as a peon. When he saw all the artists working, he said, 'Hum bhi bana sakte hain' (I too can sculpt). So he brought a big block of wood, mango-tree wood, because it is soft, and carved it. It was a magnificent carving. All the artists got enthusiastic, saying, 'We treated him like a peon but he's a sculptor!' When he had done a sufficient amount of work, we felt that he should have a show at the Jehangir Art Gallery. So the show was held. But there was an untoward incident that happened. It is very clearly imprinted upon my mind. Batliwala did not like it. Batliwala said, 'He's a peon. Why are you making him into an artist?' So, to put him in his place, when we all came back from the show, he told him, 'Chalo sab jagah pe jhadu maar do' (Come on, sweep the whole place). This was to remind him that he was a servant and not an artist. But Raman had no problem. He swept the place. He was then asked to make tea. He made tea. But we felt very bad. It was his opening and this was the treatment he was being given.

Many foreigners used to come to the Institute. There was a Swiss woman who came once. She saw Raman Patel's work and said, 'Why are you wasting your time here working as a peon? Marry me and I'll take you to Switzerland.' So he went away. He came back after several years with the work he had done in Europe. But it was very academic. Because this lady had told him, 'You don't know how to sculpt. You don't know how to draw.' So she put him in an academy and educated him. But while doing that, he lost his real talent. The primal artist in him was gone. He tried to do an exhibition again, but this time nobody liked his work very much. So he said, 'You people don't understand anything. I have studied in Europe. I even speak English now.' People told him, 'We are not discouraging you. What you're saying is all true, but the fire inside you is gone.' He left after that and we never heard of him again.

Alyque Padamsee

Soli Batliwala was a bit of a manipulator and stemming from the queen that was Madhuri, he was Polonius, her able adviser; and sometimes a bit devious. He used to play favourites but I don't think he was a bad guy. A lot of people at that time hated Soli. But personally, I never had a bad experience with him.

The Lead Actor: Ebrahim Alkazi

Photo credit: Prakash Kanhere

Ebrahim Alkazi was the son of a Saudi Arabian businessman and trained at the Royal Academy of Dramatic Art. He worked for many years at the Bhulabhai Desai Memorial Institute before moving to Delhi in 1962 as Director of the National School of Drama, a position he held till 1977. He was arguably the most influential theatre director of his times, bringing a new vision and technical discipline to Indian theatre. He trained many well-known stage and film personalities such as Vijaya Mehta, Om Puri, Naseeruddin Shah and Rohini Hattangadi.

Alkazi directed over fifty plays, including three of the most important in modern Indian theatre—Dharamvir Bharati's *Andha Yug*, Mohan Rakesh's *Ashadh Ka Ek Din* (One Day in Ashadh) and Girish Karnad's *Tughlaq*. He also directed several Greek and Shakespearean plays in English. He is the recipient of all three Padma awards, and the Sangeet Natak Akademi Fellowship for lifetime contribution to theatre.

Girish Karnad

The only time I met Alkazi was when I went to see *Eurydice* in Siddharth College. We were in the gallery—me and my friend Caveh Munshi. And some college boys came along and started drumming on some surface and singing a song just before the play was about to begin. And this very angry person walked out of the wings and stormed up and Caveh said, 'That's Alkazi. Now you'll see drama!' And he came and blasted the life out of them, and these kids, mere seventeen-eighteen year olds, just shrivelled up in front of him. That was quite a performance. That was the only time I saw him. Actually the next time I saw him was on a train to Delhi where I was told he was going as a Director of the National School of Drama. I was on the same train, going for my Rhodes Scholarship interview.

But Alkazi's contribution to our understanding of theatre was immense. From where I came, the tradition I had known was of natak companies performing in proscenium theatres. Then in Bombay, Ashok Kulkarni and I saw a lot of Marathi plays. You know, *Katyar*

Kaljat Ghusli (The Dagger that Pierced the Heart, a Marathi play by Purushotam Darvhekar) and all those successful plays. But theatre was really opened out to us by Alkazi. Particularly his productions like *Miss Julie*, *Antigone* and *Eurydice.* It was not just how he used the space. There were all kinds of things that baffled me about these plays. For example, in *Miss Julie*, there was a scene where Jean is listening and Miss Julie is giving a long sentimental speech. She is crying and he is looking at her and some sentimental music is going on. She stops crying. Jean takes out a box of matches, puts a cigarette in his mouth and strikes a matchstick, 'Chhhck'. At that exact moment, the music stopped and the lights came on! The mood suddenly changed. I was thunderstruck. I was also very confused about how the lights could grow brighter and dimmer. The fact that they could be controlled the way fans are didn't occur to me. So I asked Ashok and he asked Meghnad Desai. His one claim to fame is that he explained what a dimmer was to Ashok Kulkarni! So anyway, we were that innocent. This was on the technical side. Then there was the psychology of something like *Miss Julie.* It was completely new.

I would like to trace my own development as a playwright to those early influences. For one vacation, I went to my brother's house in Banaras and I was reading Rajaji's *Mahabharata*. It was just three hundred pages but it was a very intelligent man's summary. And there I read both the Yavakrita story, which formed the base of *The Fire and the Rain*, and the Yayati story which just excited me. Perhaps at the back of my mind, there was Alkazi's *Antigone*! And I thought if Yayati was younger than his son Puru, what could've happened with Puru's wife, Chitralekha? So all this poured out and to my utter surprise, I wrote it in Kannada. It was just pouring out in Kannada. I was like a stenotypist. Literally in about two-and-a-half weeks—about twenty days—I had finished writing the play. And I was really shocked. I remember when I came back from Banaras and Ashok came to see me at Belgaum station, I told him I had just written a play and that too in Kannada, he was just as shocked.

'What! Why! I thought you'd write in English.' But I knew then that I would only write plays in Kannada.

So, seeing Alkazi's plays triggered an impulse that took me back into my own background. It didn't take me out. One great thing that I learned from *Eurydice* and *Antigone* was that this was what you could do with your myths! Suddenly, it was clear to me what was wrong with our pauranik plays, our mythological plays. Although I couldn't have phrased it that well at the time, I knew that one of the problems with the pauranik plays was that they all dripped with bhakti. And the whole point of bhakti ultimately is that salvation comes from god. So no tragedy is possible. Harishchandra may go through the worst kind of agonies but you know that at the end of it, god will appear and save him. Quite apart from whatever is said in the *Natya Shastra* about tragedy being unacceptable, one of the reasons our pauranik plays are so sentimental and incapable of tragedy is that you know at the end of it no one will die. No one will suffer. All the suffering is actually a test of your faith in god. And I suddenly realized that there were sections of the Mahabharata, like the story of Yayati, where such salvation was not given. So the modelling of *Yayati* was very much an influence of Alkazi, of Anouilh. For instance, in all of Anouilh's plays, the debates and discussions take place between two people. Two people argue, one person goes, another person comes. That is how it is in *Yayati* also. In *Tughlaq*, I had to deliberately break away from this. These influences would not have come from reading the plays. They came from seeing them played out on stage. My first play *Yayati*, really the whole confrontation between Chitralekha and Yayati, is straight out of *Antigone*—the older man and the younger woman, the younger woman saying, 'I insist on my rights,' and the older man saying, 'No, be reasonable,' and so on. Although it happens in the fourth act, I must acknowledge that it was Alkazi's production of *Antigone* that impacted it.

I think Alkazi's contribution to our work was not where it took us but what it took us away from. The dominating figure those days was George Bernard Shaw. So a modern play meant a living room. In the

Marathi or the Kannada version, a sofa and two chairs and a servant dusting the furniture and then answering the phone and delivering all the necessary information was its reflection. This was absolutely derivative of George Bernard Shaw. That was modern theatre to us. And Alkazi took it away. He said, 'No, that's not it.' The great advantage to us was that he looked to Europe, leaving England aside. He did *Hedda Gabler.* He was interested in European playwrights and their plays, particularly with female actors. That was a complete education for us in theatre.

Alyque Padamsee

The Bhulabhai Institute left one scar. Alkazi after a while felt that the plays that Alyque Padamsee, Sylvester Da Cunha, Deryck Jefferies were doing in the Theatre Group were not real theatre. And he then said, 'I am going to walk out.' He was the President of the Theatre Group at the time. He had called a meeting on the terrace of Bhulabhai. It was a very memorable evening. It was like the Potsdam convention at the end of World War II. He said, 'I am going to talk to you and give you some news.' At that time I think about a hundred people had gathered on the terrace. Sylvester Da Cunha, Gerson da Cunha, Pearl Padamsee, Usha Katrak, Kersi Katrak, Deryck Jefferies and his wife—many people.

Alkazi said, 'There can be only one leader. That means, if you want good work consistently, there must be a single leader. I don't think there should be other directors in the Theatre Group. I should be the only director. I have been to the Royal Academy of Dramatic Arts.' (As a matter of fact, so had I). He felt that he was a trained person in theatre and there was too much amateur rubbish going on. So he said, 'Either I will take over the Theatre Group or form my own separate unit, the Theatre Unit. And people are not free to join. I will select people.' In the case of the Theatre Group, anyone could join and as long as they had done a play before, anyone could direct. He said, 'No, your experience maybe wrong! Which means you will direct a lousy play.'

So then there was a big discussion and one young man stood up and said, 'Elk, you're talking about theatre as though it is religion. We are here to enjoy our life. This is all a façade.' Alkazi went red in the face. He said, 'You call it a façade? This is my life! I have devoted my entire life to theatre and you're calling it a façade?' He really screamed the word! We all remembered that word for a long time to come. Façade. And the poor guy who had said it shrank back into his seat. And that is how the two companies were formed.

Alkazi also did workshops besides theatre, in which theatre people were taught dance. I remember Kathakali being taught. I did that course and was the worst dancer you'd ever see in your whole life. He'd do three-month workshops and during that period it would be every day. He was a slave driver and thank god for that because we all learned the discipline of theatre from him. But he was also a bit of a straight-laced guy. He didn't like laughing at rehearsals or stuff like that. Many of us got into trouble, including me because I love fun. I used to laugh. I liked to enjoy myself. I love theatre, I live for theatre, but not in an overtly solemn way. I thought theatre was to enjoy in rehearsal, if you're playing a serious part you play it seriously, you come off, you may have a drink, crack a joke with friends and have a good time. It's not religion! But Alkazi felt it was religion...and in the church you don't laugh.

Shyam Benegal

When Alkazi broke away from the Theatre Group, he started his own Theatre Unit and that was located at Bhulabhai because it wasn't too far from where he used to stay. He used to stay at Kemp's Corner in a little apartment, where he had also created another terrace theatre, on top of his building. Alkazi was a man of many parts. He was almost a Renaissance person in that sense. He also wrote poetry. I befriended him because I used to versify a bit myself. So he invited me to his place and I sat and read out my poems to him. He then gave me a critical analysis. This was in 1956, the first time I visited Bombay.

Alkazi was a great perfectionist. He was a great disciplinarian and he handled his theatre with a tremendous amount of control. So it would always be a controlled performance, done in exceptionally good taste. He was, until he stopped doing plays, a very remarkable theatre producer. It was one of the pioneering generations of this country for modern theatre. For someone like me, a person who had come from the outside and was in his early twenties, it was all overwhelming. I felt like I was in heaven! It was such an incredible learning opportunity and experience.

Kusum Haider **(née *Behl*)**

Alkazi was an outstanding teacher. In retrospect I think, however brilliant a director he was, he was an even better teacher. If you were a student of his, it could only be an unforgettable experience, because all that learning inspired you to search for more knowledge and experience. I still use the same exercises in my teaching as he did. From all that he taught me, I can say that, because of him, I developed an eye for the visual arts. Being in a production of his was a huge learning experience that has certainly helped me to impart to others. I learned that all arts have a meeting point. Music, art, sets, movement, all form a cohesive whole. This experience enlarged one's horizons and opened up the mind.

Satyadev Dubey

There was an Irani shop outside Alkazi's house and sometimes Alkazi would join us, but he always reprimanded us and said, 'Don't waste your time. You must read. You know how much we have read.' And of course, we knew about his history. He had done RADA for three years along with his wife. So I mean he was perfectly trained. The point is, these little pep talks did help. And we kept doing these acting exercises which he gave. We were given scenes to perform and I would always be in the director's shoes. But later Alkazi reprimanded me because I was trying to improve the actors' English. I wanted them to speak like me and I was told that was not how English was spoken. Later I decided that English could be spoken in many ways as long as the pronunciation was correct. In the Indian context, we don't have to speak like the English, like Bapsy Sabavala and all those people.

Pooh Sayani

I think Alkazi was, in a sense, a benevolent dictator. And theatre was his whole life. He didn't approve of the way the Theatre Group was running, in the sense that everybody was an amateur, that everybody had a job and that they would come there only in the evenings. For him theatre was a very serious thing.

The Space, the People, the Plays

The question with which this oral history project was initiated was this: To what extent was the existence and availability of spaces like the Bhulabhai Desai Memorial Institute responsible for the spurt in new theatre activity of the sixties, seventies and eighties? In this chapter, interviewees recall the specific qualities of the space at Bhulabhai Desai Memorial Institute, the manner in which these particular features had impacted their work, the kind of environment—conducive or otherwise—that the presence of the other artists working there created, and finally, how being participants in the activities that happened in the space, chiefly the plays that were rehearsed and performed, affected their own growth as theatre people. For example, it was because Satyadev Dubey dared to stage Dharamvir Bharati's *Andha Yug*, a play that had originally been written for the radio, that it came to be hailed throughout India as a modern classic, and was translated into several languages including Bengali, Manipuri, Assamese and Marathi.

Satyadev Dubey

The Bhulabhai Institute…I have heard Bade Ghulam Ali Khan sahib sing over there: 'Ka karoon sajni aye na balam'. I also saw Mina Chitnis do a production in which Hari Jariwala, who later became the star Sanjeev Kumar, acted: *All My Sons* (Arthur Miller). It was done on the lawns. The lawns have a history of their own. I want to say something about the lawns. When I joined Theatre Unit, I came to know that Alkazi had produced *Oedipus Rex* (Sophocles) and he had performed it on the lawns. The lawns were also where Vijaya Mehta and P. D. Shenoy had a talk and Shenoy persuaded her to go back to Marathi theatre, which she did, and became perhaps its first star. At that time, every actress seemed to copy Vijaya.

I would like to remember P. D. Shenoy here. He influenced me immensely. He was a man who quoted liberally from Shakespeare. He took a class when Alkazi was not there. Alkazi had instructed him that there should be musical improvisations. I have always had a very bad ear for music but Alkazi used music in his productions extensively. He listened to a lot of different kinds of music and had a good ear for it. Now, every time I hear a piece of music, I instantly begin to wonder what kind of play or scene I could use it in. That has become second nature.

So in the improvisations that were done in Alkazi's workshops, a girl called Sunita did one and then P. D. Shenoy asked Narendra Sheth to do one. I have seen a number of brilliant improvisations in my life, but the one that Sheth did that day is one of the most delightful I have ever seen.

That reminds me of Gurnam Singh. He was quite close to me. I was once taking an improvisation class at the Institute, and he was in it. I tried to teach exactly what Shenoy had taught us earlier, which was that improvisations are meant to help the actor discover things inside himself, to surprise himself. An improvisation is not acting. Alkazi would often have to go abroad and Shenoy became the sole teacher for the group of people acting with Theatre Unit. In retrospect, I realized that the only flaw Shenoy had was that he tended to see too much in people. He would often praise actors for their potential.

I remember Shenoy once started reciting Keats in class. I think it was 'My heart aches and a drowsy numbness pains / My sense as of hemlock I had drunk.' I think that was the one. I remember how much I got out of his recitation. I remember his voice. There was another poem he once recited—a Walt Whitman poem. The opening line was 'Out of the cradle and listlessly walking' or some such thing ('Out of the cradle endlessly rocking'). I remember that poem because

Shenoy did both the voices in it. I have never been able to find that poem. Anyway, I tried very hard to recreate it while teaching it to myself. But couldn't.

I also remember an incident where Shenoy and I were having lunch at an Irani restaurant, not near Bhulabhai but somewhere else in town. I asked him what he felt about the things he had done. Shenoy very coolly said, 'A sense of satisfaction.' That was also the conversation in which I learned that he had read some of Einstein's original lectures. And I didn't have any background in science. The other instance I remember happened on one of our walks when he explained the second Five-Year Plan to me. I distinctly remember saying that it was a very good plan but if it failed, it would give rise to inflation—which it did.

I also remember when I got Shenoy to see my film *Aparichay Ke Vindhyachal* (Mountains of Unknowing) and he didn't like Alaknanda (Samarth) at all just as he hadn't liked her when he had seen her in my *Band Darwaze* (a Hindi adaptation of Jean Paul Sartre's *No Exit*). And he said, 'Burn the film. There is nothing in it.' After that we went out for a drink and got totally absorbed in talking to each other. This is something some people resent. They cannot bear to see two people talking earnestly, with total concentration, immersed in conversation. They get irritated. In this case, one gentleman got very irritated and he became abusive. Surprisingly, in spite of my temper, I kept cool. This man, after a point, started getting upset about the fact that I was so cool. So what he did was, he took out a lot of money from his pocket and shoved it into my pocket. So then I told Shenoy, 'Let's go out.' We finished drinking and stepped out and I told him, 'I will complete the film because I think Alaknanda has given a marvellous performance.'

The tragedy was that Shenoy ultimately joined S. Mukherjee and not being a money-minded person, he charged him a very small fee. He became enamoured by Joy Mukherjee who was a potential star at the time. Anyway, Shenoy had this failing for stars. Actually, I wouldn't call it a failing because he knew so much that he could help people with. He helped Joy Mukherjee make that film—I don't remember its name. He even knew about lenses and all that. Because that is something he commented on when he saw my film. He said, 'You have not used the right lenses.' I, of course, didn't understand what lenses were all about. But that was Shenoy.

Sulabha Deshpande acted in *Band Darwaze* which was a runaway success. I had used the same man whom Alkazi had used for *Oedipus Rex* to build the set. And I had these rounded steps which were very good. I have to thank Mr Soli Batliwala for the furniture which I used. It was from the Bhulabhai Institute itself. The sofa set and the chair. All the play readings of *Band Darwaze* as well as all the rehearsals took place at Bhulabhai. Its success was because I would read out the play to anybody who was willing to listen to it. Therefore, when we finally performed the play, I knew it by heart.

There is another side story attached to this. Gurnam Singh, who was busy with Rajesh Khanna at the time, was cast in my play as the man who looks after hell. But for some reason he couldn't do it and Amrish Puri, who had acted with me earlier, stepped in. His presence was truly frightening because he had practised not blinking his eyes. For this role, he had asked me, how do I play a blind man. I had told him, 'Just don't blink.' Sulabha Deshpande and Alaknanda were cast in the play. Sulabha Deshpande didn't know what a lesbian was at that point. When she found out, she had qualms about doing the role but she did it. Alaknanda was, of course, a very good actress. But in this case, I didn't let her anticipate me at all. Everything she did in the play I told her, and she'd give me a thumbs up. That is also the quality of fairness that Alaknanda had. That is why I took her for the film also. Everybody in *Band Darwaze* knew their lines in thirteen or fourteen days and then we did the play and performed it at Tejpal.

By some accident, I was looking for an actress to play Gandhari for my show of *Andha Yug* in Calcutta. I mentioned Sulabha Deshpande and Pu La Deshpande said, 'Oh she is very good.' Sulabha said she didn't know Hindi. I said, 'Just listen to me. Don't try and catch my voice or do anything with your voice. Just let it be.'

Sulabha Deshpande is the only actress I know who made the backstage people cry when she was cursing Krishna. The audience cries very easily, but not the backstage people. Sulabha made them cry.

When Girish Karnad first came to meet me at Bhulabhai, I was doing three one-act plays. I did them on the terrace of Bhulabhai. Girish came to see them. One was written by Sagar Sarhadi and produced, directed and enacted by V. K. Sharma. It was called *Khayal Ke Dastak* (When Ideas Knock). The second was a play I had directed earlier in 1956 called *Shaadi Ka Prastav*, translated from Chekhov's *Proposal*. The third was a play I had directed in 1958, *Thodi Der Pehle, Thodi Der Baad* (A Little Before and a Little After). It was obvious that I had read *Time and the Conways* by J. B. Priestley and it was influenced by that. Girish came to see the plays. He congratulated Sagar Sarhadi and V. K. Sharma and then came to me and said, 'I didn't know I was meeting a famous director who was also a potential playwright.' I remember he told me later that he had written a play based on Yayati and his inspiration had come from Rajagopalachari's retelling of the Mahabharat.

I was directing a play called *Sapne* (Dreams), translated from a (Albert) Camus play. I found that all the movements I was devising were going round and round. I was just not able to get the choreography right. It so happened that Shombhu Mitra was performing in the open air at the Cricket Club of India. So I went to see the performance because my Gujarati friends said you have to see this. And I saw *Raktakarabi* (Red Oleanders) and also *Putul Khela* (Doll's House). What I realized in *Putul Khela* was that the actors were not always moving across the stage. They would sit, come close to each other and there was this marvellous scene—the bed scene as I call it—where the husband and wife are on the bed and they are talking. In that scene I suddenly realized what was wrong in the production I was doing of *Sapne*. In next day's rehearsal, I changed everything—made the actors stand still much more and in a composition which I'm sure I borrowed from *Putul Khela*, I got them closer together and tightened the talk. It worked beautifully.

Dharamvir Bharati saw this play because he had seen an earlier play that the Theatre Unit had done, Samuel Beckett's *Waiting for Godot*, which had made some ripples. The *Times of India* critic had praised it. Since this news had gone around, Dharamvir Bharati came to the Institute to see the play. There was nobody there except my friend Abdul Shakoor, who is no more. These people were moving around and Shakoor being naturally inquisitive asked them, 'What are you looking for? Can I help you?' So they said, 'We have heard about Alkazi and the Theatre Unit and so we came, just wanting to know more.' Shakoor said, 'But we also do Hindi plays. Why don't you come and see our play? It's on tomorrow.' As it happened, the Bharatis had shifted to a place behind the Bhulabhai Institute near the Parsi General Hospital. So they were staying within walking distance of the Institute. They agreed to come and *Sapne* was done. They were shocked because there was no front curtain or anything. Dharamvir Bharati came backstage and congratulated me and said, 'This is the first time I'm seeing a play without a curtain in front and all that sort of thing.' By that time I had read *Andha Yug*. So I said, 'Please give me the rights of *Andha Yug*. I want to do it.' So he said, 'Sure. You want to do it, take it. The rights are yours.' That's how I did *Andha Yug*. But I must tell you where.

Alkazi had already accepted the offer of the Sangeet Natak Akademi to head the National School of Drama in Delhi. There was a farewell party for him. People were worried about what was going to happen to Theatre Unit after him. Alkazi in his parting speech eulogized me and said, 'Why are people worried about the Theatre Unit? Satyadev Dubey has already started a new play.' That was Ugo Betti's *The Queen and the Rebels*. Later on he said, why don't you do *Andha Yug*? I said, 'I want your terrace. Will you allow me your terrace?' At that time, his flat was vacant and I was using the flat, sleeping over there and doing all my recordings there. That's how I did *Andha Yug* on Alkazi's terrace.

But there are stories about how we did it. One day before our dress rehearsal, a young boy, Kadar, an architect, very sincere and genuine, fell and fractured his ribs because it had rained. So I asked V. K. Sharma to play Vriddha Yachak. The set was very simple because I used the facilities on the terrace for it. There was this water tank. Sharma had to stand on the water tank. So my friend Gohil wrote down his lines on the railings of the water tank. We also wondered who should play Ashwaththama. Mina Chitnis—Manavendra Gajananrao Chitnis—suddenly got panicky and didn't want to do the show. So finally, I was forced to do the first show myself. Amrish Puri was doing Dhritarashtra. Bharati came to the next show where he saw Mina Chitnis performing Ashwaththama. He was very impressed. Everybody was impressed. That's how *Andha Yug* started.

The lady who had acted in *Sapne*, Iqbal, had been acting in Wasi Khan's *Ret Ki Deewar* (Walls of Sand). By the time that play ended, Iqbal had lost her voice. So we had to eliminate her from the cast which was very sad because she was a very fine actress. So we were looking for another actress. I remember we were walking down. There was an Irani shop near the Institute. A lady was walking past it. Since I vaguely knew her, I asked her whether she was interested in acting. Her name was Neena, not Neena Kulkarni mind you. She was quite adventurous. So I said she should try to do the part of Gandhari. She agreed and we rehearsed with her and she did a very good job of it. Narendra Sheth was Yudhishthir—a very fine Yudhishthir. Gurnam Singh played Kripacharya. I used his Sikh appearance for the role.

I'll say something now about *Macbeth* (William Shakespeare) which Alkazi directed. He wanted Nargis Cowasji to play Lady Macbeth. In an earlier play, *Arms and the Man* (George Bernard Shaw), which Derek Bond directed, she had played Luca, the maid-servant, and she took away all the glory with her sheer presence. Pheroza Cooper who was RADA-trained, knew all the tricks of acting and was a very good actress. But Nargis Cowasji did hardly anything on stage. Her mere presence was exciting. Now she had gone away somewhere and meanwhile she had been double cast by a lady called Frieda Toin whose husband was also acting in the play. Wasi Khan did a marvellous job getting the set painted. I was staying in Goregaon at the time with Bhavani Prasad Mishra. So I would sit in the train working on my speech. I was playing the messenger. Alkazi decided to do Macbeth himself.

Macbeth was a total disaster. It was a very finely conceived production but everything went wrong with it. In the fighting sequences the swords bent. The two swords never met each other. I remember, with resentment, that the Theatre Group people—they were the rival group—kept laughing. And the thing is they were happy doing a play like *Little Hut,* for which they called Adi Marzban to direct. It was a sex comedy. And they would compare it with *Macbeth*. I had a lot of fights with some of my friends. 'How can you compare these two plays? Okay, this is a failure. But it is a failure on its own terms. It is not *Little Hut* which is quite an ugly play.'

Alaknanda Samarth

A little more than a decade after Independence, Mr Alkazi called on my parents. With courtesy and respect, he said he'd seen me on stage in a comedy, and wanted to offer me a role in his company and assured them I would be looked after, chaperoned and protected. A promise Mr and Mrs Alkazi kept. My brave parents were at ease.

Safety and a lack of anxiety is my overriding memory of Theatre Unit. Evening rehearsals were in a large room at the Bhulabhai Desai Memorial Institute. There was a bare acting area and facing it were two or three rows of chairs. Sometimes we worked at the Alkazis' flat round the corner. There was professional silence, respect for fellow actors and a devotion to theatre—values I carry within me even now. I went home by bus around nine-thirty or so, accompanied by Minoo Chhoi or Shakoor who saw me to my door.

Of the work I did there, *Miss Julie* was catalytic. Strindberg's play is a lethal act of class vengeance, a neo-Jacobean, sado-masochistic dance of desire between the teenage daughter of an aristocrat and their manservant, and his wife. Mr Alkazi was Jean, Farida Sonavala was Kristen, and I, Julie. It was an English translation.

The 'blocking' was unfussy and done quickly. But what emerged was a series of heightened, distanced, restrained images. Here are three:

1) Sinking to the ground, ending up on my back with head downstage stifling a scream with the back of my hand, Jean standing beside me, looking down.
2) Seated with flowers at a table centrestage with Jean standing to my left, holding up bloodstained hands.
3) The final exit, an excruciatingly slow, steady walk on high heels through a guillotine-like door onto a ramp horizontal to the lit cyclorama.

What I learned then was how to organize and structure a role, image it, frame it within the terms of reference of the director and pitch it. Lessons for life. Mr Alkazi was superb at tapping the visual power of a text. Roshan Alkazi designed the costumes. I'd never worn a décolleté gown, heels, gloves, an Anna Karenina fur hat! She showed me how to build a character from an item of costume, create the stance and walk. This has been a lesson for always.

I worked with British actors John Ridley and Derek Bond, and with Kusum Behl. Profound influences were Zul Vellani and his wife Nimmo. Zul was my co-actor. His charisma was palpable. Nimmo was alluring, rippling, flowing. She took me under her wing and gave me an entrée to the Urdu Progressive Writers Association. 'All this English is okay but come and listen to Urdu poetry,' she said. Theirs was a passionate, bohemian poetic salon. I was timid, but my parents said you should go and hear Urdu. It's beautiful.

Miss Julie didn't get great reviews in Bombay as I recall. It was a sensational hit in Delhi. I remember St Stephen's students, British and US expats, theatre folk, artists being there. It opened up a new world to me. The Alkazis remain my theatre family.

Band Darwaze, directed by Dubey, swept everybody off their feet. My parents got phone calls. Atre (P. K. Atre, editor of the

Marathi daily *Maratha* and a prolific playwright) phoned. He was bowled over and wrote about it. Dyaneshwar Nadkarni, of course, a champion of Mr Alkazi's Theatre Unit called them. Sai Paranjpye must've seen it (Sai and I spent a lot of time together in those days. I was fascinated by her being half-Russian). Dr Lagoo wrote in his memoirs and talked to me four years ago about the revelation the play had been. Amol Palekar must've been there but I don't remember meeting him afterwards. All of Sulabha's theatre colleagues were there. To this day, people who've never seen the production describe details of it to me. Girish Karnad told me he hadn't seen it but had heard it described by a friend as if he'd seen it! 'No, I did not see your *Band Darwaze*, but it has attained the status of a legend in Indian Theatre. I grew up with it.' Never has 'not seeing' a production been described as such a formative influence. It's what the great playwright, my friend Mahesh Elkunchwar, wrote to me just a few days ago: 'Even today people say, I didn't see it, but it's as if I've seen it. As if I was there.' My cousin Tanuja told me she's never forgotten the way I licked my lips in the address to the audience!

There were many film stars, screenwriters, film directors in the audience. Rinku Tagore whom I bumped into after decades reminded me of it. Tanuja, the Kapoors, including Shashi, Jennifer, Shammi, scriptwriters like Tanveer Faruqi, Snehaprabhabai Pradhan who phoned me and invited me over for tea with her and her dogs! She gave me such unadulterated, loving, supportive praise; I'll never forget even in my darkest moments. They all came backstage or on stage in the Indian way. Also in the audience were the Anands. Dubey had just played a small role in the English version of *The Guide* with Dev-sahib. He was there, 'Goldy' Vijay Anand, and probably Chetan, though I don't remember seeing him personally. Iqbal Mehboob Khan was there. Anyway out of that came two jobs for me: one was to dub *Teen Devian* (Three Ladies, dir. Amarjeet) with Dev-sahib in English. I dubbed Kalpana. The other was to do the Lal Quila Son-et-Lumiere for Chetan Anand. I played the watermelon seller and my laugh rang out in that Son-et-Lumiere for years!

In all the praise that has been showered on *Band Darwaze*, what's never mentioned is the impact Dubey's production style, choice of play, and translation had on the independent film people. It must have surely influenced some screenwriters. Dubey in 1964-65 had a corrosive laugh, a savage impatience with the prevailing system and with himself.

He commanded a chaste, muscular Hindi. He offered me a role in an Urdu translation of Sartre's *No Exit.* Having just returned from five years in the West, I'd never acted in Urdu. First he cast me as the lesbian Post Office clerk and then changed it to the socialite murderess. So Sulabha Deshpande and I switched roles. He played the army deserter. All three are dead. In Hell. Amrish Puri played the Valet/ Death.

Every language is a map with bleeding, porous borders. It's not bandaged. *Band Darwaze* helped my growth at the deepest level of language as consciousness. Dubey paid meticulous attention to syntax, the substratum of text analysis. 'She's India's only properly trained actress,' he always said of me to my embarrasment! We didn't take ourselves seriously. To this day, people who've never seen the production, describe it to me in detail. Why did it sweep everyone off their feet? Because it was the moment language shifted palpably and visibly on the Bombay stage and so gave rise to a new, inclusive audience. The audience changed. That's a revolutionary act in theatre. It doesn't happen twice. It happened in *Band Darwaze.*

***Kusum Haider* (née *Behl*)**

The Bhulabhai Desai Memorial Institute was the bungalow of senior Congress leader Bhulabhai Desai. The estate had two bungalows set at an angle and was surrounded by lush lawns. Madhuriben lived in Hasman, the private bungalow near the road. The rehearsals of Alkazi's plays took place in the large hall of the Institute which opened out to a large verandah and garden. Soli Batliwala, who managed the Institute with Madhuriben, had set the rent at Re 1 a day.

I got to know about the Bhulabhai Desai Memorial Institute through a neighbour who used to act in Mr Alkazi's plays. Her name was Farida Sonavala. She now lives in Delhi. I had just finished my Senior Cambridge exam from the Convent of Jesus and Mary in Byculla. I was fifteen and underage to join college. I had to occupy myself for a year. So my parents agreed to let me join Mr Alkazi's School of Dramatic Art at the Bhulabhai Desai Institute. I lived in Gold Cornet on Naoroji Gamadia Road. The Institute was a good twenty-five-minute walk away on Warden Road.

We had a variety of sessions on voice production, speech, movement and improvisation. Mr Alkazi often took individual classes. We learned Hindi and Kathakali, and had music and art appreciation classes. The improvisation classes were conducted by Mr P. D. Shenoy—a fabulous teacher. In the days of the Theatre Group, before the Theatre Unit was formed, Mr Alkazi used his own terrace at Vitthal Court, 151 Cumballa Hill for performances. Mr Shenoy, whose first name was Purushottam, was one of the most well-read people I knew. He introduced us to the works of Kierkegaard, Camus and Sartre. Then people started doing their plays. We would go to the Strand Book Stall. I had no money but I would go and look at those books anyway. We put money together to buy Sartre's *No Exit*.

The atmosphere at the Institute was unique. A kind of golden age with all the arts coming together, with people engaged in a genuine quest for artistic expression. It was a period of flowering, intense activity and complete focus. People were very modest and self-effacing, without any ego problems. There was a certain kind of innocence. Art, music, dance and theatre intermingled as nowhere else that I know. There were hardly any rivalries or gossip. These were earnest, fresh and innocent days.

My deep interest in contemporary Indian art today is due to my relationship with artists and interaction with people like (M. F.) Husain, Tyeb (Mehta) and Gaitonde who left a permanent mark on me. There were other people at Alkazi's school. Cedric and Rohini

Santos and the da Cunhas were all supporters of the Theatre Unit. There were senior actors like Bomi Kapadia, Nergis Cowasji, Pheroza Cooper, Hilla Cooper, Usha Amin, Kersi Katrak, Zul Vellani, Minoo Choi, Mina Chitnis, Zohra Sehgal, Derek Bond—an Englishman—Zarine Engineer, Alaknanda Samarth, Satyadev Dubey and many others.

Great plays like *Medea* (Euripides), *Hedda Gabler* (Henrik Ibsen), *The Father* (August Strindberg), *Yerma* (Garcia Lorca), *St Joan* (Jean Anouilh), *Murder in the Cathedral* (T. S. Eliot), *Suddenly Last Summer* (Tennessee Williams), *Macbeth* (William Shakespeare) were performed. I had parts in *Macbeth, Antigone* and *Eurydice*. I played two of the lead roles. For the performance of *The Father*, Soli Batliwala presented a hundred rupees for the production.

Some plays were performed at the Institute which could accommodate about one hundred people in the big room downstairs. But Alkazi had also found a place in Jai Hind College. *Antigone* was first performed in Hindi translation at the Institute and then at Jai Hind. *Eurydice* was performed at Jai Hind. The audience was mainly people who were maybe friends of the actors. A lot of them were intellectuals of Bombay like Karl Khandalawala and Mulk Raj Anand. A couple of them were foreigners, like Rudy von Leyden—he was a great personality. One rubbed shoulders with people who were written about by everybody.

Finally, Madhuriben auctioned off the building on the suggestion of Soli Batliwala, and the flourishing centre was buried under the monolith of residential apartments. It is unbelievable that there were people engaged in such diverse passions under that one roof. The Institute had been right at the centre of the city's cultural history, starting a new chapter for the arts in India, exploring and encouraging a plethora of experiments. All the world was the Bhulabhai's stage. It was a place that started a cultural explosion and like lightning it lit fires everywhere in India. It was a period of excitement and discovery. At sixteen, for me, it was the most meaningful time of my life. I felt I was part of a movement that had taken a direction and everything in the arts could only follow from that initial awakening.

Alyque Padamsee

The Bhulabhai Desai Institute wasn't very structured like the NCPA is today. You just went to Solibhai for anything you wanted. Soli Batliwala was Madhuri Desai's right-hand man. He would just say, 'The space is free on so and so day, come and use it.' It was very bohemian. But at the same time, the work was very dedicated and disciplined. The Institute would open at about ten in the morning and go on till about eleven in the night. As far as I can remember, there was one upper level and one lower level. The lower space was not very well-designed. I always remember coming into Bhulabhai and feeling depressed because it was all dark. But once you got to the next level where the terrace was, you felt free as a bird. The terrace was very beautiful because at that time, there were hardly any high buildings around. So you had a lovely view. You couldn't really see the sea because Madhuri had built a two-storeyed building in front of it. But from the corners you could catch a glimpse of it and feel the sea air! I think the salty sea air of Bhulabhai inspired many of us. It was a huge place. And in nooks and corners little romances developed.

Of the many people who worked there, I think Hima Devi was one. She was a great dancer and a big name in dance. Later, she moved into theatre and trained a lot of actors, particularly in English theatre. She was a stickler for enunciation. She would always say, 'Don't suffer from lazy lips.'

Akbar (Padamsee) and (M. F.) Husain were a part of the painters' group. And we were the theatre people. But there was a lot of intermingling and that was the beauty of the Bhulabhai Institute. It was a place where artists of different languages in theatre, of different schools of painting, poetry came together. Nissim Ezekiel was there. Everywhere there would be workshops going on, even dance workshops. I remember even Akbar and Husain organized some informal workshops of sorts. Not the kind where you'd have to sign here and pay there but the sort where you said, 'Okay let's meet tomorrow evening and talk about art.' There was always a kind of very pleasant gadbad going on there. Conversations, rivalries, controversies…that was the beauty of Bhulabhai.

At that time Akbar, who is now this grand old statesman and spokesman for the art world, was doing paintings for one of which he was arrested by the police (A case was filed against Akbar Padamsee for his painting *The Couple*). It was a very famous case with the progressive artists. So we were all in all quite a rebellious crowd. I did a play that was banned. It was Partap Sharma's *A Touch of Brightness.* We were invited to the Commonwealth Arts Festival in London. It was the first Commonwealth Arts Festival and we were the only Indian group invited. It was a great honour and so we rehearsed and rehearsed. We had a wonderful cast. There was Vijaya (Khote at the time who met Farokh Mehta in the play and they fell in love and got married), then there was Zul Vellani, superb actor, there was Pearl (Padamsee), Mina (Manavendra) Chitnis who was the son of Leela Chitnis. And then, at the last minute, somebody told the home minister that this play was about the red light district and we were taking it to London to show Maharashtrian women portrayed as prostitutes to the whole world. Our air tickets were booked, everything was done and two days before we got on the plane, the home minister confiscated all our passports. Partap Sharma, who recently passed away, was a wonderful person and a brilliant playwright. He fought the censor board for seven years and finally the high court told the censor board they couldn't censor plays like that.

The Theatre Group to which I belonged is the oldest English theatre group in India. It was established in 1941, and was the only group of Indians who were doing plays by Shakespeare and other English and American playwrights. It was started by my elder brother Sultan, known as Bobby Padamsee. Alkazi joined it and the great actor and radio personality Hamid Sayani joined, and Deryck Jefferies who was a great technician, great at lighting and all that, also joined. They all came together with Bobby Padamsee and formed the Theatre Group. Alkazi and many others sprang from that group. Dubey sprang out of the Theatre Unit which Alkazi formed after he left the Theatre Group. Dubey was the shishya then, and Alkazi the guru. There were many others in the group. P. D. Shenoy was one of them.

Alkazi, popularly known as Elk, was the one who got the space for Theatre Group in the Bhulabhai Institute after negotiating with Madhuri Desai. It was a wonderful space in one of the most influential parts of the city on Bhulabhai Desai Road, named after her father-in-law. We used to call the area Scandal Point, I don't know why. Anyway, Alkazi got the premises there for Theatre Group. This was in the sixties. Alkazi did some wonderful plays there. He was mainly into the classics. The only modern play he did was *Waiting for Godot.* This was done on his own terrace. He had this very neat and cozy terrace theatre. Very intimate. Although it was on the terrace, traffic wasn't so bad in those days. Alkazi was the doyen. He was the man who really brought the Bhulabhai space into the Bombay art world. No doubt about it.

Before the split, I remember Kersi Katrak did an excellent enactment or what you might call a visualized play reading or what we used to call 'visual enactment' of *The Trojan War Will Not Begin* by Jean Giraudoux. This was done on the terrace and we had an invited audience and we ran many shows. It was a fantastic production. It was an insight into the world of politics and love. The play is about Helen of Troy in Paris and how the Trojan War is caused. Brilliant play and he had some very very fine actors. I myself did a few improvisations in that space on all sorts of topics.

Yes, the Institute was a wonderful place where we'd meet in the evening and do rehearsals and chat. There was a café around there so we could order samosas. And tea was always available; theatre people can't do without their chai. And most importantly, we would have wonderful discussions there.

Shyam Benegal

I will never forget the first time I came to Bhulabhai Desai Institute. There's a special reason for that. It was at the height of the battle for the city of Mumbai to be included in Maharashtra, the Samyukta Maharashtra agitation. This was in 1956. There was a lot of police firing at different spots in Bombay, particularly at Flora Fountain and Colaba. I can never forget that because mine was the last train to come into the terminal at VT (Victoria Terminus) station. I had come from Hyderabad where I used to live. I was a student at college. I was interested in dance and music and other things that I had only read about. One of the people who appeared to me to be a very exciting figure of the time was the doyenne of modern dance, Martha Graham. I had come specifically to watch her perform in Mumbai. She was performing at the Birla Matoshree Sabagriha next to Bombay Hospital. I think the public performance was there. But there was also a workshop, which happened to be at the Bhulabhai Desai Memorial Institute. The Institute used to be run as a kind of workshop and a theatre space and a studio space with a whole lot of little cubicles where the famous progressive artists of Bombay used to paint. When I came, I didn't know any of this. I was just coming to see Martha Graham.

That was the first time I went there. But her performance happened to be on a day when there were curfews and all kinds of dreadful things happening to the city of Mumbai. I was supposed to go for the performance in the evening and I couldn't go. I missed it. I was wondering if my entire trip was going to be in vain. I was stuck because trains would not even go back. Then I remembered there was also going to be a workshop. But that was for an invited audience. Still, I decided to go. So I walked to the Institute from VT. Thankfully, there was no violence on the way. And finally, I did manage to get in to see her workshop.

I remember being very impressed by Bhulabhai. It was quite an extraordinary place. There was a lawn below and next to that there were cubicles where most of the great artists of the second half of the twentieth century had their studios. Gaitonde had a studio, M. F. Husain had a studio, Mohan Samant had a studio. Then, on the first floor, was Ravi Shankar's music studio. And there was a whole lot of space given to theatre for classes, workshops, rehearsals. This space used to be handled by the Theatre Unit. And the terrace of Bhulabhai was the theatre. It was a little space created by Alkazi and Alkazi was the head of the Theatre Unit. This was a break-away group from the Theatre Group.

Besides the artists who worked at Bhulabhai Desai Memorial Institute, there were all the people who visited for lectures and discussions and so on. That was quite something. We haven't had a repetition of that ever. Today, you can't get artists together in one place like that. It was something very unique that happened to Bombay at the time.

When I came to settle in Bombay towards the end of 1958, then of course, one used to go there quite often to see the Theatre Unit plays, all those magnificent productions that Alkazi was doing. The Greek tragedies, *Eurydice*, plays with Kusum Behl who later became Haider, Alaknanda Samarth and all the other famous names of English theatre.

There used to be a Hindi section in the Theatre Unit that used to be run by a person called P. D. Shenoy. He was an utterly fascinating and extremely intellectual person. It would be an absolute pleasure sitting with him because he would have wonderful ideas and would open up many worlds for you by simply talking to you about music, literature, and all sorts of other things. He had an all-embracing mind. He used to live in the suburbs, and he was very different from the rest of the people at Bhulabhai. His background didn't match with the rest of them. The rest were all South Bombay people with mostly Indo-Anglian backgrounds in terms of education. Shenoy was different. And Shenoy therefore had a fuller sense of everything. And the person who got most enthralled by him was Satyadev Dubey!

In 1962, Alkazi was invited to Delhi to run the National School of Drama. So the Theatre Unit was left without a head. The person who took over Theatre Unit was Satyadev Dubey. Shenoy also had to leave to start the Filmalay Acting School. But the impression that he had made on Dubey was an enormous one.

Gerson da Cunha

Bhulabhai Desai Memorial Institute was a great rehearsal space. But most of the shows took place in other places because there was not enough space for pucca green rooms or for a proper set or for a large enough audience. Just the audience that could be accommodated on the terrace was not enough to cover costs.

I was a member of something called the Theatre Group, Bombay. It was run by Ebrahim Alkazi. But there came a moment when the kind of plays that Alkazi wanted to do began to differ from the kind of plays that other people in the group wanted to do. So he thought the best thing to do would be to part company. So he formed the Theatre Unit. Some of us moved from one to the other. That is how I was introduced to the Bhulabhai Desai Memorial Institute. It was through the Theatre Unit. And then through that, other people in the theatre group also became involved. The Unit needed premises from which they could work. And the Bhulabhai Desai outfit offered them that space—which was really generous and kind of Madhuri Desai and Soli Batliwala. The Theatre Group had their premises at Kulsum Terrace in Colaba.

Everybody who was in any of the arts would have met each other at the Bhulabhai. I recall meeting P. L. Deshpande at Bhulabhai. He was a completely unforgettable character. The beautiful thing about Pu La Deshpande was that in addition to being a towering figure in theatre, he was also a very fine person. He was a warm person who always talked to you like an equal, never talking down to you from his great height of theatrical achievement.

There was a great deal of coming and going at the time. We used to say, 'See you at the Bhulabhai.' As far as actual productions go, the one I remember most vividly is a visual enactment that Kersi Katrak did. A visual enactment is halfway between a play reading and a full-scale production. There are costumes, there is a set, there are lights—all fairly suggestive and vestigial, not complicated. And importantly, the players carry scripts. But it was extraordinary how soon the audience forgot those scripts. So Kersi Katrak directed a production of Jean Giraudoux's *Tiger at the Gates.* It was a remarkable play and Kersi cast it very well. He had a lot of excellent people in it. Frieda and Antony Toin, my sister and Anisha, Kersi himself, my brother Sylvie, me. It is a visual enactment that people have not forgotten to this day. All the rehearsals and more than one performance took place at Bhulabhai.

We saw Alkazi's *Waiting for Godot* and *Murder in the Cathedral.* It was a collaboration with Husain and became quite famous. For the first time Husain had designed a theatre set. I also remember seeing a (Anton) Chekhov. Maybe it was *Uncle Vanya*, again perhaps done by Kersi on the grounds of the Bhulabhai. *Tiger* was done on the terrace.

The great thing about Bhulabhai was that it produced a confluence of many arts. There were sculptors there, painters, poets, theatre people. It was therefore a wonderful fusion of minds. I don't think any of us realized the impact that the Bhulabhai Desai had on all of us. I don't think any of us can quite estimate the value of those exchanges. It is a matter of huge regret to many of us that the Institute came down and that ugly building took its place. But it is possible that Soli was as responsible for the closure of the Institute as he had been for running it for so many years. He must have looked at the future and thought this place cannot go on the way it is with no real revenue stream, so best sell it when there is a decent price that one can get. I think he was of that view. It is possible that I may be entirely wrong. But there came a moment when indeed the concept of the Bhulabhai was at variance with the environment. I mean that times had changed, costs had grown. There were competitive calls from other venues of theatre. So the financial problems may have been a thought. I don't think that they overtook the Bhulabhai at the times I remember. But any good manager looks at the future all the time and how long really could an organization like that survive? I realize that it was run on the funds of the memorial trust but that kind of funding cannot go on for ever.

Today, I see spaces where you can perform but I don't see spaces where you can meet as we did at the Bhulabhai Institute.

Prafulla Dahanukar

Bhulabhai Desai Memorial Institute was a fantastic place for the arts. It was full of energy. You can say cultural energy. There was a big hall on the ground floor with three or four rooms flanking it. Many artists had rooms there. Ravi Shankar had the first one. The Theatre Unit office was also downstairs, but they used to rehearse on the terrace. There was a long passage on the terrace. That's where the artists' studios were. The doors of the studios were never locked. Nothing was ever stolen from there. (M. F.) Husain's studio was next to mine. Bal Chhabda used to visit him often. Tyeb (Mehta) also had a studio but he and Akbar Padamsee came later.

Rajesh Khanna visited the Institute. I attended his wedding. He recognized me. I asked him how. He said, 'You've forgotten. I was Jatin Khanna to you. We used to have tea with you. We didn't have money so you used to stand us tea.' He used to do small roles, servants and things like that, in IPTA plays. Sanjeev Kumar also used to be there with IPTA and A. K. Hangal. I remember these three clearly.

I first met Satyadev Dubey there. He was working with Alkazi then. We became great friends. He came and stayed with me a year before he died. I'd even designed costumes for one of the plays he rehearsed at Bhulabhai, *Ashadh Ka Ek Din*. It was staged at Tejpal Auditorium, sometime in the sixties.

Ravi Shankar opened his Kinnara School there in 1962 to teach sitar. He produced a programme called Melody and Rhythm which he staged all over the country. Shiv Kumar Sharma used to play the tabla. He accompanied Ravi Shankar. He was a seventeen-year-old stripling then. He often tells me I'm the only person in Bombay who knows that he used to be a tabla player. Waheeda Rehman, Hema Malini, Sonal Pakvasa (Mansingh) used to come with their gurus and practise there.

Gaitonde would visit my studio regularly. He was my teacher from the J. J. School of Arts. His father, who didn't want him to be an artist, threw all his works out of the window. He lived in Ambawadi, opposite Majestic Cinema. He asked me if he could keep his work in my studio. I said why just keep? You can work in my studio, no problem. He was not only my teacher. He was my friend. He used to come in the morning at eight o'clock and work till two o'clock. I used to go in at twelve and stay till eight or nine or ten. When he left the studio he'd go to see a film. He spent most afternoons watching films.

Downstairs there was Piloo Pochkhanawala and Davierwala. They were both very well-known sculptors. Beside them was Mhatre who worked in enamel. Also B. Vitthal the sculptor. There was also a German photographer—I've forgotten his name. He used to teach photography—how to develop pictures and all that. There was the film-maker Rathod who used to show us his documentaries. Shyam Benegal would shoot there. The yoga guru Iyengar used to come on Saturday and Sunday mornings. Fifty or sixty outsiders would come to the Institute to learn from him. In the evening the stage was given over to theatre people. It was all very well organized. The atmosphere was charged from morning till night.

I had a bad habit. When I painted I sang. When I stepped back to see what I had done, I would stop singing. Husain used to shout across, 'Chup kyon ho gayi Prafulla? Gati raho, gati raho, hamein bhi inspiration mil raha hai' (Why have you stopped singing Prafulla? Keep singing, keep singing. It is inspiring me.). The studios were separated by wooden partitions. You could hear everything people were saying.

When we had nothing to do, we used to go downstairs to watch rehearsals and listen to the music. The Kinnara people were my friends, all Ravi Shankar's secretaries—Penny Easterbrook, Kamala Chakravarty. Secretary meant girlfriend. They lived with him. His school ran from about 1962 to 1966.

P. L. Deshpande rehearsed two plays at Bhulabhai, *Varyavarchi Varaat* (Procession in the Air) and *Tujhe Ahe Tujapashi*. I had a singing role in the first play and of a society lady in the second. He would come for rehearsals in the evening and go away. The third play he rehearsed there was *Sundar Mee Honar* (I Will Be Beautiful) in which his wife Sunita played the lead. She was the real force in his life. She put him together. Otherwise he would have merely been one of those entertainers.

Bhulabhai closed in 1969. The family sold the land to a builder.

Akbar Padamsee

When I went to Paris in 1950, there was no Bhulabhai Institute. When I came back, in 1952 or '53, it was there. I heard about it from my brother. It was on Warden Road. He said it was a fantastic place so we both went there.

It had been started by Madhuri Desai. When she was in Switzerland, she met Soli Batliwala who was the cultural officer. They became friends and she told him that she was about to start this centre and asked him for his help. She used to live right across the road from the Institute. With Soli's help, she contacted all the artists, including theatre people. The most prominent one among them was Alkazi. He used to conduct his rehearsals there, have shows there. Husain was there, Gaitonde was there. Jatin Das was there. They all had their studios there. They even offered me a studio. But I said I lived next door, so there was no point in me blocking a studio when I had my own studio within a ten-minute walking distance of the Institute. I used to live in a building called Tahir Mansion at the corner of Nepean Sea Road. I used to walk to the Institute every evening and spend time there. Tyeb Mehta's wife, Sakina, had started a bookshop of art books at the Institute. There were books on dance, music and theatre as well. They were very rare, special books.

Meena Naik

I grew up in Mumbai watching professional plays. My older sisters, Rekha and Chitra, who later became famous stars of the Marathi screen, began their careers on the Marathi stage. Rekha acted in sangeet nataks like *Ekach Pyala* (One Drink, No More) and *Saubhadra* (Subhadra's Wedding) with illustrious actors like Shanta Apte,

Baburao Pendharkar and Nanasaheb Phatak. My other two sisters were dancers. They were part of the Sachin Shankar Ballet Troupe. I used to go with them to watch their rehearsals. I must have been about eleven or twelve years old at the time. I'm talking here about the early sixties. The ballet shows would often be accompanied by puppet shows from Yugoslavia, Russia, Czechoslovakia. So my adolescent years were rich with these varied theatrical experiences.

Sachin Shankar's rehearsals used to be held at the Bhulabhai Memorial Institute. I would accompany my sisters there to watch the rehearsals. My memories of the place were of a bungalow and a man called Solibhai who would be wandering around in it in a white pajama, dagli and spectacles. He'd watch rehearsals downstairs then come up to Masterji's room. There was a large hall on the ground floor and several small rooms above it on the first floor. One of them was given to Madhavrao Master, the puppeteer. The room used to be chock full of puppets—stored away in boxes, hanging all over the place. He had even built a small puppet theatre there. So when I went for my sisters' ballet rehearsals, I'd watch for a while and then wander off upstairs. Masterji would come at around three in the afternoon and would stay till about nine. There was another elderly man with him called Babuji Mistry. He was, as his name suggested, a carpenter who had been with the Prabhat Film Company before he retired. Masterji also had piles of books—all in English. Masterji didn't know a word of English but he would study the pictures and instruct Babuji, who would make puppets accordingly.

I would love spending time with him and manipulating his puppets. I learned everything about puppets and puppetry there, in that room in the Bhulabhai Institute. The artist Gaitonde used to work in a room next to Masterji's and I had heard Ravi Shankar used to play in some other room. For one of Masterji's shows, Ravi Shankar had given the music because the show called for classical music. It had three sitting puppets—one playing the tabla, one the sitar and one something else I can't remember. I loved being in that place overflowing with so much culture.

My entry on the Marathi stage was with a very small role in a play called *Yama Harla Yama Jinkla* (Yama Has Won, Yama Has Lost). This play was directed by Ramakant Deshpande, Pu La Deshpande's brother, for the Bharatiya Vidya Bhavan inter-collegiate competitions and I was awarded a special prize. Madhav Watve used to come to watch the rehearsals of the play. Later, when he decided to do *Natakkarachya Shodhat Saha Patra* (Luigi Pirandello's *Six Characters in Search of an Author*), he had not been able to find an actor for the role of the step-daughter. When he saw me, he decided I fitted the role and asked me if I would do it. I readily agreed. So there I was in my first big role standing side-by-side with stalwarts of the Marathi stage like Arvind Deshpande and Lilavati Bhagwat. Madhav Watve belonged to Vijayabai's (then Khote) group, Rangayan.

My work on the professional stage brought me in touch with Vijayabai directly. I did the costumes for *Mata Draupadi* which she was directing for Sahitya Sangh Mandir. Around the same time, Vijayabai was also directing *Bai Khulabai*, Vyankatesh Madgulkar's adaptation of Jean Giraudoux's *The Mad Woman of Chaillot* for Rangayan. She was going to use masks in the play. I made the masks. The rehearsals for the play used to be at Bhulabhai. There was a terrace on the second floor—not small but not as large as the hall downstairs—where we used to rehearse till nine at night.

Ratna Pathak-Shah

I do not remember seeing a play at Bhulabhai. But I remember being there many times as a child of about eight or ten. Satyadev Dubey did rehearsals there. My mom (Dina Pathak) was acting in some play and she too would rehearse there. Other things like poetry readings and speeches too used to happen there and I was a part of that too, although my memories of those things are vague. There were poetry readings, dance programmes, talks on painting and at some point, even some workshop was held there. It was theatre related so I landed up for that too. But what I do have a very strong memory of is the kind of space it was. It was very informal and there was no real sense of distance between performers and the audience. If I am not mistaken, there was a kind of stage.

Bhulabhai was not a commercial venture. It focused on experimentation and understanding of theatre. A variety of performances took place there. None of the plays ran for a long time. They were mostly one-offs. Even the people who came there were completely different from the kind of people who came for the Gujarati commercial theatre. The actors and directors were different. They were concerned with putting forward ideas rather than producing plays that ran for many shows and made a lot of money as the general trend was in Gujarati theatre at the time.

Arun Kakade

Vijayabai knew Soli Batliwala. Because of him, we were able to work at the Bhulabhai Memorial Institute. We had been given a small space there. Also, there was a huge space at the back that was turned into a sort of godown for us. We would keep all our material there, all our sets, everything. We used the small rehearsal space, we got to use the terrace space, the lawn—we used every space available for rehearsals.

According to me, it was the ideal centre for the arts. All the arts had come together there. Gaitonde worked there. There were a couple of sculptors. Ravi Shankar practised there. Vijay Raghav Rao was there. So we'd go watch them practise, rehearse. When we rehearsed, they would come and watch us. There was a lot of give and take. Dubeyji was there. It was an extremely important cultural centre. When we did shows, Gaitonde and others would come and watch. We had to pay an extremely nominal fee for the godown space, nothing else.

I think we worked at Bhulabhai for about seven to eight years. We did a lot of plays there. We would do the larger (Vijay) Tendulkar plays in Bharatiya Vidya Bhavan on Sunday mornings. We would also perform at Sahitya Sangh every once in a while. It was an open-air theatre at first, before the indoor auditorium was built. We performed around Dadar, even Vile Parle. I always pushed for shows. Vijayabai believed in stopping after five shows but I believed in pushing shows and I did. I did about fifty to sixty shows of *Sasa Kasav* (The Hare and the Tortoise), about seventy shows of Tendulkar's *Me Jinklo Me Harlo* (I Won I Lost). We even did a fifteen-day long tour of Vidarbha. I took on contract shows and channelled that money into these other shows. When we performed at Bhulabhai, there would be about forty to fifty people in the audience, not more. Most of them would be our sympathizer members. We didn't have any money. So we told all our friends that we would bring them three new productions every year for which they would have to pay a membership fee in advance. As a result, we were pushed to turning out new work consistently. Slowly, a kitty formed. I think the membership was about Rs 15 for a year, and about Rs 25 for a family. This was more than enough money for us. This was around 1960.

We used as much as we could of the space at Bhulabhai. When we performed on the terrace, we used lights and everything. When we felt that plays like *Sasa Kasav* and *Me Jinklo Me Harlo* needed to be performed on a proscenium stage, we shifted there, because these plays would not have fitted in at Bhulabhai. The space would have been insufficient. But we performed Tendulkar's *Maadi* (Female) there, we performed (Eugène) Ionesco there. We performed all our small plays there. But then we began to use Tejpal more and more.

I don't remember seeing Alkazi's work at Bhulabhai, but I do remember seeing a show of *Andha Yug* in the terrace theatre at the top of Vitthal Court. The way that terrace space had been visualized, the way it had been used in the space design for the play was brilliant. I don't remember other groups working at Bhulabhai. I only remember Rangayan and Theatre Unit. We had an extremely limited, exclusive audience. Getting off at Grant Road station and walking to Bhulabhai wasn't easy. So our audience was only those people who believed that watching theatre of this sort was a must. In those days, South Bombay was the centre of theatre. Later it shifted to Dadar, a more central place. Now it has gradually inched further and further north. The whole movement has gotten decentralized.

When Rangayan split, it was because Vijayabai said our aim was to do five shows of a play, no more. I disagreed. I felt that this was all right when we did plays written by foreign playwrights. But with an Indian playwright who approached us with his play, how could we stop at five shows? Would he feel motivated to write another play after that?

PART TWO

Walchand Terrace

Photo credit: Vinesh Gandhi

Walchand Terrace as it stands today.

Walchand Terrace has played a very important role in the history of the Mumbai theatre of the early seventies. The building belongs to the Lalchand Hirachand group of companies, of which one partner, the late Vinod Doshi, was a great patron of the arts, particularly of the vibrant, young, non-commercial theatre that had taken shape in the earlier decade. This theatre had previously found a gracious home in the Bhulabhai Desai Memorial Institute, but was rendered homeless when that property was sold to a developer. A theatre that worked on shoestring budgets, which often came out of the pockets of actors and directors, was not in a position to hire theatre spaces that charged large fees. Despite this, theatre would have continued to survive as it always had done. However, meanwhile, Vinod Doshi generously offered the use of the ground-floor space in his family's property, Walchand Terrace, to the two leading lights of the new theatre—Arvind Deshpande and Satyadev Dubey. Most importantly, it came with no strings attached and soon became the central meeting point for the city's Hindi and Marathi theatre.

Walchand Terrace was conveniently located on Tardeo Road in south central Mumbai. It comprised a large hall and two smaller rooms which allowed all activities connected with a play under production—discussions, readings, rehearsals and translations—to be conducted simultaneously under one roof. Gradually, like-minded theatre practitioners from Delhi, Calcutta, Bangalore and other places began to use it as a base when they visited the city—always sure that rehearsals for an interesting new play would be going on there or, at the least, an animated discussion about issues in theatre. This allowed for an energetic cross-pollination of views and ideas which, in turn, contributed to the growth of theatre.

The Benefactor: Vinod Doshi

Photo courtesy: Maitreya Doshi

Vinod Doshi was the eldest son of Lalchand Hirachand Doshi and nephew of Walchand Hirachand, the founder of the Walchand Group of Industries, which included India's first modern shipyard, first aircraft factory and first car factory. Vinod Doshi was Chairman of Premier Automobiles Ltd. (now Premier Ltd.) of the group and a former president of the Confederation of Indian Industry.

Even as a college student Doshi had been keenly interested in the arts, particularly theatre. Later, some of the most illustrious names in the world of music, dance and theatre were to be regular visitors to his home—Neela House, off Pedder Road. Doshi passed away in October 2008 at the age of seventy-six. Since then, the Vinod and Saryu Doshi Foundation, in association with Premier Ltd., have been celebrating his passion for theatre by sponsoring an annual five-day festival of plays in Pune, which has grown immensely popular over the years.

Amol Palekar

I was witness to the love with which Vinod handed over Walchand Terrace to Dubey and told him to use it freely. It happened during a small party at Vinod's place. Dubey was saying, 'Our greatest problem is rehearsal space. It's impossible to come by in Bombay.' Vinod said, 'Is that all? Come. Start your rehearsals in Walchand Terrace from tomorrow.' And the rest is history, as they say. The things that were done at Walchand Terrace, the things that happened there, all these constitute one of the most important chapters in the history of the experimental theatre movement.

It was Dubey's suggestion that I should cast Vinod Doshi in *Vallabhpurchi Dantakatha* (a Marathi translation of Badal Sircar's Bengali play *Ballabhpurer Roopkatha* [The Tale of Vallabhpur]). Vinod was a big industrialist. I wondered if he would be able to spare time for a play. Dubey told him Amol is doing a Marathi play and would like you to act in it. Are you willing? Vinod said I know nothing about acting. To which Dubey said that is Amol's responsibility. So Vinod did a role in the play. It was a charming performance. He did something else too for the play. He offered to do the sound effects. Sound was Vinod's passion. Walchand Terrace later became Shashank Walchand Studio. But before Shashank got into sound in a big way, recording sound had been Vinod's passion. We used to spend entire evenings at his place listening to the things he had recorded. The first time we heard the singer Reshma was with his recording of her programme on Pakistani radio. This was during the *Vallabhpur* days. He was crazy about music. He used to go around recording all sorts of programmes and play them to his friends.

We sat in Vinod's bedroom and prepared the soundtrack of *Vallabhpur*. He had put a reverb on the sound of Raghuda's ghost which enters at the end. This was quite a new thing back in those days. It created a surreal atmosphere. When he heard the final show was to be at the open-air Rangabhavan Theatre at Dhobi Talao, he was thrilled. He said, 'Just watch how I send Raghuda's last laugh all round the auditorium.'

'What do you mean "send"?'

'It'll begin on the left of the audience, travel back, go across behind them, come out on the right and fade away.'

'How will you do that?'

'Wait and see.'

With Shashank's help he then put up twelve speakers. He had an independent switchboard made. It was called a piano switchboard or some such thing. With that equipment the sound of the laughter started on the St Xavier's College side, went behind the audience and faded out near the police headquarters. The applause when that happened was deafening.

The call of vultures was required for Vijay Tendulkar's *Gidhade* (Vultures), which Dr Shreeram Lagoo was directing at Walchand Terrace. Vinod took the responsibility for recording that sound. He used to go and sit for hours at the Parsi Tower of Silence, waiting to get the vulture calls he wanted. He realized, as did everyone else, that what he had recorded didn't sound particularly like vultures, nor did it sound as ferocious as we wanted vultures to be. He said these are absolutely authentic sounds, but clearly they are of no use to us. So, as I recall it, we sat in Vinod's bedroom one night as he created different sounds. He selected some other sounds altogether—nothing to do with vultures—mixed them, processed them and produced something that gave you goosebumps. These technological processes were not as easy to execute in those days as they are today.

Sunil Shanbag

Vinod Doshi, who had given Dubey Walchand Terrace in the first place, remained a very close friend and supporter. Many of the post-show parties would happen at his place. They didn't happen every time, but there were a lot of them. And at Vinod's place, they were very lavish. Very comfortable. He had this large house just off Peddar Road—Neela House. He had a lovely flat and he would just throw it open to everyone. There would be the best food and the best alcohol. We would stay on till very late. People used to fall asleep there and Saryu Bhabhi wouldn't mind at all.

Vinod used to also double up as a sound person for many theatre groups. He used to record sound for them. He was a very enthusiastic sound recordist. And he would get the best recording equipment because he used to travel a lot abroad. In those days, we used spool tapes; so all your music was played back on very large spool machines. To have a set-up in which you could record sound, speak into a microphone etc. at home was quite amazing. I remember I saw my first video tape at Vinod's house. I couldn't believe it. I remember he put this huge thing into a machine and said, 'Now watch this movie.' And I was like, 'Oh my god! To actually watch a movie on a television screen!' This was sometime in the seventies. Between '74 and '79 we spent a lot of time at Vinod's place.

Saryu Doshi

Walchand Terrace was a piece of property that had been purchased by the Walchand Group for their officers. So when the building was built, the flats were sold at very nominal rates to all their officers and they had kept this one floor on the ground for their offices or anything else that the space might be required for. That is why it was available.

It was a big hall that you could compartmentalize for making offices if need be. There were smaller rooms on the side that could be used as cabins. There were toilets and a small kitchenette too. It was all in all, maybe, about 1,200 to 1,500 square feet.

We had once gone to see a Hindi play, I think it was (Girish) Karnad's *Yayati*. After the play, we met Jaswanti Tahiliani. Her husband was Admiral Tahiliani of the Indian Navy. She said, 'All these people are coming over to my place, why don't you come along?' We were free, so we went along. She had a flat in line with the Taj at Apollo Bunder. Everyone from the cast and Theatre Unit was there. Soon everyone was chatting, laughing, shouting and reciting poems. After a point, Vinod and Satyadev got talking and Vinod expressed his interest in theatre. Satyadev began to tell him that the biggest problem theatre was facing was that there was no space for rehearsal. That is where the idea of Walchand Terrace began.

I knew Vijaya (Jaywant-Khote-Mehta) from my school days. Shashank, Vinod's brother, was doing something for her at the time. We had gone to see her play *Chairs.* That was where we met Arvind Deshpande and he expressed the same sentiment—experimental theatre had no place to rehearse. We began to meet all these people quite often and we chatted with them and got to know them better and they all started coming to our house. Soon we got very closely involved with their theatre. So Vinod said let me see what I can do.

Vinod used to have an office in Walchand Terrace, but then they had to move to Construction House, and the Walchand Terrace space had fallen vacant. So he said to Satyadev, 'I will give you this space but I cannot promise it to you for a long time. You can use it till such time as we require it.' Whether he promised the same thing to Arvind, I don't know, but Satyadev moved into that space and started living there. Then slowly, over the next four or five years, it developed into an adda. People knew they could count on meeting each other there and that there would always be something going on. And that is how it became an important hub. Vinod had given the space to Satyadev out of the generosity of his heart. He had no clue that he was doing something 'important'.

How important a part Walchand Terrace would play in the development of experimental theatre was not evident to us at the time. It was only when Girish Karnad dedicated a play to it that we realized it. He wrote to Vinod saying, 'I would have liked to dedicate this play to you but it would have embarrassed you greatly. So I have dedicated it to the place you gave to us.'

I think it was in 1971 or '72 that Shashank said he wanted the space for his studio. That was when Satyadev was asked to release it. After he lost Walchand, Satyadev moved into our house. He stayed with us for three-four years.

The Lead Actor: Satyadev Dubey

Photo courtesy: Theatre Unit Archives

Satyadev Dubey was at the centre of Hindi and Marathi theatre as head of Theatre Unit at Bhulabhai Desai Memorial Institute, Walchand Terrace and Chhabildas School Hall. He was born in Bilaspur in Madhya Pradesh and graduated in English from St Xavier's College, Mumbai. He had dreamt of being selected for the college cricket team; but when he failed to make the grade, he moved to theatre, inspired, particularly by his fellow student and friend, Vijay (Goldie) Anand. Besides doing new plays in Hindi, Marathi, Gujarati and later in English, he was instrumental in creating a network of playwrights and directors across the country, thus infusing new energy into Mumbai's theatre. He was also a guru to at least four generations of young actors and directors.

Dubey was a recipient of the Sangeet Natak Akademi Award (1971) and the National Award (1978) for best screenplay. He passed away in December 2011, at the age of seventy-five.

Sunil Shanbag

Dina Pathak was one of the people who had visited my residential school, Rishi Valley, to do theatre with the kids there. I was about fourteen when I got to know her. I did my first Hindi play with her. As we got to know each other better, she asked to me come over and meet her daughter Ratna (Pathak-Shah) during my holidays. I did that and we became great friends.

On one of the many afternoons I spent at Ratna's place, the doorbell rang, and a slightly crazy-looking gentleman walked in. He said, 'Ratna beta, do you have any serious reading?' She said, 'Let me see Dubey Kaka,' or something like that. He said, 'I'm looking for comics.' She gave him some comics and he went inside and that was it. As he was passing by, she quickly introduced me to him. He said hello and went away. I didn't see him for the rest of the afternoon. That was my first encounter with Dubey. This must have been in 1973.

About six months earlier, during my holidays, Ratna had said, 'There are some plays happening at Tejpal.' We both went to see them. I remember we got student concession at the time so it was very cheap for us. I saw two of Dubey's plays, and I remember being completely blown. The first was a play called *Anushthan* (Ritual for a God). It was very, very abstract, a very physical-theatre type of play. It was very intense, rigorously choreographed, very tight. There were about twenty to twenty-five of us in the audience. When it got over and the lights came on, we looked at each other and then we clapped. Nobody knew that the play had ended. It was that kind of a play.

I didn't go to see *Aadhe Adhure* the next day. We went on the third day to see *Hayavadana.* This play just completely blew me. I couldn't believe that this too could be a form of theatre. It had amazing performers. Amrish Puri and Amol Palekar played the two men. Sunila Pradhan played the woman. Dinaben played Kali Ma. So it was a big cast and quite an amazing performance. Then, as we were leaving, Ratna hurriedly pointed Dubey out to me as the director of the plays we had seen.

About a week or ten days after that afternoon at Ratna's place, she called me and said, 'Listen Sunil, Dubey's casting for a play and he wants to know if you'd be interested.' I had a lot of free time on hand. So when this offer came, I said, of course I want to act in this play. I wanted to work with Dubey, not knowing what I was letting myself in for! A couple of days later, I got a call from Amrish Puri. In that deep voice of his he said, 'You stand on the road and I'll pick you up.' He used to ride a motorcycle with a side-car in those days. He stayed quite close to my house in Santacruz, near the station, but he used to work as the branch manager of the Employee State Insurance Corporation, Colaba. That was his day job. In the evenings he did theatre. He had not made it in films at that time. He was one of Dubey's main actors.

Dubey was doing a play called *Garbo,* written by Mahesh Elkunchwar. Dr Lagoo had done it in Marathi, but it hadn't worked very well. I was taken to this old house in Andheri, in Dhake Colony, which turned out to be Sunila Pradhan's house. But she was in the process of shifting to a spanking new bungalow in the Juhu-Vile

Parle Development Scheme. So we rehearsed at her old house for about a week and then shifted to her bungalow. In those days there was civilization only up to Cooper Hospital, Juhu. After that there were the Air India buildings and then it was almost like a wilderness.

Dubey simply took over Sunila's house. Her parents lived with her; but once Dubey came, they would go upstairs. The house had large rooms. Dubey would turn up and then just take over. Once he came over, nobody was allowed to speak loudly. Sunila had dogs who would bark incessantly and that would drive Dubey crazy. So they had to be shut up. It was almost as if the house existed for Dubey and not the owners! But yes, that became a very important rehearsal and party space for a good five or six years.

I got to know the 'beautiful people' of Juhu through Dubey: Protima Bedi, Kuki Anand, Parveen Babi. I saw all those relationships coming together and unravelling before my eyes, the LSD trips, all of it. So my view of cultural life in this city at that time was completely through Dubey. He always needed a companion wherever he went. For the first five or six years, I was his companion. I went everywhere with him. I remember my mother saying to him one day, 'Okay Dubey, we have donated our son to you.'

It was only after we started working at Chhabildas that I started getting a sense of the larger theatre scene. We weren't working in isolation any more. Dubey knew a lot of people, of course. He had a lot of contacts. But that phase was when things had broken down a lot for him. He was really trying very hard to rebuild Theatre Unit because the old Theatre Unit had gotten completely fragmented. People like Amol (Palekar), for instance, had moved away. I remember Amol was associate director for *Hayavadana*. In fact, after a point, Dubey let go of it and Amol used to run it. It was my first experience of Dubey's work and some time later, I started doing sound for *Hayavadana.* That's when I started travelling with the troupe. Amol had moved away, he had formed his own group. Chitra Palekar had also moved away. Similarly, a lot of other people had moved away to work independently, or had fallen by the wayside or whatever. Also,

Dubey used to quarrel with people all the time. Today he'd be friends with someone, the next day they'd be out of his life.

Perhaps the breakdown of Theatre Unit coincided with the loss of the Walchand space. I got to know about Walchand not through Dubey, but Sunila. She would tell me about it. Dubey had this big thing about not looking back at the past, the glory days, etc. But I used to wish I had started working with him five years earlier. Because one always felt that he had crossed his real peak after that. You heard such amazing stories about the things that happened at Walchand. But every generation feels that way, that they missed the moment, the golden age. But there is no such thing as the golden age, right? So he would mention Walchand in passing but never really talk about it. There must have been bitterness. I'm sure there was some; because from what I heard, he had run that place. He was like a little zamindar of the place. Then they had to take it away and I don't think the circumstances of the taking away were particularly pleasant. Within the Walchand family there was a division of assets or whatever you might call it. And the person who got the space wanted to do something else with it.

Dubey would never talk about Bhulabhai either. He just refused to look back. Sometimes in fact, I wish he would talk about the past. Not as a nostalgic trip, but from a historical point of view. There may have been conversations. For instance, until the very end, he would talk about this one person called P. D. Shenoy, who had been a great influence on him. But that was at the Bhulabhai Institute. He talked about the individual, never about the space.

In that transition time when I started working with Dubey, he was actually trying to create venues for himself. He was performing where he could. Tejpal was one of those places. It was a big space for us—a 600-seater. We would barely have twenty-five to thirty people in the audience. But Dubey used to get it reasonably cheap. He was very friendly with the manager. The technical person at Tejpal was Dharamsey Merchant, who became a very close colleague of Dubey's for a few years. In fact Dubey got him to be the first manager at

Prithvi. It was a kind of Becket situation—Dubey placed him at Prithvi and then, over time, Dharamsey became, justifiably so, more loyal to Prithvi. When Dubey had a scrap with Prithvi, Dharamsey chose to be with Prithvi. So it was a typical Becket situation.

I also remember doing performances at Ravindra Natya Mandir, again, a big hall. One night, we performed at Bhaidas Auditorium in Vile Parle. It was a very, very rainy night. The city was flooded and about six people showed up. We were doing *Garbo.* Fortunately for us, one of the people in the audience was the actor Premnath. He sent a cheque for ten thousand rupees to us the next day saying, 'This is to cover your losses.' So when Chhabildas came, it was a huge change.

During the transition period between Walchand and Chhabildas, the performances dwindled. I don't know how Dubey managed for money in those days. He always had some money coming in from his family property in Bilaspur. But he had a big support network in Mumbai too.

Amol Palekar

How I came into theatre and met Dubey is quite a story. I am an actor by sheer accident. Dubey was rehearsing (Girish) Karnad's *Yayati* and had cast Chitra (Palekar) in it. My sole job then was to ferry her to and back from rehearsals. I remember my first meeting with Dubey vividly. There was a godown behind Babulnath temple which belonged to the Indian National Theatre (INT). Dubey was rehearsing there. Till then I had only heard of him. When I arrived, I saw a thick-haired, short-statured, boyish man dressed in shorts. One of the first things I noticed was the thick cane he was carrying as he paced the floor restlessly. This was my first impression of Dubey. A weird-looking man in weird clothes, waiting to rehearse a play with a cane in his hand. I met him later at the Bhulabhai Institute and in several other places because at that time he hadn't found a place to settle down in. Walchand Terrace had not entered his life. Then, when he was casting for Gynandev Agnihotri's play, *Shuturmurg*

(Ostrich), he asked me if I would act in it. Before I could say yes or no, he added, 'Please don't be under the impression that I have seen some great talent in you. It's nothing of the kind. I've been observing you and you seem to have a lot of free time on your hands. So why don't you use that free time for something better?' I felt like saying yes to his proposal because I had seen his work and his method of working. I still remember the first show of *Yayati*. It was staged in the open air at Rangabhavan. Girish Karnad had come to see it. I realized I was seeing something very different from what I had seen till then in Marathi theatre. I wouldn't have been able to say then what the difference was, but I sensed it strongly.

Dubey was a terror. His actors used to literally tremble before him. I have personally seen his mere entry into a room making the best talents break out in a sweat. But I never had that kind of fear of him; perhaps because I did not aim to become an actor. At the same time, it is also true, though it is difficult to say why, that Dubey gave me a lot of love. Despite being young and inexperienced, I was one of the few people who could tell Dubey not to shout so much because it scared poor Gajanan Bangera out of his wits, making him forget his lines. That I could say this and that Dubey would quietly hear me out was perhaps one part of our relationship.

Although Dubey was short-tempered as a director, he would also go deep into a play and patiently explain the ideas behind it very logically, down to the smallest nuances. What I felt then and feel even more intensely now, looking back, was that Dubey's biggest contribution was the generosity with which he gave what he had to everybody who worked with him. He would shout, curse, occasionally even throw a chair at you, but behind it all was his passion for getting his idea across. 'How is it that you don't understand what I'm trying to tell you so desperately? Please understand what I'm saying and bring it into practice.' That is why even when actors feared him (and I have seen some sob quite openly), none bore a grudge against him. His intense love for theatre was there for all to see.

Dubey taught us to love the word. He used forms like essays and poems to do this. When we saw other plays and had hot discussions about them at Walchand Terrace, Dubey would make us analyze precisely why we had liked what we had liked or why we had thought XYZ's performance had not worked. He would make us tear the play to shreds to get at what we had felt about it. This produced in us a sharp awareness of every dimension of theatre. This would happen at Walchand Terrace every day, all 365 days. This was around 1967-68.

In 1969, Dubey asked me to direct *Vallabhpurchi Dantakatha,* a translation of Badal Sircar's *Ballabhpurer Roopkatha.* I had already learned Bengali. My first solo show of paintings was inspired by Tagore's *Gitanjali.* I had felt then that I should read it in the original rather than in translation. I loved learning languages, so I learned Bengali. Knowing this, Dubey had asked me to translate the play into Marathi. 'We might do it,' he had said. I got to know later that he had wanted, for a long time, to do a Marathi play and this was going to be the first. When he read my translation he decided we would definitely do it for Theatre Unit and he asked me to direct it. I was taken aback. I was barely three plays old. I protested that I didn't know the first thing about direction. He said, 'So what? At the most you'll do a bad job. Do it.' Later he said, 'Let's do one thing. We'll direct it together.' Seeing me looking pleased he said, 'And listen. We will be jointly credited for direction with my name coming first since I'm senior to you, followed by yours. But I don't intend doing a thing. You will be solely responsible. When you are ready, I will see it. If it's a bad job, I'll throw it out and make a fresh start. If this is acceptable to you, direct it.'

There was no reason why I wouldn't accept the deal. I started rehearsals and Dubey kept his word and didn't turn up for a single one. But he did inquire on and off if I needed anything, and if I had any problems. I recall him telling me in the course of these conversations, 'Remember one thing Amol,' he said, '*Vallabhpurchi Dantakatha* is not a farce. It is a situational comedy. A farce is over-the-top and that's the fun of it. But don't turn this play into a farce.'

I asked him if something I had said or was doing had given him the feeling I might do this. But he said it wasn't that. He only wanted me to keep what he had said at the back of my mind. It was in these subtle ways that he kept giving the play direction. When he finally saw it, he told us we had done a good job. I asked him if he wanted to change anything. He said he didn't. He only wanted to know when we should stage it. It so happened that the State Drama Competition was coming up soon. We entered the play for it and won all the prizes.

Once an organization called India Cultural League approached me to select and direct any play I liked as their entry for the State Drama Competition. I told them I would have to take Dubey's permission before giving them my answer. When I asked Dubey for permission, he said the question of permission didn't arise. 'Someone has asked you to direct a play, so say yes.'

'But which play should I do? I haven't a clue.'

'Is that right?'

With that he went into the inner room of Walchand Terrace and came out with a script. It was Surendra Verma's *Draupadi.* 'Read that and direct it if you like it.'

This was Verma's very first play. He had sent it to Dubey for feedback. I read it and liked it. Dubey said, 'Do it then.' Here was an established director and someone who ran a theatre group to boot, handing over a good new play for me to direct for some outside organization. I know of no other man in his position who would have done something like that, not then, not after. The most notable thing about this Marathi production was that it came before it was done in Hindi. It took Hindi theatre people a long time to recognize the new playwright.

After *Draupadi*, Verma read out his second play to me. It was, in Marathi translation, *Suryasthachya Antim Kiranapasun Suryodayachya Pahilya Kiranaparyant* (From the Last Ray of the Setting Sun to the First Ray of the Rising Sun). I liked this play too and again the Marathi production came before the Hindi. When I started rehearsing the play, Dubey said to me, 'You must form your own group now. You won't grow in my shadow beyond this. And let this play be the first under your group's banner.'

Very few people would allow a young group member to move out in this fashion, set him free and encourage him to grow under an open sky. In all my experience of how theatre groups operated, whether it was in Bombay, Pune or Nagpur, I had never come across such generosity. It was unique to Dubey.

Gerson da Cunha

I recall Satyadev Dubey vividly. He was a close associate of Alkazi's. Theirs was an extraordinary relationship because Dubey had, very much, a chip on his shoulder about English-language theatre vis-à-vis Indian-language theatre. Despite his great antagonism to English, he ended up directing and producing many plays in English. But I recall him vividly because he was a person you could not easily forget. He was an enormous bundle of energy. He was always ready for an argument but not a violent one. His arguments would be a contest of ideas. Dubey's great contribution in the end was as a playwright, but his productions were not to be dismissed by any means. He was a great director. He was a very creative director. For example, take *Dear Liar* (Jerome Kilty). There is the exchange of letters going on between George Bernard Shaw and Lady Patrick Campbell, and Dubey, as chorus of the play, suddenly arrives, saying to the actor playing Shaw, 'The Queen my lord is dead,' which is the news that the messenger brings at the end of *Macbeth*. Here, of course, the news is that Lady Patrick Campbell has died! The creative gap that he bridged by bringing the two together was the kind of thing that Dubey was capable of. I didn't see this play at the Bhulabhai but at the Experimental Theatre at NCPA.

Saryu Doshi

Around 1973, when Walchand Terrace went to Shashank and Dubey was staying with us, he had decided to take up a job with Lintas. He had also decided to give up his column in the papers. On learning this, my son, who was only eleven years old, was shattered! Dubey was his idol. He said to him, 'You are taking up a Lintas job?'

Satyadev did take up that job. I am not sure what happened, but it didn't work out. Then, for a while, he decided to work with Mahesh Bhatt. After that he had sort of moved away from us, maybe out of resentment that Walchand was not there for him anymore. He went to Shyam (Benegal) and Nira's and he was there for a while. So he was also in a state of flux, going through some instability in his own mind about what he wanted to do, where he wanted to take his life from then on.

When he was living with us, he would keep saying things like, 'Now that I have no space', 'Now that the space is gone', almost as though the space had been his and we had taken it away! I think when he moved away, he was also trying to show us that he was getting on with his life, that he was shifting his loyalties, which I think was quite childish of him. That was Dubey. But he always counted us amongst his close friends. On his birthday he would invite five or six of us women to lunch!

Every Sunday people would come over to our place, so many of them, from around eleven in the morning to eight-thirty at night, talking, discussing, fighting. I remember this one time Dubey got very drunk and said something to me that I didn't mind but Vinod got very angry over. So Vinod said, 'You are not going to talk to my wife like that.' Dubey screamed, 'What do you mean, she is also my friend!' They had a huge fight over that, and Dubey walked out and we had to send people running after him to bring him back. I think that was the first break in Vinod and Satyadev's friendship. After that, somehow, it was never the same.

All in all, however, that was a very nice time in our lives. That bohemian lifestyle was very important, especially for Vinod, because otherwise he was in a very stultifying corporate atmosphere. Finally, he also became the corporate man. That atmosphere was so overpowering, that you had to conform!

Girish Karnad

When I came back from Oxford, I saw a lot of the actor Farida Sonavala in Bombay. She told me there was this person, Satyadev Dubey, why didn't I go and see him? So I went and met him at Bhulabhai Desai. It was not a propitious meeting. Satyadev was fairly antagonistic from the word go. Snarly. He wouldn't tell me what was bothering him. We talked for about ten to fifteen minutes and suddenly he turned around and said, 'What's the point of writing all these plays in English? Who are you writing for? How can you express Indian culture in English?' So I said, 'I don't know, but I haven't written them in English. I have written them in Kannada.' Suddenly, his face fell. He looked as though he'd been beaten. He looked around and said, 'Okay, okay, you read the plays to me and then we'll see.'

I read out *Yayati* to him, translating it into English directly from Kannada. I am quite good at doing that. He listened to it and commented on the imagery. This time he was very sympathetic. He had warmed to me. Once I finished, he said, 'I would like to put this on stage.' He was the first man to tell me that my play was stageable. But it took him three more years to do it. He actually produced it in 1967. By that time, the National School of Drama had already produced *Tughlaq*. Satyadev was very angry because B. V. Karanth had delayed the translation. 'Now look, the credit has gone to Alkazi,' he said. But when he read *Tughlaq*, he was bowled over. He said it was like an RSS (Rashtriya Swayamsevak Sangh) tract. Everything that the RSS had been saying was there in *Tughlaq*.

So anyway, he did *Yayati* and to me it was a brilliant production. Sunila Pradhan was Devayani, Tarla Mehta was Sharmishtha and Sulabha Deshpande was playing the dasi. Apparently, when Satyadev had asked her to do Devayani's role, she had said, 'I am not sexy enough,' or something to that effect. Satyadev had thrown up his hands and said 'Oof these Marathi women! What can you do with them!' But with Sunila, there was no problem at all. Apparently, whoever designed the costumes for the play wanted the women to be bare-shouldered and the other women were going, 'Arey nahi…kasa karaycha' (Please no. How can we do that?). Sunila said, 'Oh, bare shoulders? Okay, bare shoulders!' So after that everyone followed suit. Satyadev was Puru and Amrish (Puri) was Yayati. I was completely enamoured of that production. A lot that was lacking in the play was made up by Amrish's presence.

Dr Shreeram Lagoo

I met Dubey at a time when a huge transformation had taken place in my life. I had returned from Africa, given up my medical practice and decided to make theatre my profession. I was doing the role of Sambhaji in Vasant Kanetkar's *Raigadala Jenwha Jaag Yete* (When Fort Raigad Wakes Up), produced by Prabhakar Panshikar's company. I wasn't terribly interested in playing Sambhaji. Dubey came for one show. He had gone into my background discovering that I had worked with Vijaya Mehta and Bhalba Kelkar, head of the Progressive Dramatic Association in Pune. This meant that I really belonged to the off-mainstream theatre. At the end of the show, he came backstage to see me. I was still in my Sambhaji costume. I had heard of him as the head of a group called Theatre Unit. When he asked me if I would act in his play, I told him I would if it was a good play. He said it was *Aadhe Adhure*, translated from Hindi by (Vijay) Tendulkar. That was my first role with him. After that everything between us was smooth sailing.

Alyque Padamsee

Dubey was always a rebel. He always said, 'Unless I have a rival, unless I have someone to envy, unless there is someone I am jealous of, I don't feel any energy. I need that khunnas!' There was something he said because of which I was very distressed at that time and there were many others who were too. He said, 'English theatre! I will bury the English theatre!' Then in his later years, I don't know if he mellowed or if he changed his mind, but he suddenly started doing plays in English. So anyway…that was good fun and we took it in the right spirit because Dubey was a very charming fellow. Very egotistical, but very charming. He might fight with you today but tomorrow he would smile at you and you would smile back and then you were sitting down to have a cup of tea!

I remember I was doing a Hindi version of Arthur Miller's *All My Sons.* We had already started rehearsals and I was working with a very brilliant Urdu playwright called Rifat Shamim and I think we had a really workable script. It was based in India. The play had been adapted. We also had some very good actors, including Shaukat Kaifi. It was called *Sara Sansar Apna Parivar.* At the same time, Dubey was doing a version with a brilliant actor who later became a very successful romantic film actor—Sanjeev Kumar. He acted in the film *Aandhi* (Storm, dir. Gulzar). So anyway, Dubey was doing a version of the same play. And we ran both the plays. I ran mine and he ran his. Mine was rehearsed at the Bhulabhai Institute. So yes, those were exciting times.

Shyam Benegal

Satyadev Dubey wanted my wife, who was not my wife then, to do costumes for his play because he felt she had great taste. So he was acquainted with Nira before she was acquainted with me. Dubey would always remind me of that! She introduced me to him. He had made a short film in which he put Nira in as one of the actors. He had actually come here with ambitions of joining the film industry. He had been to Xavier's College and he had been friends with Vijay Anand. He was even with Navketan (a production house started by Dev Anand and his elder brother Chetan Anand) for a bit. But later, he gave it up and concentrated on theatre. His interest in films continued peripherally until he got back into the thick of films when I made *Ankur* (The Seedling). Then he started to write for me. But he was making his own small films on the side. (Vijay) Tendulkar's *Shantata! Court Chalu Ahe* was made into a film by him and Govind Nihalani, who was the cameraman for my first eleven feature films.

G. P. Deshpande

My first meeting with Dubey was at Sai Paranjpye's place in Delhi. It was a drinks and dinner party. Dubey was always an avaliya—a maverick—and came to Sai's place as one, carrying a poem in his pocket. When Kavita Nagpal came to the party, he whipped out the poem and announced, 'Here's a kavita for Kavita,' and proceeded to read it. That's my first memory of him.

My second memory is of talking to him about my response to his film *Shantata! Court Chalu Ahe*. In the course of that conversation, we also agreed that the government should build a small auditorium in every district and taluka exclusively for serious, non-commercial theatre. Its capacity should be such that the professional theatre would not be attracted to it. Dubey urged me to write an article about this idea, which I did. That article, my first, was published in the magazine *Manus*. Like my first play, this too was written at Dubey's insistence. I once asked him why he didn't cast me in one of his plays. His reply was, 'I respect you so much that I would never be able to abuse you and scream at you. How can I cast you in my plays?'

When he asked me next what I was writing, I was trying to write a novel. Discussing the problem I was having with it, I mentioned that the material might find a more suitable form in a play. He urged me then to start writing the play. *Uddhwasta Dharmashala* was written in two separate parts. All the inquiry scenes were written together and all the personal scenes written together. During the time I was writing it, Dubey mentioned that he was planning to hold a playwrights' workshop. He asked me to meet him next time I was in Mumbai with what I had written.

Sure enough when I met him in Mumbai, he asked me how far I'd gotten with the play. I told him I'd written the inquiry scenes. He took me to Otter's Club and said, 'You're going to drink beer with me and read what you've written. My reaction will depend on whether you are able to continue reading after three beers or not.' I objected to the plan. I told him I wouldn't allow beer to decide whether my play was good or bad. If that's the idea, I said, I'd rather just drink the beer and forget the play. At which he withdrew all stipulations and asked me to read. So I read the inquiry scenes to him. His mood changed. 'This is a play. It's going to be a very good play. You must come to Pune for my workshop.' 'But I live in Delhi,' I demurred. 'So come from Delhi. I won't give you your travel expenses. Spend your own money and come. When you arrive you'll get one day to visit your relatives or whoever else. You will stay the rest of the time with the group. That too will cost you money which you will pay.' He then added that he wanted Dr Lagoo to hear the play, so he would schedule my reading on one of the two days when he was going to be present. 'You have a month in hand,' he said. 'Finish writing the play in that time.' 'Let's see,' I said. 'No seeing. I'm going to tell him about the play, so it had better be ready by then.'

After my reading at the workshop, Dr Lagoo asked me if I had promised the play to anybody. Of course I hadn't, because I didn't know any directors. I told him he could have it if he wished. I had some doubts about that. The response to the few readings I had done was that *Uddhwasta* wasn't a play at all. When Vidyadhar Pundalik, the playwright, came to Delhi, he too said it wasn't a play. 'Listen to me. I have some knowledge about theatre. There are some passages of bright dialogue and good commentary in this thing that you've written, but it's not a play.' I said to him, 'I am not trying to convince anybody that it is. I have written something I wanted to write. If somebody wants to stage it, why should I object?'

Dr Lagoo offered to do the play and did it. In short, what I'm trying to say is that none of this would have happened had Dubey not entered my life.

Dilip Kolhatkar

I consider Dubey my second guru along with Vijayabai (Mehta). If you see the advertisement of Shankar Shesh's play, *The Steel Frame*, you will see my name as producer. Dubey trained me to handle every part of play-making, including production. Another important thing

Dubey taught me was how to use the strengths of each actor. You had to spot the plus points of an actor within three or four rehearsals and then build on them. It was Dubey again who gave me the opportunity to do the light design for a play of his. Later, I lit every one of Vijayabai's plays. My light design for Jaywant Dalvi's *Barrister*, in particular, came in for a lot of praise.

I discovered on one occasion that Dubey was over-conscientious. Once we were late for a show of *Steel Frame*. The show should have started at eight and we arrived at nine-thirty. There had been some problem on the railway track and our train had been held up. When the organizer rushed towards us angrily, Dubey pointed to me and said, 'He's the producer.' I explained what had happened to the organizer and offered to make an announcement to that effect before the show. The show went off well. But throughout that time, Dubey did not admit to being Dubey!

Another time I arrived late from Dombivali for a morning show of a play at Tejpal. I explained that I came by train all the way from Dombivali and the train was delayed. He demanded to know if I was expecting him to sympathize with me. He said, 'You are a professional. You should know what time to leave your house. You might arrive three hours too early, but that's better than this.' Then he went on to a different track. He said, 'Talk to me about coming by train from Dombivali. In the train, you sit by the window or stand by the door with not a soul around who knows you. You get a whole hour-and-a-half to think. That's why your plays are so good. I don't get more than the ten minutes I spend in the toilet to think.'

Sunila Pradhan

My husband, Dr Vijaykumar Pradhan, pushed me into acting. I was married early and soon had two children. My husband is a doctor so he was always busy. I was getting bored sitting at home. My husband knew someone who belonged to an amateur theatre group in Andheri. They were doing a play for a competition and needed a female actor. My husband suggested I do the role. That's where it all began.

Dubey was doing *Yayati.* I was acting in a play directed by Arvind Deshpande around that time. Sulabha Deshpande would drop in during rehearsals. She was playing the role of the dasi in *Yayati*, and Rekha Sabnis was playing Devayani. With eight days to go for the first show, Rekha fell ill and had to be replaced. Sulabha suggested my name but told Dubey she didn't know how good my Hindi was. They decided to try me out all the same. I was asked to go to Sulabha's place for rehearsals. I went. She wasn't at home, but this man with unruly hair and sharp eyes opened the door to me. I said I'm Sunila Pradhan. He said, yes, I'm Dubey. Come in. He handed me a passage to read. After I read the first line he said right, come for rehearsals from tomorrow.

I went. Everybody else knew their lines and their moves. I was blank. Dubey said, 'Don't look right or left. Just sit there and learn your lines. I'm not going to direct you. Your personality suits the role. Just say the lines and I will tell you your moves.' Rehearsals began. My acting habits had been formed in the kind of theatre where we always faced the audience, whoever it was we were talking to on stage. Dubey said, 'I'm going to sit in front of you with bits of chalk. The minute you look my way, you'll find a piece of chalk coming at you.' It didn't take long for me to lose that habit.

On the night of the first show, the sutradhar entered the stage and went blank. I was waiting to take my entry. But unless he said his lines, I couldn't. And there he was circling around the stage giving himself time to remember but still nothing came. Dubey was beside himself. Standing next to me, he was hitting his head against the wall. He looked at me for a second, smiled, and continued to hit his head against the wall.

That was my first experience of Dubey—hitting me with bits of chalk and hitting his own head against the wall. Then Rekha decided to produce *Yayati* in Marathi. Dr Lagoo was to act in it. Dubey suggested I should be asked for Devayani. So I did that role in the Marathi production too. The rehearsals for this were going to be at Walchand Terrace. That's when I first set foot in that place.

We rehearsed the Marathi *Yayati*, Mohan Rakesh's *Aadhe Adhure* and Shankar Shesh's *The Steel Frame* there. During rehearsals, Dubey would sit in the small side room behind the partition. Sometimes he would even sleep. But somehow he always caught a wrong note in what we were saying. When that happened, we would hear him roar, 'Mind your sur. You are off-key.' The right key and pitch were very important for Dubey. When we were rehearsing *Aadhe Adhure*, he told me to lower the pitch of my voice by two notes during rehearsals. The pitch would then rise one note on stage. My husband told me I was speaking like Dubey. Everybody who acted in his plays sounded like him.

When I worked with other directors, they would say, all right now walk to that window, now sit, now stand. Dubey didn't do that. He would tell me to do what I instinctively felt was right. Only if he thought the move was wrong would he correct it. 'If you want to move, move. If you want to sit down, sit. If you want to stand and say a line, do that. But let the line come from within,' he would say. For him the thing that counted most was whether the feeling in the line was coming through genuinely.

His other insistence was on understanding every nuance of meaning that a given line could yield. When we were rehearsing *Garbo*, he made us read the script over and over again. For two months we only read. And I was amazed at our interpretation of the play when we staged it compared to what we thought it meant when we started. We rehearsed just lines for eight months in Badal Sircar's *Saari Raat* (Whole Night). The rehearsals were at my place. Amrish Puri would land up there at eight in the morning, because he had to go to work after the rehearsal. My family were late risers. So when he came on his bike waking us up rudely, even our dog would bark angrily at this disturbance of the peace. We'd rehearse between eight and nine-thirty, just speaking the lines over and over. 'The movements will come,' Dubey would say, 'when you understand what you're saying.' We would rehearse more in the evenings when Amrish returned from work.

Later when Amrish joined films, he bore all the costs of our plays. But he had very little time to rehearse. That's when Dubey chose to direct two sets of three monologues one after the other—Vasant Deo's *Aranya* (Forest) and Nirmal Verma's *Teen Ekant* (Three Solitaires). Being monologues, they could be rehearsed individually so time schedules of every actor could be considered.

In G. P. Deshpande's *Andhar Yatra* (Pilgrimage in the Dark), another aspect of Dubey's relationship with his actors and writers emerged. I was very quick at learning lines. I had all my lines in this play by heart too, except for one passage. I couldn't understand why I wasn't able to memorize it. Dubey asked me why, after a whole month of having the script with me, I was missing those lines. I too was angry with myself. Thinking about it I realized that the scene was badly written and told Dubey so. I didn't know G.P.D was sitting there. Had I known, perhaps I wouldn't have said what I did. But Dubey said to him, 'This is an actor's instinct speaking, so can you rewrite the scene?' It was G.P.D's generosity of understanding that he agreed to do so. And when the scene was rewritten it took me no time at all to get it pat.

But Dubey himself wasn't a good playwright. He wrote wonderful dialogue, although it was very long-winded and wordy. I acted in one of his plays, *Aada Chautal* (The Fourteen-beat Cycle), directed by Sunil Shanbag. It was not a good play. I often hinted to Dubey that he shouldn't write plays. But I'm sure, even if I'd told him openly instead of merely hinting, it would have made no difference to him.

Hemu Adhikari

We used to see all of Dubey's plays but we feared him. I remember we had gone to Birla Matoshree Auditorium one morning to buy tickets for something and Dubey was sitting outside. He was wearing a white shirt, off-white trousers, white shoes and socks and was carrying a cane. That is the image of Dubey I still carry in my head. We used to be terrified of him because he was a terror. So there was no way we were going to go backstage to meet him after seeing one of his plays.

Deepa Shreeram

Dubey was a very generous man. I recall that a young boy called Hattangadi used to come to Walchand. He was a very good tabla player. He was very keen to work with us. Dubey too had decided to take him on. But his mother called Dubey and said, 'This boy isn't studying. He just loafs around.' Dubey went over to the boy's place and told him, if you don't study, I won't let you come to Walchand. That was not all. Dubey got after him and made him do his work. If I remember right, he later joined a catering management institute. This is how Dubey helped people.

The Constant Supporter: Dr Kumudini Arvind Mehta

Photo courtesy: Malvika Chari

Dr Kumudini Arvind Mehta was an extremely important presence on the theatre scene in the city during the seventies and eighties. She particularly encouraged experimental work by the new generation of directors. She translated several plays from Marathi into English, chief amongst them being C. T. Khanolkar's *Ek Shoonya Bajirao* as *Bajirao the Cipher* and Vijay Tendulkar's *Sakharam Binder* in collaboration with Shanta Gokhale. As a member of the censor board in the seventies, she helped free many controversial plays, like Tendulkar's *Sakharam Binder*, from the clutches of conservative members.

Dr Kumud Mehta's most significant contribution to theatre scholarship is her PhD thesis, *English Drama on the Bombay Stage in the Late Eighteenth Century and Nineteenth Century*, which has been cited in several scholarly works on theatre. As the first Joint Director of the National Centre for the Performing Arts, she edited the highly influential *NCPA Quarterly Journal* to which some of the most eminent scholars in the performing arts contributed.

Achyut Vaze

Although critics are supposed to understand and support experimentation in theatre, I can't say our critics, with a couple of exceptions, did. But there were others around, not critics, who supported us wholeheartedly. Kumud Mehta was one of them. I can't remember exactly when and how I got to know her but we grew to know each other very well. She literally showered me with love. She had given me a large format spiral-bound notebook—in those days spiral binding was very special—in which she had inscribed, 'This is for your new play.' I wrote my *Pavasacha Natak* (The Rain Play) in it. She once nominated me for the (Maharashtra) State Censor Board without asking me about it. When I protested that I stood against censorship, she said that is why I have proposed your name. Similarly, she had proposed the names of many others who were opposed to censorship.

Kumudtai's home was a meeting place not only for theatre people but also for people from various walks of life—academicians, politicians, artists, all sorts. Those conversations were at a different level altogether. We learned a lot from them. That is how a movement grows.

Kamalakar Sarang

(Excerpted from *Binderche Divas*, an account of the censorship problems that *Sakharam Binder* had to face.)

The censor board meeting was scheduled to be held on the fourth of April (1972). We had planned to meet at Kumud Mehta's place the same evening. We reached around seven o'clock. There was nobody at home. (Vijay) Tendulkar came a little later. He had been toying with the idea of taking legal action against the government. He had even hinted at it in his letter to the *Times of India*, titled 'Playwright's Complaint'. If push came to shove, we would have to carry out the threat.

Tendulkar had met Adhik Shirodkar before coming. Adhik Shirodkar was assistant to the well-known legal eagle Sushil Kawlekar. He had worked with him on the *Shyama* case. They had won that case against banning the novel. After Kawlekar's accidental death, Adhik was running his practice. Tendulkar was told that if this case was fought along the lines of the novel, it would take anything from five to six years for it to be settled. This had happened also in the case of Partap Sharma's play *Touch of Brightness*. During the six years it took for the case to arrive at a conclusion, the play had gone stone cold. Naturally, neither Tendulkar nor I wanted this to happen with *Sakharam Binder*. Tendulkar was leaving for America by an early-morning flight on the sixth. So we had barely thirty hours in hand. That is why it was crucial for us to end this impasse. Perhaps we could agree to some of the cuts the censor board was demanding and get on with the play. What was the point of continuing a fight beyond our weight?

Kumudben returned around eight o'clock. Sarojini Vaidya came with her. These two members of the censor board were on our side. We wondered what tidings they had brought us. They sat before us. There was silence for some time. Every second was making my heart pound faster.

'You will have to go to court,' Kumudben said, breaking the silence. Silence descended once again. Unable to bear it, Sarojinibai said, 'So what should we do?'

'If we file a case, it'll take five or six years to be settled,' said Tendulkar.

'We can't hold the cast together till then,' I added.

'One minute,' Kumudben said walking to the phone. Sarojinibai informed us that all the members except she and Kumudben had agreed that *Sakharam Binder* should be banned after the show on the eighth. Returning after her phone conversation, Kumudben said, 'Meet Ashok Desai. I've taken an appointment with him for you for nine o'clock tomorrow morning.' We gathered from her that Ashok Desai practised in the High Court and was a highly successful advocate.

(Ashok Desai later found a legal way to cut short all arguments in the case and suddenly *Sakharam Binder* was free to run.)

Satyadev Dubey

After giving me Walchand Terrace (this was after the Bhulabhai Desai Memorial Institute wound up), Saryu Doshi and Vinod Doshi would invite a lot of people to come and see my plays. Two of them were Kumudben Mehta and her husband Arvindbhai. Saryu kept saying that Kumudben had been a stunner as a young woman. She had joined the Communist Party and so had Arvindbhai. They had done a lot of work for a lot of people, especially for the party. Once I got introduced to Kumudben, and since I was having my late nights and sometimes I wouldn't sleep at Walchand Terrace, I could come any time of the night and sleep on the jhoola in Kumudben's garden and of course, I was guaranteed tea in the morning and some sort of breakfast. Kumudben and Saryu Doshi helped me to write the application form for the Homi Bhabha Fellowship which finally, thanks to their pressure, I submitted to the committee and received.

What I remember of Kumudben was also her son who would be there, who was a very good table-tennis player. That was the time when Girish (Karnad), myself, (Vijay) Tendulkar and all, would instinctively end up at Kumudben's place, if we were not going to the Doshi house for a drink or a party. Despite her reservations, she and Arvinbhai would also join the party. Kumudben was very fond of Amol (Palekar). Instinctively going for the youngster, she thought he would bring about the much desired revolution.

Saryu Doshi

I was the one who introduced Kumudben to everyone in Theatre Unit. She had done her post-graduation in English. She used to be at the museum library editing their journal. And I used to go there for my PhD. So we would meet there every day and we became friends. Then one day I said there was a play reading happening at home so why didn't she and Arvindbhai come. Both of them came. That evening (Vijay) Tendulkar and Kumudben became friends. Then soon everyone became friends with her because she was very helpful with looking up references and things like that. But she was particularly good friends with Vijay Tendulkar. She would often ask me if I was going to the museum library because she wanted to look up references for Tendulkar and she would only go if I was going.

G. P. Deshpande

When Kumudben saw *Uddhwasta Dharmashala*, she said, 'There's so much political consciousness in Bengal, but I don't think anybody there has written a political play of this kind.' The post-first-show party was at Kumudben's house and it was a wonderful experience for me. Something rather comic happened at the party. Somebody asked me if I was related to Pu La Deshpande. Before I could answer, Dr Lagoo, who had overheard the question, turned round and said, 'He has no relationship whatsoever with any famous Deshpande of

Maharashtra.' Much as Dr Lagoo loved the play, he had no idea of its politics. For a long time people in Delhi thought the play had to do with the Emergency although it was written and staged before Emergency was declared. Dr Lagoo himself was politically rather unaware. He had wanted the Paris Commune to be explained. Only Kumudben had seen the context which ran parallel to the play. It was Siddharth Shankar Ray's cabinet. Kumudben was never very vocal about her opinions. But if a discussion started, she would participate.

It wasn't in connection with theatre that I had known of Kumudben. I had known of her in the context of Marathi literature and the English language before I entered the theatre world. I knew her as a translator of P. S. Rege's poetry. There was nobody else then who had her understanding of modern Marathi poetry. I too particularly admired P. S. Rege's poetry, and I realized she too was a fellow admirer. One of his collections was dedicated to her in the following words: 'I am sending these few poems to you. This does not mean you should translate them. Not that you can be stopped if you want to. Anyway, these few poems are for you.' Kumudben had a deep understanding of Marathi poetry, particularly poetry that was aware of its classical heritage. I had realized over the years that I too took pride in admiring a certain kind of classicism. This was probably the thread that bound us. There was no personal friendship between us besides this.

Amol Palekar

I feel even words like partner or supporter will prove inadequate in describing Kumudben's contribution to the whole theatre movement of the time. J. R. D. Tata himself had invited her to take charge of the Experimental Theatre in the National Centre for the Performing Arts. But Kumudben was always self-effacing. So one was never sure who or what she was personally, although she and her husband Arvindbhai showered me with love.

I got to know Kumudben through Chitra (Palekar) who was a friend of her son Sanjay. Both were table-tennis players and I frequently watched table-tennis matches. I have a memory which is still fresh in my mind. It was the match I saw between Farrokh Khodaiji, the champion, and Sanjay who was much younger. What a match that was. When I met Kumudben and Arvindbhai I couldn't stop talking about Sanjay's game. So our first and following meetings had nothing to do with theatre.

The Mehtas had a beautiful bungalow on Carmichael Road. They were committed communists and yet they lived in this lovely bungalow in an upmarket area of Mumbai. It looked at first sight like a paradox. Many people even commented on it snidely. But when you saw their lifestyle you knew that no such paradox existed. They were committed leftists who happened to live in this bungalow.

There were constant get-togethers happening at their place. I've attended several play readings and poetry readings there and heard some magnificent concerts of classical music. They were ready to go to the ends of the earth to hear a good concert. Perhaps the fact that I too was always prepared to do that could have been the source of their influence on me. Arvindbhai himself was a very fine harmonium player. There was an innate tunefulness in his fingers. His harmonium playing was a totally different aspect of his life as it was with Pu La Deshpande too.

One day I got a call in the bank from Kumudben. I used to work in a bank then. She asked me what I was doing that evening. I said I was doing nothing in particular. So she said, come over if you can. I didn't ask, and she didn't tell me why. That evening when I went, C. T. Khanolkar was with her. She said he had written a play which she thought I would be the best person to direct. So would I like to hear it? I was more than eager to hear it. So Khanolkar read the play, *Avadhya* (Invincible). After the reading, we had a long, invigorating discussion about it. Even later there were many other discussions at her place about the play. After I did the play, there was a furious protest against it. Madhav Manohar, the critic, had called it the first adult play in Marathi. The protesters called it obscene. The debate continued with the popular playwright, Vasant Kanetkar, criticizing it severely but from a completely mistaken viewpoint which I spoke to him about.

But Kumudben herself had spoken so beautifully about the strengths of the play and why it was an important work that I urged her to put it all down. But she didn't. I seem to remember Dubey writing a small piece about it. Also when Rajinder Paul, the editor-printer of *Enact* asked him who he thought was a promising director from amongst the younger generation, he mentioned my name and also said that after seeing *Avadhya* he had thought hell, if I had managed to direct a play like this, I'd have been a proud man.

Kumudben was also responsible for my accessing some unpublished work of Diwakar, the essayist and writer of dramatic monologues. Once again she called me in the bank and told me that Dr Sarojini Vaidya, who was researching Diwakar's life and work, had come across this material so why didn't I take a look at it. Then Sarojinibai herself called me. I went over, saw the material and decided to stage it. I wanted to do the first show of these theatre pieces in a venue that would give it an intimate feeling. She suggested I do it in NCPA's Little Theatre. That small auditorium was meant for music recitals. Nobody had ever performed a play there. And after Diwakar, I doubt if anybody else did. Kumudben was always on the lookout for new things that could be staged in Marathi and new spaces where they could be performed. We were all in search of informal spaces for performance, a search that finally culminated in Chhabildas.

I remember another thing connected with Kumudben. When I went to Kolhapur to conduct a workshop, I heard of a form of song and drama performed locally called Songi Bhajan. I invited the performers to Mumbai and organized some four or five shows in different places. One of these was in Kumudben's bungalow in the presence of some fifty odd people. They were all rolling on the floor laughing and wondering how they hadn't ever heard of this form and of the talented performers. As always, long discussions followed the performance, making the evening highly memorable.

Another way in which Kumudben supported the entire new theatre movement was by fighting for its plays against the censor board. She was a member of the board so her fight was from within. According to her, all the rules of the board were invalid, untenable. They had to be changed. When Dubey and Dr Lagoo were arguing against the cuts imposed by the board on *Gidhade*, she was there to support them. She was also the one who advised Kamalakar Sarang, who had directed *Sakharam Binder*, to go to court against the cuts the board had prescribed. And it was she who called up the eminent advocate Ashok Desai to put Sarang in touch with him. It was entirely because of her and Sarojini Vaidya, both members of the censor board, that finally its most ill-conceived and ultimately highly damaging rules were changed. I would say this was one of their greatest contributions to the cause of serious theatre.

During that entire period, the post-show parties at her place were full of heated discussion. There was food and drink but those things were incidental. What was important were the views that were expressed about the play we had seen, what was good about it and what needed to be done to make it better. For a young man like me, these discussions were like sheer riches. They taught me how to look at plays, the different perspectives that should come into play while doing so. Members of the audience who came to the parties were some of the finest minds in the city—artists, writers, poets, musicians, and people from theatre and cinema. It wasn't just I who received this bounty from Kumudben—everybody in the new theatre movement did.

Take Khanolkar's case. Kumudben's question was why should a writer of his genius have to worry about where his two square meals would come from. It was a thing of shame for society at large. She put this argument before the Homi Bhabha Committee and was instrumental in getting Khanolkar the Homi Bhabha Fellowship. It was a way of helping him without harming his dignity. Khanolkar researched our folk theatre forms as his fellowship project and it was with this knowledge behind him that he later translated *Hayavadana* into Marathi. So the starting point of this part of Khanolkar's journey was once again Kumudben.

She was also singularly responsible for giving Marathi theatre a place in the NCPA. Given its location in south Bombay, the stratum of people who lived there and attended its programmes, and its orientation towards English and Parsi plays, there would have been no chance for Marathi theatre to find a place there had she not invited and nurtured it. The thing that drove Kumudben was the urge to share with everybody all the things that she thought worth their while, whether it was a poem or a play or the emergence of a new singer. Do read this, do go there she would urge, hugely enriching other people's lives.

Her support was very valuable to me when I turned to films and my popularity grew. People started talking behind my back saying I'd become commercial, that I had turned my back on theatre for the sake of popularity. It was Kumudben who put this talk in its proper perspective for me. She said it had its roots in envy. That caused people to grow blind to the fact that I was still devoting my evenings to theatre. Ignore the talk she said, and continue with your work.

Looking back, I realize that the time when I was at the height of my popularity was also the time during which I did my best work in theatre. What might be called milestones in my theatre career, all came during that time. I felt it then and feel it even more strongly today that at critical times in one's life it is important to have your mother's or a guru's reassurance and support. I got that from Kumudben.

The Space, the People, the Plays

Walchand Terrace played two vital roles in the growth of Hindi and Marathi theatre in Mumbai: one, it provided a large enough space for theatre practitioners of various hues to come together and seek out their own expression and style; two, since no fee was charged for the use of the space, it gave directors the freedom to spend as much time as they needed to bring a play together exactly as they visualized it. Consequently, bottled up energies spilled out, and created some of the most memorable productions of the time.

Although Vinod Doshi had given the space to Arvind Deshpande and Satyadev Dubey, Deshpande hardly ever used it. This allowed Dubey to become its reigning spirit. Fortunately for theatre, Dubey's greatest joy lay in sharing the advantages it afforded. As the following interviews show, this generosity of spirit made Walchand Terrace a nucleus for much more than just the plays that were rehearsed there.

Satyadev Dubey

I had done a play called *Shuturmurg* (Gyandev Agnihotri) which Vinod Doshi saw. We had a party at Jaswanti Tahiliani's place. I had had many lunches at her place. She was always egging me on and introducing me to potential advertisers. One of the income-tax officers whom she knew, ultimately got me quite a few ads for my production. Talking of ads, I am grateful to Gerson da Cunha for giving me my first ad. After every production we used to have a party. The party after *Shuturmurg* was held at Jaswanti's home. Vinod Doshi and Saryu Doshi were there. And because I was working with

Zul Vellani, (Mansoor Ali Khan) Pataudi and his fiancée Sharmila Tagore were also there. It was a lovely party. Sometimes parties go very well. Jaswanti was all the time pushing me towards Vinod Doshi. He had seen *Shuturmurg*, thanks to Arvind Deshpande. He asked me, 'What can I do for you?' It is interesting that Saryu Doshi had already seen my play *Yayati* which had been done earlier. I had met Vinod at another party before this and he had been bowled over by *Shuturmurg*. So when he asked me, 'What can I do for you,' I said, 'Give me rehearsal space. That's what I really need.' So Vinod instinctively, because he was always over-generous, offered me his own flat. But I didn't want to intrude into somebody's house. So I said, 'People will find it difficult to come to this place and also awkward to rehearse in such a lovely place.' So then he offered me Walchand Terrace.

Walchand Terrace was at that time vacant. We got the keys and of course we were supposed to switch off the lights and fans which we never did. But one of the things about Walchand Terrace was that it was supposed to be used also by Awishkar (Sulabha and Arvind Deshpande's group) which had just started. It had been given jointly to Arvind Deshpande and me. So here was the rehearsal space. But Arvind Deshpande's actors began to find it difficult to come to this place in Tardeo. So he didn't use the place much and I had full freedom to use it. We also misused it. We used to have our drunken parties and all that there. But the most unique thing was the number of people who would come there—actually most writers like Mohan Rakesh and Badalda (Sircar). For them it was like a dharamshala. They would come and stay there and have a drink and we would be talking late into the night since we were not disturbing any neighbours. This place was like an open house. One of the rules was, stub your cigarettes on the floor because the next morning, or the same night, all the actors would clean the floor. That was an important part of the ritual.

Amol Palekar

I seem to remember that my entry into Theatre Unit coincided with Theatre Unit's entry into Walchand Terrace. Dubey was rehearsing Gyandev Agnihotri's play *Shuturmurg*. He had given me the responsibility for its set and lighting. Rehearsals also began for *Chup! Court Chalu Hai*. After that, work at Walchand Terrace progressed rapidly. This was where Dubey lived. It became an adda, our rightful space. It provided Dubey with the stability that ensured that he could work at the pace at which he wanted to, to allow all his ideas to take shape.

The space became a hub where a coffee house or pub culture flowered. This is to say, you wound up there after office, chatted, discussed for an hour or two and then dispersed, each to his business. It was like the Marathi proverb, if you're looking for a missing fakir, you'll find him in the masjid. If you wanted to meet somebody in particular, this is where you'd find him, failing which, this is where you'd get every last bit of information about where he might be, working on what and with whom. In retrospect, I see this as an important contribution that Walchand Terrace made to theatre activity.

The Walchand Terrace space was on the ground floor. It comprised an enormous hall, a small cabin on the side and another room inside. The main rehearsals took place in the hall which you entered directly from the street. The cabin was the office where Dubey or Abdul Shakoor sat. People who weren't involved with rehearsals would also sit there. This is where Theatre Unit's administrative work was done. The inside room was where smaller, individual rehearsals took place.

I have a memory of this small room which is very important to me. This was how it happened. As soon as *Chup! Court Chalu Hai* was staged, Dubey began to rehearse another play. Strangely, I can't recall the name. It came before *Aadhe Adhure* and after *Chup! Court Chalu Hai*. Oh yes, it was Adya Rangacharya's *Suno Janamejaya* (Listen Janamejaya). Before rehearsals began for it Dubey said, 'You've made a name for yourself.' He was referring to Dnyaneshwar

Nadkarni's review of *Chup! Court Chalu Hai* which we had performed at Tejpal. Two days later Nadkarni's review appeared in the *Times of India*, praising the play sky high. One line in it read, 'Newcomer Amol Palekar was very suave in his performance.' I was very happy to see my name in the paper but I had no clue what 'suave' meant. I asked Dubey that evening what the word meant. Dubey's answer was, 'Don't take what Dnyaneshwar Nadkarni says seriously. Forget it.' But then, before rehearsals for *Suno Janamejaya* began, he said, 'It's all very well; winning praise for your first role. But now it's time to start learning acting. Let's get down to the ABCD of acting.' After that Dubey literally taught me how to stand, walk, speak, enunciate words and project the voice so that it reached the last row. We never used mikes for our plays. Dubey was very insistent that actors should reach the last row in the auditorium without shouting. He taught me all this. And the inside room was where it happened. He would rehearse me by myself there, but I had to pretend that the other actors were also there. So I had to know their lines. I would have to let enough time pass for those lines to be said before saying mine. He did this with every actor. That's how *Suno Janamejaya* was rehearsed and I was trained as an actor.

In this way, from six in the evening onwards, different things would be happening in different corners of Walchand Terrace. There would be poetry readings, play readings and discussions about them on a regular basis. Theatre writers, directors, actors from all over the country would drop in there and we got the opportunity of listening to their ideas and opinions. Pratibha Agarwal, Mohan Rakesh, Shyamanand Jalan were some of the great theatre people from outside Bombay who often spent time at Walchand Terrace. A charmed theatre atmosphere was created there and as we soaked it in, our horizons expanded.

The contribution of a space like Walchand is unimaginable. It cannot be quantified. Everything that happened there had a role to play. At Walchand, you just had to arrive. There would be a carpet from one wall to the other and a series of pillows lined up. Whoever came could sleep there. Rehearsals would be on. Sometimes you got woken up to join in, sometimes not. It was meant to be for both Arvind Deshpande and Satyadev. But because Arvind had a home, it became Satyadev's domain. Vinod had told Arvind, 'I have employed you to do theatre. You are my officer but you just do theatre.' Who would come up with a gesture like that! (Vinod Doshi had given Arvind Deshpande a job in Premier Automobiles, which he held almost till the day he died prematurely, of a heart attack.)

Before television came on the scene, that is before '82, theatre was what one did. Theatre wasn't only what was happening in Bombay. We heard echoes of what was happening elsewhere in the country too—of the work Shyamanand or Badal Babu were doing in Calcutta and the work other people were doing in Delhi. Walchand was where you got a sense of what was happening around the country and where you felt the need for theatre. We translated each other's work. It was not competitive. Translation is a way of trying to take possession of a work. That energy was tremendous.

When I directed *Vallabhpurchi Dantakatha* in 1969, I had discovered an actor called Eknath Hattangadi. I always make a point of mentioning his name because, in my opinion, he was one of the greatest talents in theatre. I have not seen another to compare with him. I had seen him in a Konkani play and realized he was something else altogether. So when I was casting for *Vallabhpur*, I decided to take him. When Dr Lagoo saw his work he asked if he could cast him in *Gidhade*, which he was rehearsing at Walchand Terrace. Eknath Hattangadi had a full-time job and found it difficult to make time for rehearsals. But I told him he absolutely had to act in *Gidhade*. His next superb performance was in *Uddhwasta Dharmashala* and then C. T. Khanolkar's *Avadhya*. In *Uddhwasta Dharmashala*, he didn't even move from the table at which he sat throughout, with only the top half of his body showing. Yet the effect of his performance was incomparable. He should have got more good work. He would have made a huge contribution to Marathi theatre. But it didn't happen.

Hayavadana had a stellar cast. Besides me as Devdutt, Amrish

Puri as Kapila and Sunila Pradhan as Padmini there were six smaller roles. Kali Mata was played by Dina Pathak, and my god, what a performance that was! I used to watch her from the wings. She used to order paan to give herself a red tongue. A sweet friendship developed between us which continued with the films that we did together. The Bhagwat was played by Chandrashekhar Kamerkar, who was a rousing singer. Then there was a very talented actor named Dilip Gangodkar. He played Hayavadana. He had an extremely flexible body, a requirement for the role. For the same reason, I cast him in *Gochi* (Trap, a Marathi play by Sadanand Rege) for which I was attempting to evolve a physical language. The remaining three roles were of Devdutt's son, played by a child actor called Nandita Aras, and the two dolls played by Priya Tendulkar and Kalpana Lajmi. They were both schoolgirls. Later, Sushma Tendulkar replaced Priya and did many shows.

The music for *Hayavadana* was done by my friend Vijay Kelkar. It was quite magnificent. But it became one of the points of criticism later. It was said that the music did not belong to any classical music gharana nor did Kelkar appear to have any sense of folk music. I had the opportunity to see B. V. Karanth's Kannada production of the play. It was beautiful. Karanth had done the music and he played the Bhagwat. The music and his singing became the focal points of that production. He literally carried the play on his shoulders. Dubey didn't want the music to be central to the play. It was to be in the background and come forward only when the play between the three main characters required it to do so. It didn't have to belong to any particular region. That was Dubey's decision.

There was one important element in Dubey's production that later productions followed. In the original play the actors wear masks, exchanging them to indicate transposed heads. Dubey wanted facial expressions for his production, so we used to exchange costumes instead, and change our body language. The *Hayavadana* rehearsals went on for five or six months. Meanwhile, Dubey was doing other work too. He could do this because he had a space like Walchand

Terrace. In my opinion, Dubey's golden period belonged to Walchand Terrace.

Although Walchand Terrace had been given to Theatre Unit, it wasn't the only group that rehearsed there. The space wasn't available to me to rehearse *Gochi*, but when I did *Avadhya* for the India Culture League, I rehearsed it from beginning to end at Walchand. One of the biggest contributions of this space was the luxury it afforded us of taking as long as we needed to get a production stage-ready. We rehearsed *Gochi* for nine months and not once did any of my cast ask me when we were going to open the play.

The other great advantage of Walchand Terrace was that the finest literary minds would frequent it. One day while we were rehearsing for the Marathi translation of *Pagla Ghoda* (Mad Horse, a Bengali play by Badal Sircar), Khanolkar had dropped in. He sat watching our rehearsal. When we broke for tea, I confessed to him that there was a small nursery rhyme in the play which I had been unable to translate into Marathi. He said, 'How does it go?' I recited it for him and explained its significance in the play. I also told him what depth of meaning Badalda had suggested through the rhyme. Then he said, 'Recite it again, will you? The original Bengali.' I did. Then he said, 'Recite it again.' In this way he made me recite it five or six times. Then he said, 'Give me a piece of paper.' He took the paper, drew out his pen and translated the rhyme at one go. What an amazing translation it was! He hadn't merely got the sense of it, but the rhythm, metre, everything. Only a man of Khanolkar's genius could have done something like that. 'How wonderful this is,' I said. To which he said, 'Glad you've liked it,' put his pen back in his pocket and left. These are the many small gifts that made Walchand Terrace culturally such an important space.

Evam Indrajit was a significant milestone of the Walchand Terrace years. People often argued then, as they do now, about how good or bad an actor Dubey himself was. But it has to be said that his performance in *Evam Indrajit* was superb. Indrajit had literally entered Dubey, specially the poems. Anybody who watched his Indrajit would be left in no doubt that he was a brilliant actor.

Another play that Dubey did in the Walchand Terrace years was *Anushthan*. The play wasn't talked about much nor was any note taken of it later. It was written by Gyandev Agnihotri. After its first reading at Walchand, the general opinion was that it was too verbose, abstract and abstruse. But Dubey said, whatever it is, I'm going to do it. He cast total newcomers in the play and began by putting them through physical exercises. He was trying to discover how flexible their bodies could be made and in which way they could be used. I made sketches of the set and showed them to the group. Everybody loved them but Dubey said, 'I'm not going to use a set for this play at all. You've been saying this is an abstract play. Then why are you trying to give it a concrete shape? I want to see if I can express its wordiness purely through physical movement.' The idea of giving physical shape to words interested me and this experiment of Dubey's was responsible for giving direction to my ideas for *Gochi,* the play I was going to do.

I broke up and reconstituted *Gochi* radically. That kind of thing had given rise to one of the major arguments of the experimental theatre of those days. The issue was how far a director could go in tampering with the writer's script. I discussed the problem with the author of the play, the poet Sadanand Rege. He said, 'Do whatever you think is best.'

The late Jayram Hardikar was a very talented actor, whose body suggested the same brute strength as Amrish Puri's. I used him to represent the male principal in *Gochi*. Similarly, I cast Juili Deuskar as the female principle. She was femininity personified. I tried to use the combination of their two voices for effect, his deep bass and her high contralto. An important feature of *Gochi* was using Chitra, Dilip Kulkarni and Dilip Gangodkar as a kind of Greek chorus which is constantly there and yet not there, witness to the event, participating in its joys and sorrows and yet holding itself aloof.

We were certain that we needed to go beyond the proscenium for this play. We did our first show in Sujit Patwardhan's garden in Pune. Our first show in Bombay was in Purandare Hall on an upper floor of Sahitya Sangh Mandir, Charni Road. But we reversed the space. This means the audience sat on the stage and we performed in the auditorium. Then we performed in the parking lot of a housing society and in the canteen of the Life Insurance Company. This search for informal spaces, which began then, culminated when the Chhabildas School Hall space was acquired.

Shyam Benegal

By the time Dubey came to Walchand Terrace, I knew him very well. So of course, I would visit him there sometimes. He was a nomad. At the time he was living right there. And I lived on Pedder Road so it was next door. Vinod Doshi who owned Walchand Terrace was very actively into theatre. He was a great encouragement to Satyadev Dubey. One play that was rehearsed at Walchand and has stayed with me was Girish Karnad's *Hayavadana.* It was a magnificent production. It became very popular. It must be counted as the finest of Dubey's productions and the finest to have been rehearsed at Walchand Terrace, as also being one of the last.

Girish Karnad

Walchand Terrace was a very important place for me. For those four-and-a-half years, it was like going back to school again. Everything was happening together. Someone was fighting, Dubey was shouting, someone was rehearsing, people were falling in love, people were falling out of love, getting married, everything was happening simultaneously. Actually, my most vivid memory of it is arguing intensely with (Vijay) Tendulkar one evening, both of us quite solidly drunk, and then falling asleep. When I woke up the next morning and looked on my side, there was no Tendulkar. I looked to the other side and there was Badal Sircar! And I thought, God! I've had too much to drink last night! But apparently, Badalda had come by some train at two o' clock in the morning, and turned up here. Those four years were just extraordinary and came at the right time.

Even Alyque (Padamsee), who didn't like us very much, and he and Satyadev had some differences, would drop in every once in a while to see what was going on. And it was so centrally located. Tardeo! That was unbelievable.

Deepa Shreeram

I got acquainted with Walchand Terrace when rehearsals for Dubey's Hindi production of *Aadhe Adhure* started. Dubey had me in mind for the elder sister's role in the play. My Hindi was very good so I'd agreed to do it. He read it out to me. I asked him what about auditions. He said, forget auditions. It's enough if you intend doing theatre seriously and committedly. I don't want you coming to me with excuses like there's a naming ceremony at home or a wedding in the family to take time off from rehearsals.

(Amrish) Purisaab had his job. Jyotsna Karyekar had her clinic. She would have to keep it closed for rehearsals which were in the evenings, and often continued late into the night. In one scene, I had to collapse and sob. Dubey kept saying my sobbing was false. He wanted to hear me really sob. He was so insistent that I really cried. That evening Vinod Doshi had come for the rehearsal. He was about to leave before we did that scene when Dubey asked him to stay and watch it. Having an audience strengthened my motivation to cry and I cried with all my heart. That's how I got to know Vinod Doshi, the man who owned the place and because of whom we were there.

At the end of rehearsals, we would all end up at Vinod's place for drinks. Dubey would take all of us along to his parties. Once, Lt Cdr Shahane threw a New Year's party for us. After we left, Dubey stood on top of a car and said, 'I have something to declare: I am drunk,' which was more than obvious. But that's the night when an argument started between Dubey, Shreeram and Shrikant Lagoo, the owner of one of Mumbai's celebrated jewellery shops. Shrikant said, 'I'll bet you anything you're never going to do *Gidhade.*' Shreeram had been blown by the play and had been saying for a long time that he was going to do it. Then everybody got agitated. A challenge was thrown at Shrikant. Would he back the production if they went ahead and did it? He said he would and the entire production was planned that night, there and then. Eknathdada (Hattangadi) was a relative of mine. He was in the play and would be very upset each time he had to spew one of the obscenities that filled the play. But he was a fantastic actor, and what a voice he had. Shreeram would tell him, do a few shows and quit if it really gets to you. The play isn't going to do many shows anyway. But once he started performing, he was quite amazing. The obscenities sounded like they were second nature to him.

Personally, I had not understood the play at all. I once sat Shreeram down and asked him to explain it to me. Why did he think it was such a great play? What was so great about it? When he was through answering my questions, I realized (Vijay) Tendulkar had not written it merely to create a sensation.

Then there was the question of the red stain that had to be put on the back of my sari to indicate that I had miscarried. There was censor trouble over that. I remember we were doing a show in Thane. Shreeram said the censors had agreed to no cuts so we were doing the play as it was. The only concession we were making was with regard to the red blood stain. Our solution was to make it blue. Shreeram made an announcement about it. 'At one point in the play, you will see a blue stain on Manik's sari. You are requested to see it as red.' The audience burst out laughing. But when I actually took my entry, there was pindrop silence.

There was another play, *Main Suar Hoon* (I Am a Pig) that I was part of. Dubey had a friend called Nanduji (Nandkumar Mittal). He was a share broker—short, fat, and constantly chewing paan. When I asked Dubey where he had fished this play out of, he said he'd challenged Nanduji to write a play. Nanduji had said he would write if Dubey agreed to direct it. So Nanduji wrote this play. Committed to directing it, Dubey was thinking, what a fool I am. So he turned his anger against himself into the title of the play, calling it *Main Suar Hoon*.

Ashok Sathe, Dilip Kolhatkar, Bapu Limaye were some of the people who would frequent Walchand Terrace. All of them formed theatre groups in their own neighbourhoods. There was Gossip at Vile Parle and Mitra Mandal in Thane. Dilip Kolhatkar started a group in Dombivali. When people like Girish Karnad, Kumud Mehta, Tendulkar, Shreeram got together, there would be wonderful discussions which made it a very enriching experience for me.

There was a large main hall at Walchand and two side rooms. When a rehearsal was going on in the hall, there could be a play-reading going on in one of the two side rooms and someone else could be sitting in the second room translating something. The best thing was, there was nobody around to tell us not to do this or that. If there had been restrictions, we would never have managed to do the work we did.

Dr Shreeram Lagoo

Walchand Terrace was Dubey's fiefdom. I had no idea who Vinod Doshi was. Later, this place became practically our home. I used to live in Vile Parle in those days. Rehearsals would start late and continue into the night. Afterwards Dubey and I would loaf. We'd eat bhelpuri and gorge on icecream. That was our dinner. Then we'd return to Walchand and flake out. Girish Karnad spent a few days in Bombay; but didn't have a place to go to. Dubey said why look for anything else, stay at Walchand. So he did.

Meena Naik

When Dr Lagoo came back from Africa to do theatre full-time, he directed *Gidhade* for Theatre Unit. He asked me if I would play Rama, Umakant's wife. Dr Lagoo was playing Umakant. Rehearsals for the play were held at Walchand Terrace. That's how I began going there. This place had a large hall as you entered and a room at the back where Dubey lived. By then I had got to know Dubey very well. He had done *Aadhe Adhure* earlier in which Bhakti (Barve) was acting. She was a very good friend of mine. That's how I got to know Dubey. And that's how Dr Lagoo cast me in *Gidhade*. I would always be included in the first show parties that his friend Vinod Doshi used to throw for Theatre Unit members, friends and associates at his house.

During the time we were rehearsing *Gidhade*, Dubey was talking about doing *No Exit* in Marathi. He wanted me to play the role Alaknanda Samarth had played. It required some daring to play that role. I didn't even quite understand it. I was only about eighteen then. Dubey said we'll do it when you've matured a little more. But it never happened. I haven't acted in a single play directed by Dubey.

I kept going to Walchand Terrace for rehearsals. Dr Lagoo was as rigorous in his direction as Vijayabai (Mehta) was. The role I was playing was also a little beyond my experience and understanding. I was playing a barren woman. Also the play was full of violence, cursing and abusing. I wasn't used to hearing such words. I used to feel shocked. But my parents never stopped me from acting in the play. During rehearsals which we did in the Walchand Terrace hall—it was a longish rectangular space so we would use the length of it—I would go and sit on the steps outside as soon as my part was done because I couldn't bear to hear those obscenities.

When the script went to the censor board, they asked for all the abuses to be edited out. Dr Lagoo said the play wouldn't be worth doing then. He called a meeting with everybody involved with the play. He said we would simply go ahead and do the play as it was written, asking us to be prepared to go to jail if we got arrested for it.

We started doing shows at Tejpal. Various members of the censor board would come to see the play—Sopandev Chaudhary, Sarojinibai Vaidya, etc. And there would be another round of discussions which Dr Lagoo and Tendulkar would attend. So it went on. Meanwhile we were doing shows and receiving contradictory reviews. Some praised the play while others said why should this aspect of society be shown on stage. But every show we did was fully booked. This was most unexpected for an experimental play. But apart from rehearsing for plays, the Walchand Terrace atmosphere was extremely stimulating. Dubey was always there and others like Tendulkar, Madhav Watve, Kamalakar Sarang, Arvind Deshpande would drop in and there would be constant debates and discussions about theatre from which I learned a lot.

Sunila Pradhan

From the time I entered Walchand Terrace for rehearsals of the Marathi *Yayati*, I was struck by its potential for being turned into a performance space. The large hall would have made a beautiful intimate theatre with a seating capacity of around fifty. The acoustics were marvellous. It would have been much more comfortable than Chhabildas for actors and audience. It could have been air-conditioned too. If the idea had been suggested to Vinod at the time, I'm sure he would have considered it.

I count that period at Walchand Terrace as our golden age. During that time we were doing two productions a year. Immediately after *Yayati*, Dubey offered me *Aadhe Adhure*. Then we did Shankar Shesh's *The Steel Frame*. In all I have done thirty-three plays with Dubey and Amrish Puri, but I still feel the Walchand Terrace period was our golden age.

Ratna Pathak-Shah

My chief memory of Walchand is of rehearsals for *Hayavadana*, in which my mother, Dina Pathak acted as Kali. I think that is the most magical production I have seen. I was just enthralled by the whole process. Dubey with his incredible rehearsal style which was sixty per cent shouting and forty per cent very detailed work on the actors' speech. I think that was my first exposure to how speech could come alive on stage and how performances were created.

I remember a rehearsal where the two doll puppets were being rehearsed. Kalpana Lajmi and Priya Tendulkar were the puppets. They were rehearsing how the puppets should move, how they should become limp and of course, Dubey having hysterics because what he wanted was not coming across! But I remember being completely blown away by the way he rehearsed.

I remember being there for rehearsals of *Yayati* too, in which my aunt Tarla Dalal acted. But I was too small then for anything to make sense to me except that Dubey shouted a lot! And I also remember discussions about the costumes. That was perhaps my introduction to the importance of costumes for the effect of a play. My lifelong interest in costumes was probably spawned by the *Yayati* rehearsals. That is something that has lasted me a lifetime. I also remember my mother creating her own costume out of little bits and pieces for her role as Kali. It was amazing how it worked and how she was transformed into a completely different personality. The *Hayavadana* rehearsals at Walchand showed me that this business of putting together a play was extremely hard work. But that hard work was extremely pleasurable too! The enjoyment Dubey derived from the process was always much greater than what everyone else experienced during performances.

Walchand Terrace was a space where people would hang out. They would come during or after rehearsals, would sit around and the whole planning of how things were to be done took place there. There was Hemant Rege running around with cups of tea. There was Abdul Shakoor, an elderly person who helped in the organization. Dubey worked very well with people like that. He had trouble with actors who threw their weight around. He also had trouble with people to whom he could not get his ideas across too easily. Most days after rehearsal there would be one major argument about something or the other which would spill over into someone's house and turn into a dinner and late-night discussions about theatre! These pre- and post-performance sessions in our house have been a part of my growing up.

Being in *Hayavadana* was completely liberating for my mother because by then she had been getting bogged down by the whole Gujarati commercial theatre business. It is a killing experience, I can tell you that. If you have done one or two typical commercial Gujarati plays, it becomes unbearable. I realized this when I was a kid and knew that that was not what I wanted to do.

Walchand was dominated by Dubey's work although Awishkar also rehearsed there. *Gidhade* was rehearsed there, and so was the Gujarati production of *Sakharam Binder*. I was a part of that production. I used to hang around a lot. It was produced by a co-operative that they were trying to form—my mother, Giresh Desai, Tarla Mehta and Dubey were in it together. All these artists would contribute their labour and talent and if any money was made, it would be split. There was no producer. Of course, it did not do well at all!

Alaknanda Samarth and Ebrahim Alkazi in August Strindberg's *Miss Julie*, directed by Ebrahim Alkazi. Photo credit: Mitter Bedi

Alaknanda Samarth and Satyadev Dubey in *Band Darwaze*, translated from Jean-Paul Sartre's original *Huis Clos*, directed by Satyadev Dubey.
Photo courtesy: Alaknanda Samarth

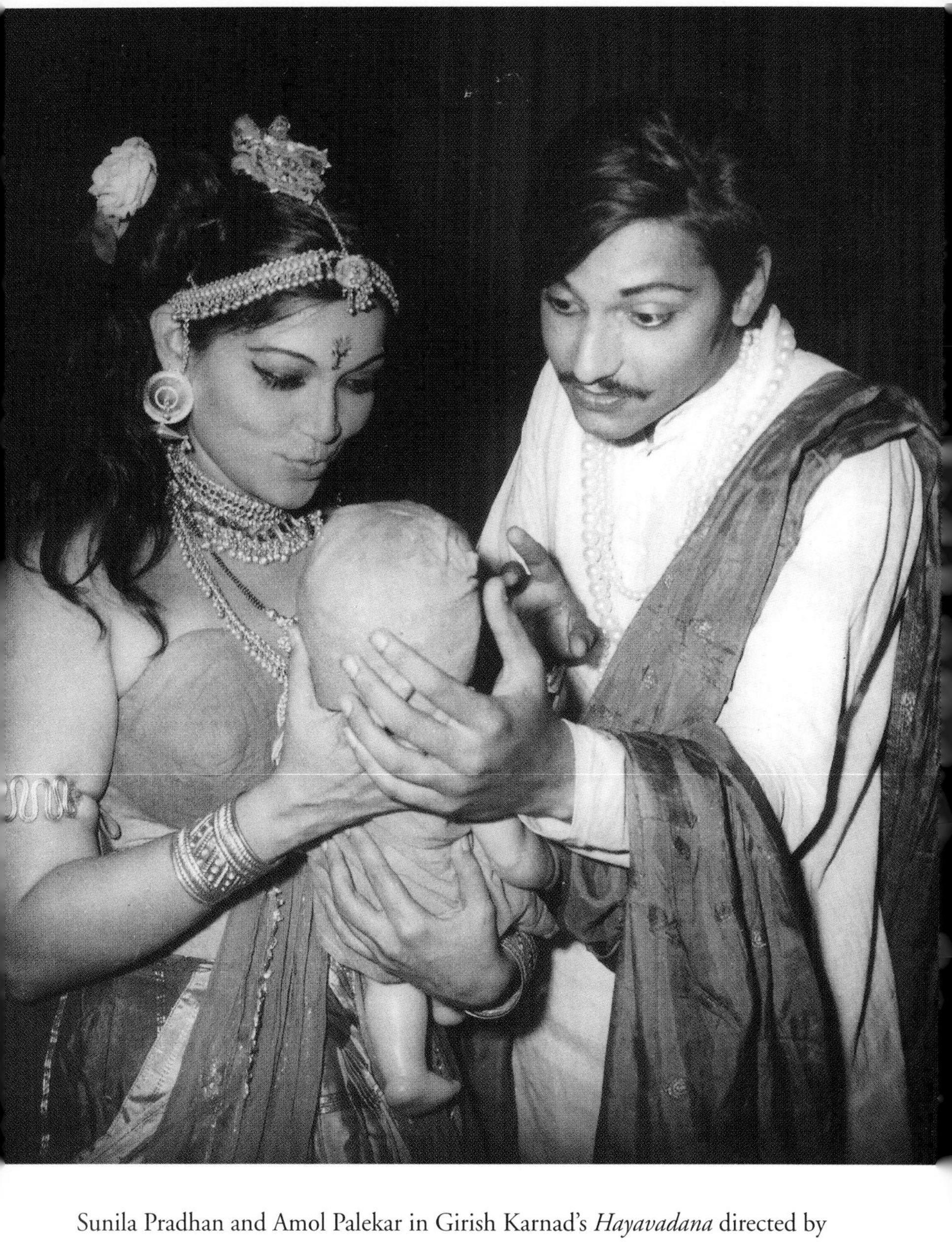

Sunila Pradhan and Amol Palekar in Girish Karnad's *Hayavadana* directed by Satyadev Dubey. Photo credit: Theatre Unit Archives

Sunila Pradhan and Amrish Puri in Mohan Rakesh's *Aadhe Adhure*, directed by Satyadev Dubey. Photo credit: Theatre Unit Archives

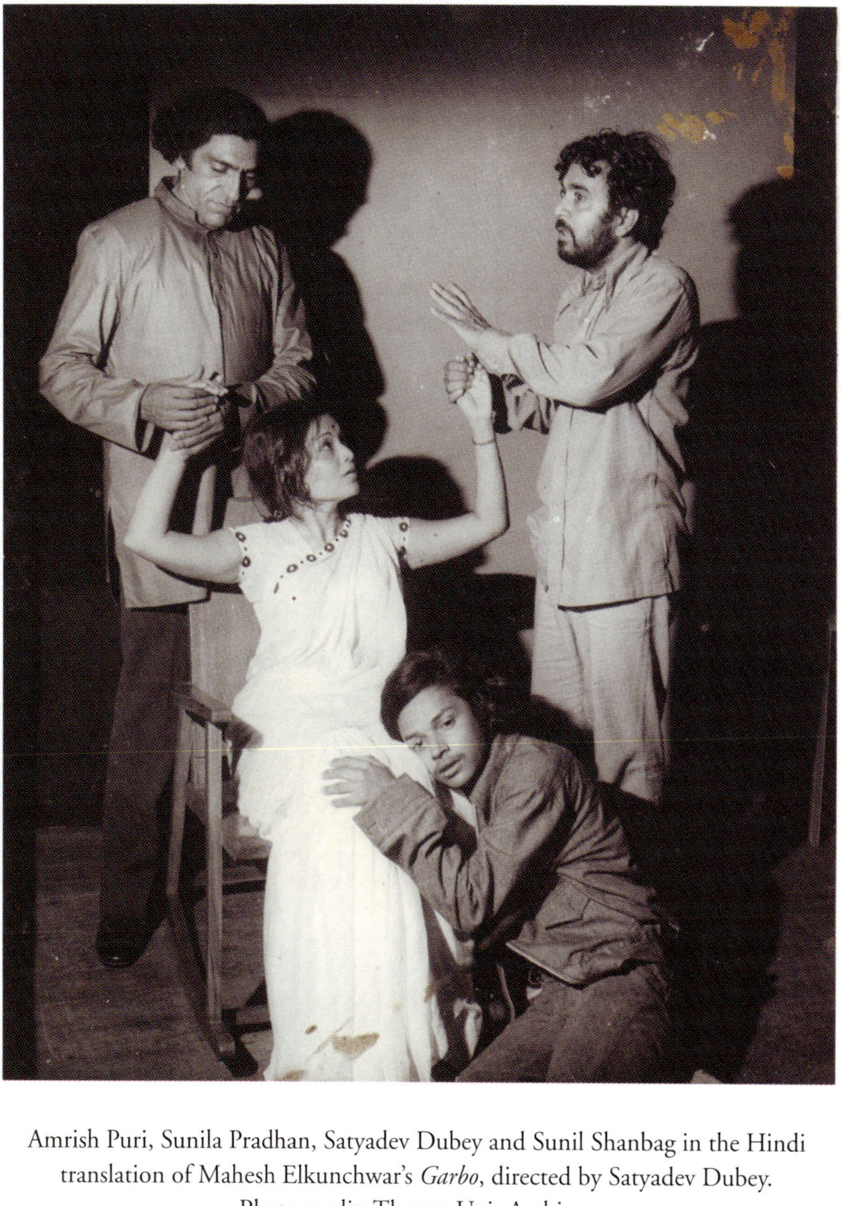

Amrish Puri, Sunila Pradhan, Satyadev Dubey and Sunil Shanbag in the Hindi translation of Mahesh Elkunchwar's *Garbo*, directed by Satyadev Dubey.
Photo credit: Theatre Unit Archives

Rekha Sabnis and Dr Shreeram Lagoo in G. P. Deshpande's *Uddhwasta Dharmashala*, directed by Dr Shreeram Lagoo.
Photo courtesy: Dr Shreeram Lagoo

Devendra Saralkar, Shruti Muzumdar and Rajan Bhise in a run-through at Chhabildas of *Mitali Papni*, written by Rajeev Naik, directed by Vijay Kenkre.
Photo credit: Antarnatya Archives

Jyoti Dogra in *The Doorway*, written and directed by her.
Photo credit: Ameet Malapur

PART THREE

Chhabildas School Hall

Photo credit: Vinesh Gandhi

The Chhabildas Boys' High School.

If you get off at Dadar West station on the western railway, walk down the road and take the first right turn, you are in the narrow, crowded Dadar Vachanalaya Marg, where the Chhabildas Lallubhai Boys' High School is located. It is a large, flat-faced building that once housed the Awishkar Theatre Group and provided a space for rehearsal and performance to whoever wished to do plays that did not fit the formulae of commercial theatre. Sulabha Deshpande was a teacher at the Chhabildas Girls' High School. Her brother-in-law, Madhav Sakhardande taught at the boys' school. In their hunt for an affordable space to perform, Awishkar appealed to the school management to rent the hall out to them for its activities. The management agreed and Awishkar became a tenant of the auditorium.

Showing the same generosity of spirit that Satyadev Dubey had shown with regard to Walchand Terrace, Awishkar allowed the use of the space to any theatre group that wished to rehearse and perform there. This allowed it to grow into a vibrant hub for new theatre activity. The space had its limitations, but its convenient location and inexpensive rental made it a very attractive proposition for theatrewalas with many ideas and no money.

Pioneering experiments in theatre like Vijay Tendulkar's *Ghashiram Kotwal* could not be staged here, but G. P. Deshpande's *Uddhwasta Dharmashala* could, and was staged there. When Awishkar lost the space to the school management's commercial interests, there was a general feeling of betrayal. However, by then, theatre too had lost the charge that it had shown in the sixties, seventies and eighties and theatre groups were increasingly looking for better equipped spaces for performance. The liberalization of the Indian economy was instrumental in altering the balance between creativity and money, thus bringing the curtain down on the legendary Chhabildas movement.

The Anchor: Arun Kakade

Photo credit: Vinesh Gandhi

Arun Kakade is eighty-three years old, but his physical energy belies his age. He has been the sole administrative pillar of the oldest active theatre group in Mumbai—Awishkar—since its inception in 1970. His fascination for theatre began in his college days in Pune, and continued after he relocated to Mumbai and started working with Vijaya Mehta's theatre laboratory, Rangayan. In 1970 he, along with Arvind and Sulabha Deshpande, parted ways with Rangayan and founded Awishkar. Arvind Deshpande died prematurely in January 1987, after which Kakade ran the group's activities single-handedly in the Chhabildas School Hall space they had rented. In 1992, they lost this space and Awishkar moved to a municipal school in Mahim. Arun Kakade continues to oversee the activities of the group from this new base. His services to theatre were acknowledged by the theatre community when they elected him President of the 94th Akhil Bharatiya Marathi Natya Sammelan.

My Years with Theatre

I have been serving Marathi theatre for about sixty years now. I worked for the first four years in Pune and have been working for the last fifty-six years in Mumbai.

I worked with Rangayan first. Rangayan laid the foundation for the Marathi experimental theatre movement in Mumbai. It provided a way of looking at theatre and a discipline. But to go even further back, Bhalba Kelkar of the Progressive Dramatic Association (PDA) in Pune was my first guru. He taught me that, given the kind of theatre we aspired to do, we might be able to ensure its longevity only if we made it group-centric rather than individual-centric. Someone had to stand behind the creative work to nudge it forward. If nobody did this background work, no work would be done in the foreground. I have been the background man for the last five decades. Without my kind of work, the group would not stand, the play would not stand, the show would not stand, the artist would not stand.

Post-Independence, when we began looking at theatre, we were influenced by Western ideas. We had a clear position regarding the kind of theatre we wanted to do. If we wanted to expand the possibilities of our medium, we would have to experiment. If we wanted to maintain the direction and consistency of our work, we would have to form a group. I learned how to hold on to an objective and work with consistency while I was in PDA. Unfortunately, Rangayan split towards the end of 1970 and in 1971, we formed Awishkar. We started off with a production that was extremely grand. Never in the history of Marathi theatre had anything been done on this scale. This was *Tughlaq* (Girish Karnad). There were seventy actors in the play. Damu Kenkre did the set, Pt Jitendra Abhisheki did the music and Tapas Sen did the lighting. Arun Sarnaik played the main role. It cost us Rs 80,000—a huge amount for those days.

Vinod Doshi was of great help during this time. Not only did he do a splendid job of acting, he also had all the weapons made at their factory at Satara Road, near Pune. When Vijay Tendulkar said he wanted to translate the play into Marathi, he put up Tendulkar at the Satara guest house.

We performed *Tughlaq* at Ravindra Natya Mandir in Mumbai and Balgandharva Rang Mandir in Pune. Initially, we didn't think it could be accommodated at the Sahitya Sangh Mandir, but we managed to put up the set by pushing all the skirting to the top. This enabled Tughlaq to be seen when he stood on a height at the end.

I now come to the Chhabildas Boys' High School Hall. Madhav Sakhardande, Tillu and a couple of others—all sympathizer members of Rangayan—were teachers there, while Sulabha Deshpande was a teacher in the Chhabildas Girls' High School. Tendulkar, Sulabha, Madhav and I went to meet the school committee. We told them we would like to rent the school hall to perform our plays. They agreed to let us use it. Before this, they used to rent it out for music recitals, meetings and other programmes. They calculated the average income over the last ten years for us. We assured them that we would not pay them a paisa less than that. We also assured them that we would share whatever we made with them, because we were not a profit-making group.

We discussed how to utilize the space. We spoke at length about other groups like ours who were desperately scrambling for space to perform. This led to our decision to welcome all such groups there. There were at least seven or eight of them at the time, including Rekha Sabnis's, Hemu Adhikari's and Dubeyji's.

We opened the space with (C. T.) Khanolkar's *Pratima* (Image). The cast comprised Dr Lagoo, Amol Palekar, Deepa Lagoo (then Basrur) and Sulabha. When Jaidev (Hattangadi) came from the National School of Drama, he performed *Changuna* (the Marathi translation of Lorca's *Yerma*). Dubeyji performed *Hayavadana* (Girish Karnad) with Amol (Palekar), Amrish (Puri), Sunila (Pradhan) and Bapu Kamerkar in the cast. We did *Saari Raat*. Dubeyji performed *Aur Ek Garbo* (Yet Another Garbo, a Hindi adaptation of Mahesh Elkunchwar's Marathi play). They also did *Achha Ek Baar Aur* (Okay, One More Time, a Hindi adaptation of Mohit Chhattopadhyay's Bengali play). Bahuroopi performed *Rajacha Khel* (The King's Play/ Game, a play by Vrindavan Dandavate), directed by Dilip Kolhatkar and Unmesh (Achyut Vaze's group) did *Chal Re Bhoplya Tunuk Tunuk* (Come Little Pumpkin Hoppity-hop, a play by Achyut Vaze). These were the groups that performed in Chhabildas during the first year. Once people realized that they could do work of this sort there, the groups grew in number, and a strong current of new plays began.

We had prepared a chart, which I still have and which we published in *Ranganayak* (the memorial volume of essays Awishkar brought out to mark Arvind Deshpande's first death anniversary). It indicated how many plays were done and gave a detailed diagram of the architectural plan of the space. All the dimensions of the space were given. We charged Rs 50 as rent. The ticket rates started at Rs 5 and went up to Rs 15 by the time we moved out. All the details of the economics of running the space were given in the book.

There was a small verandah that ran the length of the hall, where we stored all our material. We made an office behind the hall. There was a small stage there under which, again, there was some storage space. Our costume trunks and all our other stuff were stored there.

When the school broke up for vacations and no shows were being staged, we even constructed sets there. Otherwise we used the large quadrangle outside the school for this. During school term, all our work had to be done after six in the evening, when the students went home. The most important condition was that, no matter what we did the previous night, the hall had to be handed over to the school next morning in pristine condition. It had to be spic and span. Sitaram (Kumbhar) messed up once. He cleared the sets but left tiny nails strewn all over the floor. The principal gathered them in a bowl and stood waiting for me. He simply said, 'Please see to it that this doesn't happen again.' After that day, I would make it a point to be the first to get to the theatre to ensure everything had been cleared away.

We didn't use Chhabildas only to rehearse and perform plays. We also organized workshops for children and adults. Jaidev conducted three theatre workshops every year. Guru Parvati Kumar trained children in dance every Sunday. There was always something or the other happening in Chhabildas.

We did a lot of plays in the beginning but gradually, very gradually, the number of shows decreased. Every movement has its ups and downs. Besides which, there were other reasons. First, the consistency and force with which new writing was done once, subsided. Second, as new opportunities beckoned, people went away and the groups disintegrated. But we always welcomed new groups. We made sure the place was open to whoever wanted to perform. We were criticized for this. People said, 'Anything and everything goes at Chhabildas. There is no quality control.' But we felt that new theatre people with no experience needed to be given that experience. How were they to grow otherwise? The high lasted for about four years. We hadn't planned for success or failure. We had no idea Chhabildas would become so popular. But highs or lows, it was important to take both in one's stride. And anyway, it wasn't a bad thing that the movement petered out. That needs to happen to any movement for it to regain its force. I think we should take these lows in our stride and keep going.

When we started Chhabildas, we saw it simply as an effort to create an opportunity for all those who wished to participate in the movement to come together. We had noticed that there was a lot of theatre activity happening in pockets all over the city. We felt this needed to be channelized. That is why we decided to open the space to all. But it was easier said than done. There were a lot of fights over dates. Everyone wanted the weekends. Those who got Thursdays would get very annoyed. On Thursday evenings, families watched the popular film-music show, *Chhayageet.* People living around Chhabildas would switch it on exactly at the time our shows started. We would have to shut all the windows to keep the sound out. This happened a number of times with Jaidev Hattangadi's *Changuna.* Just as we had problems with our neighbours' noisiness, rarely but occasionally, they too would complain about the noise we created with our activity. But they were mostly supportive. Sometimes someone would shout from across the street, 'Enough of this now!' But that was it. They never made trouble for us. They never made any official complaints to the school.

During the two years before Chhabildas, we had sympathizer members who paid a regular subscription. That was when we did *Tughlaq*, *Bai Eke Bai* (A Woman, That's All) and *Saari Raat*. But once we got Chhabildas, maintaining separate accounts for the members and for the administration of the space became too much trouble. So we wound up the idea of sympathizer members and depended mostly on advertisements. Initially, ticket-selling licenses, performing licenses and police permissions were not required. We simply paid the municipal tax. According to government rules, Chhabildas did not count as a proper theatre. There were no fixed chairs, no doors, etc., so we did not fit into their definition of a theatre. They told us we were free of all these official procedures. Neither the BMC nor the police gave us any trouble. In fact, I remember a BMC official coming to me and saying, 'Kaka, you haven't paid the tax for six years.' So I asked him to bring all the papers, prepare the statement and made all the payments.

Today, looking back, I realize there were many discomforts that came with the space. The wooden staircase that led up to the hall was old and rickety. The iron chairs were uncomfortable and the seating on the floor was tough on elderly knees. No snacks were served at the hall during the interval. The canteen nearby sent snacks and tea for the actors and crew but the audience had to go downstairs where the famous batata-vadawala did brisk business. There was no air conditioning, of course. But with the high ceiling, fans and a wall lined with windows, one could get by, except during peak summer. An expert had told us that the space had good acoustics. Everything could be heard everywhere. Also, we had had a bamboo canopy made right above the stage that prevented sound from reverberating. So despite all its discomforts, Chhabildas, which could hold almost 200 people, was still a good space to have.

We had discussed renovating the place a bit. We had thought we would redo the staircase. The toilets were absolutely horrible. Those could be repaired. We offered to make all the changes, spending from our pockets. The proposal was put before the school committee. But the problem was that the committee had a three-year term. As long as there were teachers and members on it who valued and supported our activity, there was good communication between us. But some new members created trouble for us. Once, a teacher complained at the school's general body meeting that Chhabildas had become a hotspot for prostitution and drinking. The biggest problem was that we had a contract that needed to be renewed every year before April. The threat of it not being renewed hung over us every April. As the management became less and less interested in supporting us, they made it more and more difficult for us to work there. Eventually, in 1992, they told us they wanted to develop the space commercially and we should vacate it within a month. But yes, they did let us use the space for eighteen long years, for which we must be grateful.

It must also be admitted that audience numbers had reduced greatly over the years. I remember some shows which had just ten or twelve people in the audience. Television and other sources of entertainment were perhaps partly responsible. But the quality of the newer plays had also dropped. Prithvi Theatre had started. A lot of experimentation had begun on the commercial stage too by then. A number of actors, writers and directors from the experimental theatre had moved to commercial theatre and were exercising a certain discipline there, changing the ways of working there. They were trying to deliver productions of a certain quality. So the audience must have found that attractive and moved there. Because so many artists from here moved there, a sort of vacuum was created here.

When we left Chhabildas, we handed over all the equipment we had gathered over the years, lakhs of rupees worth of wings, lights, skirting, etc. to a Chhabildas teacher who had worked with us and acted in our plays. We asked him to take over and run the place. About ten or twelve shows happened after that, but the nature of the place changed rapidly. He hiked the rent. When we were running it, we always believed that no matter who performed there, their play was our play, too. It was a part of the movement that was ours together. But that changed with this man. The approach became commercial. That upset theatre people. About two years after the place shut down, I got a call from Hemu Adhikari. He said, 'Kaka, the people at the school kept everything else but our group still has the lights we bought.' So I asked him to donate them. He said that would be unaffordable. So I asked him to sell them to me at a reasonable price. He agreed. So now the lights that we use at Mahim (the municipal school where the Awishkar office and performance space shifted from Chhabildas) are those lights.

Immediately after Chhabildas shut down, I started three centres, first at Karnataka Sangh, Matunga, second at Vile Parle in collaboration with the Lokmanya Seva Sangh, and third at Goregaon. I ran them for three years. But they became financially unaffordable, so I had to shut them down. The government never took notice of what went on at Chhabildas. They did not offer any financial help. The only money we received was a small production grant from the

Sangeet Natak Akademi and a small salary grant from the Ministry of Culture. But we never actually used those salaries for ourselves. We signed and accepted them and then gave them to Awishkar.

After Chhabildas, we tried to acquire a space from the government, but it didn't work out. The Mahim space was the only thing we managed to secure. We have been working out of that small space for the last twenty years. The Maharashtra government had apparently made a cultural policy that a small 200-seater theatre should be built in every taluka. But that plan doesn't seem to have been realized. Also, how many of us practitioners are really interested? The Pune Municipal Corporation has built a small theatre in front of Balgandharva Rang Mandir. Nobody knows what is happening there. And yet I firmly believe that if a well-maintained, well-located, subsidized and therefore, affordable space comes up, it would generate a lot of activity again.

We have always supported new writers. We did plays by C. P. (Deshpande), we have done plays by Chetan (Datar), Ira (Irawati Karnik). Achyut Vaze has written a new play after all these years and we are producing it. But somehow I don't see anyone with Tendulkar's vision on the horizon. I don't think one needs to get disheartened by that though. Someone will step forward. It is this hope that keeps me going.

The Initiator: Sulabha Deshpande

Photo credit: Vinesh Gandhi

Sulabha Deshpande is one of the finest actors of the Marathi-Hindi stage and cinema. She began her work in theatre by directing plays for the students of Chhabildas Girls' School where she taught for many years. Her performance as Leela Benare, the protagonist of Tendulkar's *Shantata! Court Chalu Ahe*, directed by Arvind Deshpande, is a landmark in Marathi theatre. She directed the verse play *Pratima* written by C. T. Khanolkar, with which the Chhabildas space was inaugurated. But perhaps, her most experimental work was the Marathi adaptation of Franz Xaver Kroetz's one-woman play *Request Concert*, which she evolved and performed at Chhabildas in collaboration with directors Rustom Bharucha and Manuel Lutgenhorst. One of her most enduring contributions to theatre has been Chandrashala, the children's wing of Awishkar, which she started when the group acquired the Chhabildas space. Chandrashala has been a training ground for generations of child actors, some of whom, like Nana Patekar and Urmila Matondkar, went on to become stars.

How It All Started

The Chhabildas Hall was a fairly large space. In order to give it a more intimate quality that would better suit the plays we expected to do there, it needed to be contained in some way. As it stood, it had a stage at one end and chairs on a few raked platforms at the other end. There was also a gallery running down its length and a large room at the back.

We curtained off the stage because it was too small for plays, and too distant from the seating arrangement and, instead, created a floor-level performance area in front of the curtain. This brought the chairs closer and left enough space between them and the performance area for a durrie-covered space on the floor for youngsters and late-comers. The gallery was used as a lighting cabin and in other different ways. For instance, when the acting space was used lengthways, you could seat half the audience in the gallery and the other half on the other side of the acting area. All decisions about how to configure the space were taken collectively by our group.

The space had one major problem. It was on the second floor and you had to climb four flights of stairs to reach it, something that elderly people found exahausting. But the advantage was that back in 1974, when we were allowed the use of the hall, the rent was quite low. We could afford to pay it from the gate money we collected at Rs 3 per head. When we were asked to leave in 1992 after eighteen years, things had changed. The earlier management committees had been very sympathetic to what we were doing, particularly after we started Chandrashala, our children's wing that tied in with the objectives of the school. The school students were given free entry to our workshops. Arvind (Deshpande) was able to give a lot of time to setting up the space. He had given up his laboratory job and was concentrating on doing professional theatre. He and (Arun) Kakade Kaka were the two pillars of the project. Later Vinod Doshi gave Arvind a job. He told him he could wind up work whenever he needed to leave early for his theatre commitments and not worry about what his colleagues and superiors would say. He said he would deal with that. That's how the Chhabildas space was developed.

Unfortunately, the committee that took over in 1992 was not sympathetic to our work. When they decided they would not be able to continue allowing us the use of the hall any longer, they gave us no reason at all. But we suspected the reason was to do with money. The space could potentially make them a lot of money if they rented it out for weddings and other such events. However, while the space stayed with us, it was filled with energy, because we invited all the theatre groups who were doing plays to treat it as their own.

We had been collecting equipment like lights and wings with small donations, often made by members of our own group, like my sister. If somebody happened to be moving to another city like Pune, he would donate his chairs to us. That's how we accumulated things. We allowed the groups to use them without charging a fee. They only had to pay for any extra lights they might require. Similarly, we had platforms and blocks that were free to use. Because of this, people were constantly coming and going, hanging around, exchanging news and views. They didn't always come up to the hall either, but gathered downstairs. So the place was constantly buzzing.

Could Chhabildas be called a theatre movement is a question that gets thrown around a lot by people who quibble with words. To my mind, it was a space that got young theatre people moving. In that sense it was a movement.

The Set-Builder: Sitaram Kumbhar

Photo credit: Vinesh Gandhi

Sitaram Kumbhar has been the set-builder for Awishkar at the Chhabildas School Hall almost since its inception as a space for theatre. Illiterate and without any previous experience, Kumbhar gradually learned the ropes from colleagues and members of Awishkar, till he became their most invaluable hand. His quiet, dignified demeanour and flowing beard has added character to Awishkar's backstage. On all celebratory occasions, such as anniversary shows, Sitaram Mama, as he is fondly called, is requested to ring the traditional three bells before the show. He is a perfectionist in his work and can be counted on to find solutions to the prickliest problems of set design.

How I Found a Career

I am from Sakhargaon in Velhe Taluka of Pune district. I used to look after a man's buffaloes to put together some money to come to Mumbai. The same man brought me to Mumbai. He had a sugarcane juice centre here, where I helped him. He had promised to get me into a mill but didn't keep his promise. So for two or three years I sold fruit, vegetables, roasted peanuts, that kind of thing. My brother, Rajaram Kumbhar began working with a make-up artist, Shantaram Vichare, in 1970. I would often visit him. Vichare advised me to start working as a theatre backstage hand, telling me I should not expect anything fancier since I was illiterate. He sent me to Kalavaibhav, a professional theatre company. He advised me to stand on the pavement outside Shivaji Mandir theatre and observe how set material was brought in, taken out and packed into a bus.

I worked with Kalavaibhav for two or three years. But the company manager would abuse a lot. So I left and restarted my business of selling fruits, vegetables and roasted peanuts from door to door. I had a brother called Parshuram who worked with Awishkar. The group had been formed in 1971. I joined them in 1974 at Chhabildas. After that I didn't go back to commercial theatre. I said I'd rather go back to the village and knead clay for pots—my traditional work—than do commercial theatre.

In Awishkar, I was paid Rs 5 per show. Actually it was Rs 30 for the three of us. Parshuram would give me five, keep ten and Bhau Gole who had been working there longer, would get fifteen. There would be seven or eight shows in a month. During the day I continued selling vegetables. A Muslim man named Nizam showed me how to tie the pulley and throw ropes over the flats to secure them. We used ropes in those days. Now we use pins. It took me three years simply to learn how to do this. I managed to subsist on what I got at Chhabildas along with my business. I didn't eat much and spent very little. In those days living was easy.

I remember the set for *Pratima*. It was beautiful. I didn't work on it. It was made by Gole and others. But when Dubey was doing *Baby* (Vijay Tendulkar), he told me, why don't you try your hand at making the set? Make a kitchen and put in a window through which Bhakti Barve can look. I asked him what I should make it out of. He said gunny sacks and to plaster it with cowdung to prevent the light from filtering through. I made the set, about four flats. It looked good. That was the first set I made.

While putting up a set, we would secure it to the wall with wire. Parshuram fell while doing this and fractured his hand. Dharamsey Merchant who was doing the lighting, took him to hospital and paid all the expenses. We were allowed to use the hall after six in the evening. We would go upstairs about fifteen minutes before that and get the set out. By eight o'clock, it was up. During the day we were not allowed to disturb the school activities.

The play I really liked was *Uddhwasta Dharmashala* which Dr Lagoo directed. It was rehearsed somewhere else but they did seventy or eighty shows of it in Chhabildas. The other thing that happened at Chhabildas was Jaidev Hattangadi's workshops. They were very popular. There would be 300-400 people wanting to join. Out of these he would select thirty or forty. He didn't like anybody interfering with his work. Arvind Deshpande would come but not interfere. Jaidev was very strict with the children but even then, they were all like family.

Pradeep Mulye got me to do a lot of good work on his sets. He taught me a lot. He made me smart. For *Durga Jhali Gauri* (Durga Becomes Gauri), there were four flats and a boat. Pradeep Mulye got me to make the shell of the boat, overseeing the work himself. He told me what to do, what not to do, how to give it a good finish. There was also a red cage that had to be let down without allowing it to touch the tube light which was above it. After trying different ways of doing it, Pradeep decided to drop the idea. I said fine. But the next day, before he got there, I put up the flats and wings and suspended the cage above. When he came I said, sit in the front and I'll show you how the cage can be let down. When he saw the demonstration, he was pleased. So we had the cage.

That's how I won everybody's trust. (Arun) Kakade Kaka always said, once you give Sitaram Mama a job, you can rest assured it will be done perfectly. Jaidev once kept fiddling with my set and moving it around. Baba Parsekar (senior set-designer) was watching. Finally he said, 'Don't ever move the set that Sitaram Kumbhar has put up, not even an inch. He puts it up perfectly.'

Pradeep Mulye taught me the importance of a good finish to the set. When Chandrakant Kulkarni's group came to Chhabildas to do a play, they had brought some striped fabric for masking. I was watching them do it wrong. So I stepped in and said, with striped material, line has to match line when you stitch the pieces of fabric together. Only then will it look well finished. So I took the cloth and stitched it that way—line to line. Even if some cloth gets wasted, it's all right. But the set must be perfect in every detail.

When I came to Chhabildas, I used to drink and eat non-vegetarian food. Kakade Kaka would always know when one of us was drunk. Working with Awishkar, I gave up those habits. My life improved a lot. I was extremely well treated. I was respected by everybody. I was an illiterate when I came here, but they made me one of them. I may not have made money, but it is my good fortune that I have worked with people who respect me and have acknowledged my good work. So I have no regrets.

The Space, the People, the Plays

The Chhabildas Hall stayed with Awishkar for eighteen years. The early years were driven by the excitement of having a new space to try out new things in. At least some directors attempted to push formal and spatial lines to see how far they could go. This was the period when issues like the curtailing of theatre's freedom of expression by the censor board and the rights of the writer vis-à-vis the director were hotly debated. In the later years, the value of Chhabildas as a space for new theatre fell when two other centres for off-mainstream theatre emerged in the city—Prithvi Theatre to the north and the Experimental Theatre of the National Centre for the Performing Arts to the south. The debates at Chhabildas became more academic now. Did the plays that were being staged there amount to a movement? Were they truly experimental or merely represented a theatre that ran parallel to the mainstream? It was these debates as much as the plays that were staged at Chhabildas that made it a vibrant centre for serious theatre in Mumbai.

Amol Palekar

Around 1970, we had been looking for an informal space that would allow us to do plays like *Gochi*. Around this time, several people were writing and doing very interesting plays which fell outside the conventions of the proscenium stage. For instance, we used to do a one-act play that Achyut Deshingkar had translated from Adya Rangacharya's original in Kannada. It had a very long name, *Ajcha Karyakram Yashasvi Karnyasathi Tumchya Sahakaryachi Garaj Ahe*

(Your Cooperation Is Required to Make Today's Event Successful). We used to stage it with *Gochi* as a double bill. It had only two characters. We staged the first show of the play in an art gallery on the top floor of Balgandharva Theatre in Pune. The audience, which was seated on one side of the hall for *Gochi*, was asked to sit on the other side for the second play. Prabhakar Padhye, the illustrious academic, was present for the show and he was furious, 'We are here as your audience. How can you move us around like this? What's going on?' Others in the audience calmed him down and it was decided that we would discuss why we had felt moving the audience was necessary after the second play ended. By then he was so thrilled with what we had done that he not only spoke volubly about the experience but also wrote about it. We continued to experiment freely because the audience was supportive.

Vrindavan Dandavate wrote three very lovely plays during those days. One was *Rajacha Khel*. Dilip Kolhatkar, the director, brought to it the raw robustness of street acrobatics. The other play was called *Upashi Khalashi* (The Hungry Sailor) and the third was *Boot Polish* in which Bhakti Barve acted. The only note that was taken of these plays was in the theatre magazine *Enact*.

Before Awishkar offered us the Chhabildas space, amateur groups like Achyut Deshingkar's, Hemu Adhikari's, Achyut Vaze's, Dilip Kolhatkar's and mine had struggled to find rehearsal spaces. The great thing was that we were all like-minded, devoted to doing a new kind of theatre. So we helped each other whenever required. For instance, when I was doing a play for the India Culture League, somebody knew somebody who gave us a room in the Income Tax Office at Marine Lines for rehearsals. Hemu Adhikari's group found a place in Shishu Vihar School in Dadar. When Mahesh Elkunchwar's *Vasanakand* (The Book of Desire) was under the censor's threat, we did some shows in Shishu Vihar. And then Chhabildas came our way.

It was decided that Awishkar would produce C. T. Khanolkar's *Pratima* to inaugurate the Chhabildas space. It was a very important play written entirely in free verse. It is unfortunate that no note was taken of it. Arvind Deshpande was supposed to have directed it. But he had been offered a job in the Walchand Group of Companies which was going to involve a lot of touring. So Sulabha directed it. Besides seasoned actors like Dr Shreeram Lagoo, Deepa Shreeram, Kumud Pawar and me in the cast, the music had been composed by Bhaskar Chandavarkar. Kumud used to sing some of the songs live. They were wonderful melodies. We did many shows at Chhabildas but unfortunately, the play didn't get the attention it deserved.

A historically important event that led to several experimental plays being done at Chhabildas was the playwriting workshop Satyadev Dubey organized in 1973. It threw up Achyut Vaze's *Chal Re Bhoplya Tunuk Tunuk* and Mahesh Elkunchwar's *Vasanakand*, both of which I directed and staged at Chhabildas, and G. P. Deshpande's *Uddhwasta Dharmashala* which Dr Lagoo directed, also at Chhabildas.

Chal Re Bhoplya Tunuk Tunuk was remarkable for the easy colloquial language that Achyut had used in it. His words were not chosen merely for the sense, but for the rhythm. It revolved around the ennui that had come to grip middle-class youth. Achyut had found a way to present boredom without being boring. This was also a challenge for me as director. Our generation was enormously influenced by Badal Sircar's *Evam Indrajit*. Achyut admitted to the influence in his play. For example, Kamal, Amal and Vimal of *Evam* appeared here as Dandekar, Khandekar and Vandekar. But there was nothing in common between the two plays beyond this. Achyut was talking of a later generation coming to manhood under different circumstances. So his play and the expression he found for its central characters were totally his own.

We staged the first show of *Chal Re Bhoplya* for the State Drama Competition and the second in the Sahitya Sahawas Housing Society. The people who saw it then have told their children how a refrain from the play, 'The bus, the bus, the bus. Where's the bus? It's not our bus,' became part of the lingo of the society for many years. We did some 100 shows of the play.

Another experiment was staging Diwakar's *Andhale* (The Blind). Prof. Sarojini Vaidya was doing research on Diwakar's writings. I received a message from Mumbai University one day asking me to meet her urgently. I rushed there. Dr Vaidya told me that she had discovered some unpublished writings of Diwakar which were incredibly important. She talked at length about the pieces she had come across, reading some of them out to me. I took possession of them all. We had known Diwakar only as a writer of dramatic monologues. But this was something else altogether. What increased its importance was the time of its writing. The pieces were all written between 1912 and 1915 or 1917. They were different from anything else he had written and way beyond their time. Diwakar was aware of this. Perhaps it was for this reason that he had made a written request that they should not be published. One of the unpublished works was a play called *Mi Apla Chalaloch Ahe* (I Am Walking On and On). It is about twenty-eight to thirty-two minutes long, not even a proper one-act length. But I think of it as a full-fledged play because of the powerful theatrical experience it communicates. It consists of six scenes. As they unfold, they reveal a man's awareness of his own sexuality which he describes as being comparable to innumerable horses galloping wildly. It was completely unheard of for anybody to express such ideas in 1912.

So we put together a selection of these writings. We created links between them from passages that we extracted from Diwakar's letters to his fellow-writers and friends in which he expressed his views about literature and his opinions on the contemporary social scene. We presented this experiment under the title *Diwakar: Ek Upekshit Lekhak* (Diwakar: A Neglected Writer). We performed the first show in the Little Theatre at the National Centre for the Performing Arts. It was the first piece of theatre to be performed in that space.

Andhale was one of the pieces in this selection. All the characters in it are blind. Actors tend to enact blindness in a clichéd way. But this piece distinguishes between several forms of blindness. For example, between someone who was born blind and someone who has become blind having known how the world looks, or one who is aware of light, even fading light, but sees no details. Diwakar has explored all these forms of blindness subtly and expressively. The blind people are inmates of a home that is next door to a church. Every day a priest takes them out for a walk and brings them back. One day he doesn't bring them back. He has died on the spot. The blind men discuss his absence among themselves, make fun of him and of religion. But soon they begin to get worried. Then they grow afraid. Gradually, their panic increases. When they realize he is dead, and there's no going back to the home, they set up a loud lament. We staged most of the shows of this piece of theatre at Chhabildas.

One might say that my exploration of sound that had begun with *Gochi* culminated in *Andhale*. Even the smallest sound has a unique importance in the lives of the blind. One of the blind people sits apart in a corner scratching her/himself. The sound of that scratching was created live, not pre-recorded as a sound effect. It was an attempt to give every sound its due weightage.

There was another piece of Diwakar's called *Bhar Chowkaat* (Right There In). The idea he had explored in it was this: a man is standing in a square with its noise assaulting his ears. If he fine-tunes his listening and is able to separate the various elements that make up the clamour, could a piece of drama be created out of them? I was bowled over by the very idea.

I did *Juloos* (Procession, a Marathi adaptation of a Bengali play by Badal Sircar) as a small protest against the Emergency. When I first read the script, I realized this play was going to be a landmark in theatre. It was no more than a skeleton, to be filled out by the director and actors to the maximum extent they could. Its theme was to show how the artist could raise his voice against all forms of repression. It was a theme after my heart. I approached Hemu Adhikari with the script. He was a leftist, an activist in the left movement and a man with a passion for theatre. He ran a theatre group called Bahuroopi. Kamalakar Nadkarni (later critic for a Marathi mainline daily) was one of its most active members. Both

Adhikari and Nadkarni welcomed the idea of producing the play under the Bahuroopi banner. The rehearsals for *Juloos* went on for months. I used to be away from Mumbai a lot in those days. Hemu used to conduct the rehearsals in my absence. Ajit Kelkar played Munna, the young man who protests. Swati Chitnis made her debut in this play. I had interpolated some poems in the play. Two were by Vasant Abaji Dahake, one by Vinda Karandikar and one by Namdeo Dhasal.

We decided to stage the first performance of the play in the State Drama Competition, although we knew it would make no mark there. But for us, it was important to do a play protesting against the state on a state platform using state funding. The auditorium was bursting at the seams for this performance. The play was designed for audience participation. At the end of the play, when the procession leaves the stage and enters the auditorium, practically every man and woman in the audience joined in. Because Emergency had been declared, several socialist leaders like Mrinal Gore had gone underground. Pushpatai (Bhave) had invited them to the show, but we weren't sure they would come, so we didn't make a noise about it. But they did. Predictably, the production did not win a single prize. However, the state allowed us to continue doing shows; perhaps because the script that had been submitted for the censor's approval was a bare skeleton of what happened on stage. Although the first show of the play was performed on the proscenium stage, all later shows were staged in informal spaces, including Chhabildas. We did one in the foyer of Jaslok Hospital and another at Mood Indigo, the annual festival of the Indian Institute of Technology, Mumbai.

Then there was *Party*. When Mahesh (Elkunchwar) read the play at my place, the most obvious thing that drew people was the guessing game it encouraged—was this character (Vijay) Tendulkar? Was that Kumud Mehta? And wasn't this Elkunchwar himself? The game tickled us. But this was only the superficial layer. What really held me were the inner layers that concerned the creative process, the falsehoods and hypocrisies of the intellectual and middle classes, and the impossibility of avoiding them in the process of creation. These ideas fascinated me. That's why I decided to direct *Party*. The play was written with the proscenium stage in mind. But we didn't confine ourselves to that. We performed it elsewhere too, doing many shows at Chhabildas.

I did not use any background music for the play. Instead, I made an attempt at using sound effects. The buzz of conversation in a party, the clink of glasses, the tinkle of ice dropped into them, the sudden silence after the noise of a party broken by the 'thuk' of a soda bottle being opened. I tried doing something else. When there is a party on in somebody's home, it happens in different spaces of the house simultaneously. The invitees split into groups and each group has its own party. I wanted to find an effective way to present this simultaneity. The conventional way of doing this is to light up each space as the action shifts to it, while others freeze in their unlit spaces. I wanted to avoid this. My solution was not to light up only the space where the main action was taking place, but to keep the other spaces in soft focus with the actors continuing their actions. So if a viewer's attention moved from the focal area to the other areas, s/he would see that the party was going on there as well. That is how I designed the whole production. *Party* was Neera Adarkar's first play. She continued to contribute to the stage for a long time after that, while moving into social activism as well. Anant Bhave also acted in it.

Meanwhile, the Marathi mainstream had become completely trapped in the proscenium arch. Even there, the only dimensions that were used in mounting a play were width and depth, never height. Even our writers didn't envisage a play that took all four dimensions—length, breadth, depth and height—into consideration. All thought was devoted to making the picture in the proscenium arch beautiful. There was also a practical reason for the way sets were designed. The Marathi mainstream is a touring theatre, so the sets had to be collapsible. They had to be constructed in a way that they could be folded up in fifteen minutes and loaded on top of the bus in which the troupe was travelling. These considerations were important for this only large-scale touring theatre in the world. But strangely, we, who were doing plays outside the commercial context, had somehow unthinkingly adopted the mainstream's way of designing plays. The set design influenced our light design too. When Tapasda (Sen) came here to do the lighting for *Tughlaq*, we realized for the first time that lights could be placed in the wings. Again, we experienced for the first time, the difference it made to how the stage and action looked when the light came from the side and behind.

Besides my plays, there were other important plays happening at Chhabildas. I consider *Uddhwasta Dharmashala*, directed by Dr Lagoo for his group Roopvedh, a milestone in theatre. He also directed *Antigone* as a protest against the Emergency. Dilip Kolhatkar's *Rajacha Khel* was another landmark, although it did very few shows. Then there was *Alwara Daku* (Alwara, the Bandit, a Marathi play by Purushottam Berde).

Another important play, for itself and for the issues it raised, was Achyut Vaze's *Sofa-cum-Bed* which Dubey directed. Achyut didn't like the changes Dubey had made in the original script, so he directed his own parallel production. For me, Dubey's production was important because, for the first time, one character was played by three actors. I found the idea of exploring the different layers of a character through three representations very interesting and more theatrical. The controversy that arose out of the two productions was less important to me. But there was one angle to this controversy which we didn't discuss as much as we should have. Dubey had refused to accept the cuts in the play that the censors had prescribed. He was fighting for the integrity of the writer's word. But when Achyut decided to stage a parallel production, he accepted every cut that the censors had prescribed. That took the wind out of Dubey's fight. If the writer was willing to accept cuts in his script, what was the director doing fighting for the non-negotiability of the writer's word? Then, as now, I feel this was a huge setback to the perennial fight for the artist's freedom of speech and expression. I made my opposition known to Pushpa and Anant Bhave and Dr Lagoo who were supporting Achyut in this debate. There were heated arguments, animated fights. Unfortunately, nothing conclusive came of them. But I continued to maintain that the battle against the censor, which plays at Chhabildas and elsewhere were fighting, suffered a setback because of Achyut's acceptance of cuts to his play.

Sunila Pradhan

We did Shyam Manohar's plays, *Yakrit* (Liver) and *Hriday* (Heart) at Chhabildas. The rehearsals were also at Chhabildas. Vihang Nayak acted with us. He was a brilliant actor. Rehearsing with him used to be a pleasure. Once there were five people present for one of the shows of *Yakrit*. Of the five, only two were ticket holders. The remaining three were Vihang's parents and wife. But we were determined to go on with the show even for two people. I remember Amrish Puri peeking out and excitedly announcing, 'Arre, two people have come. Let's start.' But one day Vihang took it into his head to have drinks at my place instead of doing a show. Vihang announced that we were cancelling the show for circumstances beyond our control and we went to my place and drank rum. But that was the only show at Chhabildas that we ever cancelled. Otherwise, we've even acted for an audience of one.

Chhabildas was a terribly uncomfortable space to act in. I'd be streaming with sweat. You couldn't switch the fans on because people wouldn't be able to hear us. I wish we could have converted Walchand Terrace into a theatre.

Achyut Vaze

The generation before ours, of (Vijay) Tendulkar and (C. T.) Khanolkar, had reacted against the earlier plays with their long-winded speeches and artificial language. They experimented with realism. But for our generation their realism had become false and irrelevant. There were many things that we wanted to say through theatre that could not be bound together as narratives. This was common to all the young people working in theatre then. In order to make theatre say what we wanted to say, we had to break down the convention of narrative. Our forms of experimentation were not pre-planned. They were the result of what we wanted to say. The how was the result of the why and the what. We didn't read theories and write plays. They came organically.

We were also influenced by what we were seeing. My plays were called absurdist, but I had not read a single absurdist play. The medium that influenced my theatre most was cinema. That is why scenes became brief. The jump from one scene to the next was quick and precise. The film society movement was strong in those days. We used to see European films without subtitles. Many ideas came to us through them precisely because we didn't understand the language.

We were also influenced by one another's work. For instance, there was a play Dubey did, called *Anushthan*. It was not talked about much, but what we heard and saw in the play affected us radically. We attended its rehearsals, saw Dubey tormenting Amrish Puri. And in the end when we saw the show, we realized how extremely subtle things were being said through well-chosen and perfectly executed theatrical devices.

Our group began by doing plays for children. I was at college in Delhi. There were no children's playscripts readily available. So I would write them. There was no affordable space to perform in. We would stage most of our plays in Purandare Hall in Sahitya Sangh Mandir although there too the rent there was beyond our reach. I remember the terrible dilemma we were in once. We had booked Purandare Hall for a show of a play called *Ek Hota Madhukar* (There Was Once a Man Named Madhukar). I had no cash to put down as deposit against the rent for Purandare Hall. There was no money in my Delhi bank account on which I had drawn the cheque. The cheque was realized only after I went back and deposited the collection we had made by canvassing our tickets. Then, on the day of the show, Balgandharva died. A member of our as yet nameless group was upset that we were performing on the day this iconic singer-actor of the golden era of music theatre had died. But we had just about managed to organize the show after forcing people to buy tickets. Cancelling it now was out of the question. We went ahead and did it. That created a bit of unpleasantness in the group.

Later, Tejpal Auditorium became available to us. Satyadev Dubey used to do all his plays there. The kind of plays that we wanted to do could not be performed on the proscenium stage. But we had to fit our ideas to it because no alternative space was available. Even Chhabildas looked like a proscenium stage. But once we began to perform there, we discovered new possibilities that the space offered.

The first play we did there was *Chal Re Bhoplya Tunuk Tunuk.* The form of the play was such that we could perform it even in the open, which we did. But shows in Chhabildas were invariably the best. It gave us an intimacy with the audience which no other space could give and intimacy was important for this play. In retrospect, I think the experience of doing the play there influenced our later productions. But back then we used to think, 'What kind of theatre is this where the heat kills you and where you can't see your way properly to the stage.' It was the most uncomfortable backstage space you can imagine. But Dubey used to say, 'Good it is uncomfortable. That is how it should be. That is why you are doing reasonably okay work, you idiots.' We soon realized that the terrible acoustics of Chhabildas, with outside sounds leaking in and the fact that we didn't use mikes, forced our actors to learn to project their voices to be heard above the sound disturbances. Of the sixty odd shows we did of *Bhoplya*, twenty-five were in Chhabildas.

With Chhabildas available to us, different forms of theatre began taking shape in our minds. For instance, we began creating sets by using modular pieces with levels and blocks that could be switched around. My impression is that this was the first time it was done in Marathi theatre and in Chhabildas. The idea spread quickly, and soon experimental theatre became equated with abstract stage sets.

The economics of doing plays at Chhabildas was a huge factor in the movement gathering strength. The rent did not strain our pockets and the ticket rates did not strain the audience's pockets. It must be remembered that we were all amateurs who did regular jobs during the day and rehearsed and did shows in the evenings. Amateurs don't have to please large, mixed audiences. Risks could be taken, new things could be tried out. That is why Chhabildas became a laboratory for theatre.

Chhabildas was also at the centre of a stormy debate which questioned the rights of the director over the writer's work. Of all my plays, the one I wrote specifically with the Chhabildas space in mind was *Sofa-cum-Bed*. Dubey directed it. He split my hero into three parts to be played by three actors. This was totally unacceptable to me. Although there were three sides to his character, it was important that they be integrated into one whole. There were other points over which we disagreed. We were at a party where we continued our argument. Dubey challenged me then. He said, 'If that is how you feel, why don't you direct it yourself?' So I did, under the name *Dhadasi Dhonduchya Dhandali* (The Shenanigans of Gutsy Dhondu). It was understood that Dubey would continue with shows of his production. But we were very happy when our play began doing better than his. This upset him terribly. The ethics of this event were discussed at great length in theatre circles. Dubey held that it was unethical to run a production parallel to one that had just opened. I held that I had only answered his challenge. Dr Shreeram Lagoo wrote a long article about the debate for *Maharashtra Times*, in which he argued that it would be unethical to withdraw a production on the grounds that the playwright disagreed with the director's treatment of it.

However, there is no gainsaying that Dubey made a huge contribution to our growth as theatre practitioners.

Dilip Kolhatkar

My first play in Chhabildas was Vrindavan Dandavate's *Rajacha Khel*. I decided to use the advantage of the open space available in Chhabildas to mount it in the round, with a circus-arena kind of set-up. The challenge was to ensure that every point of the circle would give a member of the audience as privileged a view as her/his neighbour. I choreographed the play with a lot of shifting movements. This in itself was a challenge because the play had only two actors. The set was a one-foot high iron ring made of pieces welded together and the lights were fixed all around, exactly as in a circus. Kamalakar Nadkarni was one of the actors. I forget the other actor's name. People loved the play and we did many shows at Chhabildas—at least fifteen, I think.

I also did another play by Vrindavan, *Boot Polish*, again using the freedom that the Chhabildas space offered by creating multiple acting areas. The stage made one area and I made 'roads' on both of its flanks and in the corridor outside. In this way, I put the entire available space to use. The audience sat on two sides of the acting areas and watched the play from one end of the space to the other. The boys who polished boots sang, 'This road is ours, has been for centuries; this sky is ours, has been for centuries'. At the end a beggar-woman with Hansen's Disease would enter. Bhakti Barve was playing this role. She would spend three hours doing her make-up. You couldn't look at her without shuddering.

Bhakti was an extremely successful professional actor. But the reason I asked her to act in my play wasn't to ride on her fame. Not at all. It was because we were friends. She was my benefactress. That's how we first met. When she heard about the work I was doing, she began to quietly put her earnings from two or three shows in an envelope and send it across to me. She knew our group, Unmesh, was full of empty pockets.

I also directed Vrindavan's *Kulavrittanta* (Family Chronicle) and staged it at Chhabildas. It had a cast of some forty or forty-five actors. It was a family saga. Each of those characters came with a story. So if one family group was acting at one end of the space, suddenly the light on them would go and come up in another spot where the flashback happened. I had done a multi-cast play before so I knew what to avoid and what to do.

I had acted in (C. T.) Khanolkar's *Avadhya* much earlier, before Chhabildas. The play was directed by Amol Palekar. I had five or six entries with a stage time of about fifteen minutes. But in all the three competitions we entered, I walked away with the best actor prize. There were great actors like Eknath Hattangadi and Satish Dubhashi in it, but I was the one who got the prizes. However, when Amol was considering doing the play commercially, I said I would not act in it. I didn't think the play should be commercialized because then a different kind of audience would come to see it for different reasons and what Madhav Manohar (eminent critic) had called the first adult play in Marathi would have been seen as the first salacious play. I didn't want to be a part of that. Even during the competitions, I had realized how the play could be viewed. There was a love-making scene in it, and one of my entries came directly after that. I would hear all the comments that people were making about it. That made me decide I wouldn't act in it commercially.

There was an attempt in the 1980s to establish the activity at Chhabildas as a great movement. To my mind, the ultimate test had to be the mainstream stage. Chhabildas could be your laboratory but you had to move from there to discover if an audience sitting in rows A to Z was held by your play. Each scene had to have the power to hold the audience's attention totally. They might leave the auditorium saying they did or didn't like the play. But the fact that they sat glued to their seats was the real measure of your success as a theatre person.

My attempt in every play I did was to bring experimentation into a professional play and professionalism into an experimental play. We were so experimental that if we were doing a play, we didn't feel obliged to stage it. We were rehearsing a play by a writer called Shrikant Haldule. The cast included Shrikant, Nana Patekar, Neelkanth Haldule and Mangesh Kulkarni. All the lines had been learned and rehearsals were proceeding satisfactorily. But at one point we wondered whether the play was really worth doing. How were we to decide? It was being produced by Awishkar. So we asked Arvind Deshpande to come and watch. He saw the rehearsal and agreed with our hunch. You're right, he said. Don't do it. That's how experimental we were in those days.

What Chhabildas contributed to Marathi theatre was a space where a new generation of theatre enthusiasts, keen to do something different from the conventional, could try out their ideas and learn what worked and what didn't. It provided exactly the kind of intimate space our plays called for. It was also the right size for the comparatively small audiences that came to see them.

Pushpa Bhave

By the time Chhabildas Hall was made available for theatre, Shivaji Mandir and Ravindra Natya Mandir had already come up for professional theatre. One of the promises made by the government when they built Ravindra was that they would create a 200-seater mini theatre where experimental plays could be staged and parallel cinema films could be screened. Just as experimental theatre had no place for performance, there was no place where parallel cinema films produced by the Film Finance Corporation, like Dilip Chitre's *Godam* (Godown), could be screened. I was on the FFC committee in those days. That promise was not fulfilled. And even now, when the old Ravindra Natya Mandir building has been demolished and a new one has gone up in its place, the promised space for experimental theatre has not been created. The mini theatre on the third floor of the complex seats too small a number of people for its rather high rent to become economically viable for amateur theatre groups.

To return to Chhabildas, there was therefore a crying need for a dedicated space for parallel theatre activity. Sulabha Deshpande was a teacher at the Chhabildas Girls' School. It was through that connection that the Boys' School offered its hall to Awishkar which had split from Rangayan. I understood both sides of the split. Awishkar held the view that plays were meant to be staged as often as there was an audience for them. Vijayabai (Mehta) argued that this would make the name—theatre laboratory—given to Rangayan a misnomer, because then it would be no different from commercial theatre. As it turned out, however, Dr Lagoo, who was once part of the parallel theatre movement, moved on to the commercial stage. His presence there unquestionably raised the quality of performance in mainstream plays. He introduced a realistic style of acting in commmercial plays and the effect of that is obvious even today. A few years later, Vijayabai herself moved to the commercial stage stating that she was transporting Rangayan to it.

Previously, Chhabildas Hall had been used by the school for annual gatherings and cultural events. It was a free space. But, instead of using it in that way, the Deshpandes (and I'm not blaming them—we were all in it) refurbished it as a proscenium arch stage. So once again, the plays that were performed there continued to adhere to the style of proscenium stage plays. As a result, very few plays experimented with space. *Juloos* did. *Rajacha Khel* did. But there weren't many other plays like that. So all in all, Chhabildas became the poor man's proscenium stage.

Roopvedh was one of the groups that performed at Chhabildas. I was part of it. There were other groups too. One of the good things that happened at Chhabildas was that although it was used and managed by Awishkar, it was open to any group that wished to perform there. Some groups didn't do more than a couple of plays, but often they were important attempts. *Alwara Daku* (written and directed by Purushottam Berde) is one example. Many of the people who were involved with that production are working on the commercial stage today. But back then, they did some important experiments. However, personally, I would not like to exaggerate what was happening at Chhabildas because I think we did much less than what was possible. We fell short as a movement for experimental theatre. If you considered the experiments that were being done in theatre elsewhere in the world, you would be struck by the strength of the ideas about theatre that guided them. It was through new thinking that they saw a new vision, found a new language, a new style for direction, performance and speech. Everything changed. The writers and directors of Chhabildas could never have made a claim like, 'We are metaphysical rebels.' Because there was no truly fresh, radical thinking about theatre, importance was attached to technical innovation which often amounted to pyrotechnics. Perhaps it was because the core supplied by a new thought was missing that the movement fizzled out. That is why no theatre person today says, 'Forget Chhabildas, we want to do something new.'

The essential difference between the plays at Chhabildas and those on the Shivaji Mandir stage was one of age and values. Middle-aged people with conventional values went to Shivaji Mandir. Young people who wanted to see something new came to Chhabildas because, by and large, the groups which performed there were socially progressive.

Kamalakar Nadkarni

I started watching plays from the time I was a boy. My father used to play female roles in the old-style plays and my uncle was a mill-worker. His colleagues used to stage plays on contract. So I got to see practically every play that was staged at Damodar Hall, in Mumbai's mill area. Gradually, I began to feel a distance growing between me and those plays. It seemed to me that they were irrelevant to the reality around me.

We had heard about Bhulabhai Desai Memorial Institute where a lot of exciting things were happening. But it seemed too far away to get to for us living in Dadar, although I did see two or three plays on the terrace there. Marathi newspaper critics who could have been a source of information about these happenings, were too conventional in their outlook to appreciate them. Even when one of those plays was staged at a venue that was convenient for them to go to, and they did see the performance, their understanding was too limited to grasp the ideas that drove the new theatre. So they merrily ridiculed them.

Two critics who opened our eyes to new theatre were Dnyaneshwar Nadkarni and Madhav Manohar. Their writing revealed what the new theatre was all about and changed the way we looked at theatre in general. We were, of course, directly exposed to Dubey's and Vijayabai's plays, and we were deeply impressed by them. But there was a fear in our minds about whether these people would accept us into their world, which struck us as somewhat elitist. That is why we formed our own group, Bahuroopi. Otherwise would we not have joined Rangayan itself?

Our group performed several plays at Chhabildas. Our most important play was *Juloos* which Amol Palekar asked us to do under our banner. There were some forty or fifty of us in the play. We did seventy or seventy-five shows of it all over the place. Our experience with it was that the less educated members in the audience were more moved by it than others. We got invited to many villages and small towns to perform. It was an anti-Emergency play but the government did not realize this and allowed us to go on with it even during the Emergency.

The Chhabildas space was not just the hall upstairs, but included the area downstairs which became a meeting place for us. Wherever we went and whatever we saw, we always ended up on the footpath outside Chhabildas to discuss it. That footpath was the source of information about everything that was going on in the cultural world. There were a few benches just inside the entrance. You would always find some people sitting there. When there was no show upstairs, new plays were read here, followed by discussions. It was a kind of itch to register your presence down there. You simply had to go. The discussions were never formally organized. They happened spontaneously. The result was a constant exchange of ideas and opinions. I believe this is what made Chhabildas a movement.

We keep saying Chhabildas was a space for young experimental theatre. But Vidyadhar Gokhale, who wrote several music plays in the old style, once staged a show of *Sangeet Saubhadra* (Saubhadra's Wedding, the Musical) in Hindi, complete with painted curtains. The aim was two-fold. One was to show the young people who frequented Chhabildas what the old theatre used to be like. Two was to do the same for non-Marathi playgoers who would not have followed the original Marathi play.

Hemu Adhikari

We were a group of young men from Khalsa College who watched plays and did one-acts here and there on invitation. Kamalakar Nadkarni was in the group. He had seen a lot of theatre. I had not, until the mid-fifties. Gradually, the group became more consolidated till finally, we turned it into a formal theatre group—Bahuroopi. We asked the head of the Marathi department in college, who was very supportive, to be the president of the organization. He readily conceded to our request. This was in 1960.

Meanwhile, the Bharatiya Vidya Bhavan had become an active centre for theatre in the mid-fifties. All the leading personalities of the emerging new theatre used to perform there. There was Damu Kenkre, Vijayabai, Madhav Watve, Arvind Deshpande, Nandkumar Raote. They also performed at the Mumbai Marathi Sahitya Sangh, which was again in South Bombay. The third centre was the Bhulabhai Desai Memorial Institute which had a small hall where plays were performed in an intimate style. I remember seeing a Hindi version of *All My Sons* on the lawns outside, in which Leela Chitnis had acted. It was directed by her son Manavendra. We saw many Rangayan plays and Dubey's plays there, as also at Tejpal. I particularly remember his *Band Darwaze* for Alaknanda Samarth's performance. We were very impressed by all of his plays.

We did play after play under the Bahuroopi banner, but I didn't think this was the way to go. I felt the need for some formal training. In those days a three-month course in acting and direction used to be run at the Mumbai Marathi Granth Sangrahalaya. K. Narayan Kale taught direction there. I enrolled for the course and it made a lot of difference. Kale particularly altered my whole approach to theatre. I directed all the Bahuroopi plays after 1965. Kamalakar was our writer. What we would do was: borrow a whole lot of plays from the British Council Library, choose one that appealed to us and perform it as a translation or adaptation.

Chhabildas started around the seventies. In 1972, we had done a play by Ajitesh Bandyopadhyay, translated into Marathi by Ashok

Shahane. This was our entry for the State Drama Competition. Amol Palekar must have seen and liked it. That's why he approached us with a proposal to do *Juloos* under our banner. We promptly agreed, but on the condition that a maximum number of members of our group should be included in it. Amol consented to the condition. We rehearsed the play for almost three months. We did a lot of improvisations. Amol never told us to do this or that but drew us out. He led us, gave the play direction. It was an immensely enjoyable process. We did innumerable shows of it, almost 125, including one on the grounds of the Indian Institute of Technology, Powai. After this play, Amol concentrated exclusively on doing plays for his own group, Aniket.

Towards the end of the sixties, we started an organization for amateur theatre at the Mumbai Marathi Granth Sangrahalaya, of which I was a part. So were Ashok Sathe and Ramesh Chowdhary. At that time, the Mumbai Marathi Sahitya Sangh had started a scheme called 'Thursday Project'. Under this scheme, the Sahitya Sangh auditorium was made available free of charge on Thursdays to any group that desired to stage an experimental play. Everything, like lights and sound system, was on the house. Several groups performed there on Thursdays but later, for some unknown reason, the scheme folded up.

With failed experiments like that, the question of where to rehearse and where to perform continued to bother amateur theatre groups. It was this lacuna that the Deshpandes—Sulabha and Arvind—filled with their unsparing efforts in acquiring and running the Chhabildas space. They were aided in their efforts by Madhav Sakhardande who was a teacher at the boys' school. Many groups took advantage of the space—ours, Dr Lagoo's, Achyut Vaze's, Rekha Sabnis's, Vinay Apte's and Ratnakar Matkari's. However, I have to say that Chhabildas soon became a proscenium theatre space. People would say we had pinched the proscenium arch from Ravindra Natya Mandir and fitted it in Chhabildas. The possibilities that the space offered were left practically unexplored with a few exceptions. I can think of only three examples which made a different use of the space. One was a play called *Yatrik* (Pilgrim), produced by the Indian National Theatre. The second was our own *Rajacha Khel* written by Vrindavan Dandavate and directed by Dilip Kolhatkar, in which the audience sat on all four sides. And the third was *Juloos*, again done by our group under Amol's direction.

After 1975, we, the older members of the group, got busy with our professional lives. The young people who had been part of *Juloos* continued to stage plays sporadically. But by 1980, they too had moved on and the activities of the group came to a halt.

Ratna Pathak-Shah

We did Dubey's *Sambhog Se Sanyas Tak* (From Sex to Celibacy) at Chhabildas. My most vivid memories of that place are of the green rooms. Or what functioned as green rooms. There were a couple of benches there and a very dirty mirror strung up somewhere at the back. I don't even think it was an enclosed space. The girls had to go to a smelly, dirty loo to change and that was hard to do as the costumes of *Sambhog Se Sanyas Tak* were complicated. So we had rigged up a little black cubicle at the back where we could change. There were a large number of us in the production and not as many people in the audience!

The other memory of Chhabildas is the entrance—that very dark municipal school kind of entrance and the staircase going up. The whole locality seemed to be a part of the venue. There was a long balcony which ran alongside the acting area. So, in a sense, the view exited off-stage and went into the balcony and you could check out what was running on television that day on the neighbourhood television sets. I remember Wimbledon was going on when we were performing. So between acts everyone would stand around peering into the neighbour's television to figure out who was playing against whom. We knew the neighbours' television viewing habits intimately—their tastes, their timings, everything, because you could see all of that from the stage and from the balcony. Cooking smells would also float in. You knew exactly who was cooking what. And if you were hungry, you felt pretty desperate to share that.

I remember the lighting board which we should have preserved for posterity because it was incredible. In the early days, of course, there were those dabba dimmers. Then we moved to the one with levers. But it was still a rigged-up thing. No brand names anywhere. I don't know who had put it together. In Chhabildas you improvised everything. Lights were minimal. What could you do with them? How did you produce what you wanted to? Sets were practically non-existent. When we did *Don Juan in Hell*, it was quite a job carrying the set upstairs. In fact, Sitaram Kumbhar had constructed it on the spot from where it had to be carried up. I remember that being quite an issue because it was a complicated set and the lighting too was complicated.

But before all that we did *Sambhog Se Sanyas Tak* and then *Waiting for Godot* and *The Lesson* directed by Ketan Mehta. There was a designated performance area in Chhabildas. There was no stage. It was all on the ground. Dubey loved to have actresses fall on the floor. And we had to rise from that bloody uncomfortable, really rough Kota-stone floor. In a play like *Sambhog* there was a lot of rushing around and falling and stuff. So everything had to be done on that raw floor. The audience had some kind of a raked seating system with a series of levels that gave them some kind of visibility. Sound was pretty poor because every sound from the surroundings came into the theatre. Lights were very basic—those lovely old halogen floods, the big dabbas—very, very basic stuff. Everything was very basic. The sets, if there were any, used to be constructed on the spot. Otherwise it was just black wings and black backdrops. This freed us in many ways to focus on what we were doing, the kind of plays we were doing, how we were doing them, how much were we enjoying doing them and how good we could be, more than how we would appear to the audience. That was secondary.

There have always been two kinds of theatre in Mumbai. The Gujarati and Marathi commercial theatres were run by the guys doing plays to make money. Because their focus was so sharply on making money, there was no sophistication in their productions, no sophistication of ideas and no sophistication of performance. They were crude in all three respects. When I say no sophistication, I mean there were plays with planes landing, trains passing and that kind of tamzham. But extremely crudely done.

The other was the kind of theatre Dubey, Vijaya Mehta, Arvind and Sulabha Deshpande were doing. It was a very strong point of reference for all of us growing up at the time, and I was much more drawn to that kind of work. So Chhabildas was very, very exciting and it was the only space that everyone could afford. It literally was our only hope. If you were a young group that didn't have money, but had ideas, where could you go? Chhabildas was your only space for Hindi and English theatre, for whatever nascent work we were doing. Chhabildas allowed us to try out our ideas, to make mistakes and to grow. If Chhabildas hadn't been there, I don't think we could have done the kind of work we did. Of course, the audiences were very, very small. They grew as we went along. But five, seven or ten people was the average. Everyone performed to that kind of audience. Sometimes there were discussions after performances. Dubey encouraged that quite a lot. And that was exciting.

The important thing was to do theatre which would respond to and comment on the world around us. People like (Vijay) Tendulkar and (Girish) Karnad were writing plays of that kind. So theatre as a reflection of society was an idea that was absolutely precious to all of us. Theatre was not meant for just showing off your acting skills. There was always another agenda to it. Sometimes it was overt and more politically stated. At other times it was not. But that theatre must be a reflection and a comment on our society was taken for granted by people performing at Chhabildas.

It wasn't just the space that allowed us leeway to experiment. It was also time. Although during the week we only got the hall at six-thirty in the evening, we could use it through the day on Sundays. So you had time to set up lights and if you felt that the lighting was not quite working, you could actually reject it and spend time and energy refining it. Refining performance too. I remember an absolutely wonderful day when we were doing *Waiting for Godot*—one of the first shows was staged there. Everyone was rehearsing. Sagar Arya, Sulabha Arya's younger son, was acting as the little boy. Sagar was asked to be there from nine o'clock in the morning because we needed to rehearse with him. His elder brother Sameer, who had played the boy earlier, came along and they spent the entire day at Chhabildas doing the whole play. They both knew the lines of the entire play. And they did their version of *Waiting for Godot* alongside ours. Benji (Benjamin Gilani) and Naseer (Naseeruddin Shah) would be rehearsing on stage while Sagar and Sameer were doing their version simultaneously. The same dialogue being done here by these two kids who tumbled, turned cartwheels, rushed around the theatre—all to the lines of *Waiting for Godot.* I remember they did this whole sequence between Benji and Naseer but they did it rolling over each other, like Chinese acrobats, tumbling across that whole damn floor speaking the lines of *Godot.* I can't tell you how exciting that was. I could barely watch the rehearsal of the play properly because it was so interesting to watch these two. I realized how productive it was and what a wonderful experience for young people to grow up backstage. I always encouraged my kids to do that. It was the healthiest way for them to grow up. So yes, to have a place to rehearse the whole day, to just be there in the theatre where you were going to perform, to own that space, to really build a connect, Chhabildas was the first place that did that for me.

The energy of the people who performed there was really infectious. We shared a sense of being pioneers. I don't ever remember thinking how I was going to make a living out of it. Perhaps we were particularly dumb. It was like something will turn up, and we carried on from thing to thing to thing. Not to have any kind of safety net liberated us. It made it possible for us to do whatever we wanted. And that's fortunately something we have been able to hold on to over the years. Chhabildas was very much the bedrock on which that freedom was constructed for a whole generation of us.

The only exposure I had had to theatre was the Chhabildas kind before I went off to the NSD (National School of Drama). It was a rough and ready kind of theatre and NSD, in comparison, was at the other end of the spectrum. Everything was highly planned there, sometimes over-produced, with lots of sets and costumes and access to anything you wanted. NSD had the most fantastic costume department ever, the most fantastic library and the most wonderful set store. So, if you wanted to do a play, all you needed to do was walk into any of these places and say I want this, this, that, and please set that up, and change that, and mend this, and it was all done for you. You never realized what went into putting a play together. If you went to NSD without any previous experience, you thought that's how theatre was going to be. You realized very quickly when you came out that it wasn't so at all. Which is why ex-students of the NSD, even today, find it very difficult to do theatre outside. But I would constantly be thinking of how I would do this, that or the other when I got out. There was this second track running at the back of my mind all the time. And I think that is why NSD did not prevent me from doing theatre. Otherwise NSD ends up preventing people from doing theatre. It's a great tragedy and it's something that needs to be thought about and delved into.

If you were a part of a theatre group, you had to be prepared to do anything that was required. Everyone operated sound and lights and did costumes. Operating sound in Chhabildas was another real learning experience. They used to have a spool recorder. There were no cassettes in those days; perhaps they had just started coming in. So, we used to have just that one old spool recorder. When that got spoilt, my dad donated his to Chhabildas. I don't know how many people today would know how to use a spool recorder but all of us learned to do it. Because that was our only option.

I have another personal connect with Chhabildas. My dad died in '79. He ran a shop which made clothes for men. Obviously, we had to shut down the shop. But we had a whole lot of stuff lying around and we did not know what the hell to do with it. So we held a sale in

Chhabildas. Basically, we were just trying to get rid of all the fabric, pricing it very cheap. We set up our counters in a space downstairs, and the kind of people that came to Chhabildas to buy things were not those one had come across in one's life. We didn't really know the value of the stuff we were selling—silk and high-quality Italian fabric and all that. To us it was dead stock which we wanted to get rid of. But not for the floods of people who came to buy.

I remember one particular incident of a man, probably a mill worker, who had picked up something, checked the price, then checked something else. After looking at two or three things, he selected one. I could see he was really keen on buying that. But just before he could make the payment, his wife came with their two children. Immediately, he put that thing down and went off to another counter where he could get things more suitable for his kids. I can't tell you how moved I was.

But, that is what Chhabildas did. It connected you to life. The real world was always around, part of the work you did and informed by it. That is not something I can say about any of the theatre spaces that exist today, more is the pity.

Naseeruddin Shah

I heard of Chhabildas in '73 or '74 while I was studying at the Film Institute in Pune. I think I first went there to see a performance of Dubey's production of *Aadhe Adhure* with Amrish Puri, Bhakti Barve, Amol (Palekar) and Sunila (Pradhan) in it. That first experience of seeing Chhabildas was a shock. It had none of the jazz which I associated with theatre, having been a student of Alkazi's at NSD (National School of Drama), and bowled over by the spectacle he always liked to create, and at which he was very good. But even while we were in the middle of grand productions like *Tughlaq* and *Razia Sultan*, I had seen my first Dubey play, *Evam Indrajit*. I was struck by the starkness of his staging and the austerity of his approach to theatre. I have to say I preferred Alkazi at the time. I was dazzled by him. Yet I identified more with Dubeyji, with his crumpled jeans and rugged chappals, although he was nowhere close to Alkazi, who, I thought, was the real representative of class in theatre.

My orientation in theatre—thanks to Alkazi and the fact that we had done grand operas annually at my school, and I had seen filmed theatre with Olivier—was towards the typical West End kind of thing, which I have now come to abhor. I think it was Jaidev Hattangadi, my contemporary at NSD, who talked a lot about Chhabildas. But I was pretty appalled when I saw the place. I said, 'Hell, this is theatre?'

I saw several wonderful performances there, but the supposed magic of Chhabildas continued to elude me until I finally performed there. It was a place which was hardly conducive to concentration. There were sounds from the street, sounds of television sets. You could see the neighbours' television sets when you were on stage. There was no air conditioning, the seats were uncomfortable, lighting arrangements rudimentary. We were actually performing on the floor with just black curtains and flats around. But that is where I realized that ideal conditions are not of paramount importance when you are performing a play. I saw Dubeyji rehearsing in all sorts of places, wherever he got an opportunity—in lassi shops, in buses and so on. This is one of the treasures that Chhabildas gave me—the realization that you must retain your concentration no matter what. All the disturbances, in a funny way, helped me to keep my energies together while performing. The audiences were always very thin. I think we once performed for an audience of fifteen or twenty. But they were people who cared.

I even felt encouraged to do a production in English. I don't think that was ever done at Chhabildas, with the exception of *Don Juan in Hell* which Dubeyji did later. So Chhabildas, gradually, became a tacky little heaven for me, available to people with no resources, and where you could count on a few crazy chaps to turn up to watch you perform.

I don't think anybody becomes an actor to serve theatre or to serve art anywhere. We all become actors because we are insecure people who want to be looked at. That was the reason I became an actor. Theatre always gave me a tremendous high, but I always knew I was going to earn my living in the movies. In fact, at the interview for admission to the NSD, I put my foot in my mouth by saying so. Thankfully, they didn't hold it against me. It was a dispiriting thought that I wouldn't be able to live off theatre, because the process of theatre was always so enjoyable.

I had been dying to get my teeth into directing *The Zoo Story* (Edward Albee), to perform it to an audience! Chhabildas welcomed anybody who was crazy enough to attempt something like that with open arms. I did not take myself seriously as a director. I did not think that thirty-five years down the line, I would have directed thirty-five productions. I still don't think of myself as a director. I think of myself as an actor, so my involvement then was really to display my wares. I wanted to be noticed. I wanted to be on the map. I wanted to get employment. So that was really the reason, and Chhabildas didn't ask questions. It was there for all of us. Coping with the less than ideal conditions there was a tremendous learning curve for me. And watching the spirit with which Dubeyji and others who came to Chhabildas worked was also an eye-opener. And somewhere, I think, Chhabildas was responsible for my resolve to continue doing theatre, irrespective of the conditions I encountered, as well as for helping me sharpen my communicative instincts as an actor.

The most important thing was that it cost almost nothing to perform there. You got all the help you needed. You had a bunch of crazy people around who were willing to chip in any time you asked them to. It was the kind of scene that did not exist in Delhi, where I came from. I don't claim I was very deeply into theatre in Delhi. I was in this cocoon of NSD. But I hadn't encountered this kind of spirit there. (At Chhabildas) you could just say to anybody who was part of any other group, 'Can somebody please help me?' and they would come along and do it. It was something I had never experienced before.

The NSD environment, honestly, wasn't a very healthy one. There was a star system there. There was competitiveness there. There was politics there. It bred a lot of wrong ideas, testified to by the small number of NSD students who are actually doing theatre in the city. There are hundreds of them here, but barely four or five who are actually doing theatre. And I think that's because they have been conditioned to the kind of theatre where someone else gets your costume, someone else puts up the sets, someone else does the lighting and you complain that your costume is not ironed and throw a tantrum. As against that, here was an open environment, in fact just an empty space, coming alive! You could set up the stage where you liked, you could arrange the seating as you liked and you could perform without fear of losing money or face. It was a place where you could make a fool of yourself, a place where great creation could happen. It was heaven!

I think it's a great loss that Chhabildas withdrew its support for theatre. It has taken away a space from theatre people in the city where they could be on an omni-cool platform; where they could be on common ground with co-practitioners; where they could sort of smell each other. That's the only way I can put it. There was also Dubeyji's famous statement: 'Hum theatre isliye karte hain kyon ki humein khujli hoti hain; aur jisko khujli hoti hain woh aake dekhen' (We do theatre because we have an itch and those who have the itch to watch, let them come and watch). This has made more and more sense to me over the years, although I can't claim to have the same Zen-like approach to doing theatre as Dubeyji had. Today, if I perform a play and ten people turn up, I'm sure I would be shattered. I have not achieved that kind of equanimity where simply having done the job gives complete satisfaction. I really can't imagine how he achieved that state. But then he was one of a kind.

My association with Dubeyji also helped me to find a reason—apart from displaying my acting—to do theatre. That reason was to get across. I'm not a political person, I'm not an activist, I'm not a guy with strong beliefs about anything. I have nothing to say to the world. I'm content to act as a spokesman for those who decide to use me as one and I think I'm a good spokesman. So I think that's a good enough thing. But thanks to Dubeyji, I found a reason apart from showing off to do theatre. And certainly, Chhabildas where there was nobody to show off to, has helped to shape whatever views I have.

Another thing that Chhabildas did was to finally help me realize that the damn front curtain was an archaic bloody institution. What is the big deal of making a mystery about what you are doing with actors hiding away and nobody appearing and all that kind of stuff? Then the curtain opens and the mystery is finally revealed. And I said, 'Hell! What is this?' It ceased to make sense to me entirely. Alkazi would kick our asses if we so much as peeped out of the curtain to see how many people had come. Chhabildas made me realize that the mystery of theatre has nothing to do with any of this. The mystery of theatre is the stimulation that the audience gives and so, why hide? Why try to disguise the fact that you are in the theatre. The audience doesn't need any reminding. All they have to do is look around and they know they are in the theatre. So Dubeyji's little practice of having the 'nata' (actor) and 'nati' (actress) enter—he even wanted it in *Dear Liar*, if you please, with Ratna coming late and I looking around saying 'kahaan gayi thi' (where were you?)—all of that made complete sense to me. There is no mystery, no secret ceremony that is going on here. What we are doing is not secret. We are actors who have come here to do a play. Welcome, sit down, please be comfortable, our play is about this and that and now we are going to begin. That is the way to do a play and that is the way we did plays in Chhabildas.

Mahesh Elkunchwar

When one talks about experimental theatre, one does not expect fancy places. One does expect to walk through lanes and by-lanes. One does expect the place where one has to get to, to be a small, ignored little space somewhere. One expects that there will be a couple of flights of stairs to get there, that the seats will be the most uncomfortable in the world. It's also what happens in New York if you're going for an off-Broadway play. This is how this kind of theatre had to be done. Chhabildas was exactly like that, with the additional discomfort of having outside noises filtering in. Cars honked, street vendors and children shouted. Yes, there were instances when one would get irritated. For example, you'd be watching a scene between Creon and Antigone very seriously and suddenly there would be a vadapaowala loudly selling his snack outside! But you took these things in your stride. In a way, I was even proud of the place. I loved it. Because nothing mattered if the work was good and was being done with conviction.

At Chhabildas, the immediacy of the experience, the intimacy of the experience, was very strong. One felt like a part of what was happening in the play. Witnessing theatre almost felt like a religious act, a sacred act. What I also loved was that people who mattered to me would devotedly come to Chhabildas to see what was happening there. For example, Adya Rangacharya would come, Shri Pu Bhagwat (Elkunchwar's publisher) was another such person. So I was happy that I was a part of this happening, bustling scene.

What was remarkable about Chhabildas was that it was an accessible platform, available to many. It didn't matter if what you wanted to do was going to end up being good, bad, or indifferent. People who were looking for space found it here. Also, it was centrally located. And yes, even at that time I used to think that there was some vision behind it. I thought that it was very good of Sulabha and Arvind (Deshpande) to make the space available and open to people who were interested in using it even if they weren't a part of Awishkar. So it was not simply a space; there was a vision behind it. Rangayan was much more exclusive than Awishkar. Awishkar was more open and democratic and therefore young people felt welcome there. Rangayan was more like a group of seekers who came together and relentlessly pursued their quest for a few years. When I was a part of Rangayan, we used to sometimes perform in the hall of the municipal high school in Topiwala Lane. It was a dirty, ill-lit place, shabby with cobwebs hanging around everywhere. But I was happy with it. Comparatively, Chhabildas was better.

Chhabildas began when Rangayan broke up. I was friends with Arvind and Sulabha. I had written only one play around that time called *Party* which Amol (Palekar) directed. After that I took a long break. I didn't write a single word. So I was not performed much in Chhabildas. *Party* and *Garbo,* the Hindi production, were the only two plays that were performed there. In Marathi, *Garbo* had bombed. It was considered a miserable failure. I realized it was, in a way, a badly written play. But when I saw how Dubey had edited and performed it, I learned my first lesson in editing. Dr Lagoo had done the play commercially in Marathi. So it was performed in large auditoriums. It was bound to fail. It demanded intimacy. I tried to reason with him but he assured me that it would work with his star cast. I didn't think it made sense to do the play with well-known, popular actors. Lagoo had become a fully professional actor by then and his habits and priorities had changed. But Dubey knew better. Dubey edited the play heavily and performed it in the right places with the right kind of actors.

I didn't write plays for informal spaces. The fact that they were performed in informal spaces did not influence my writing. I have never visualized my work outside of a proscenium theatre. I have always imagined it being staged in a proscenium theatre. In my opinion, every viewer always composes everything he sees in a sort of frame, which is the proscenium arch. I think it is self-deception when we tell ourselves that we are breaking the structure of the proscenium in imagining a performance space. What ultimately matters is the immediacy of the experience, which you can provide very effectively in a proscenium, and the spectator and actor being seriously engaged with one another.

Dr Lagoo's *Antigone*, which was staged at Chhabildas, had a strong impact on me. So did Jaidev's (Hattangadi) *Changuna.* I had always wondered if Lorca's play would work in Marathi, if its lyrical quality could be translated. I saw it happen in this production.

Rohini Hattangadi was very young at the time. I was young too. So I had not lost my capacity to feel moved by what I saw.

One thing I must say, one often hears the phrase, 'Chhabildas movement'. In my opinion, Rangayan was a movement, so was Awishkar. But I don't know if Chhabildas was a movement. It was a space open to whoever wanted to do honest, serious work. It was a movement for about ten years perhaps, but later it fizzled out when all and sundry began performing there. But yes, looking at the seventies, it is true that all the most important plays of the time were done at Chhabildas.

Madhav Vaze

It was the year 1972. Maharashtriya Kalopasak, the then renowned experimental theatre institute from Pune, was to launch its new project called Prayog. It was decided that a brand new one-act play would be staged on every Wednesday night of every month. It wasn't that difficult to find a brand new play to perform every week, as the magazines *Satyakatha* and *Hans* used to publish them regularly. Raja Natu, who initiated the idea, was worried about only one thing. Where could we perform? Bharat Natya Mandir was of no use to us in that, for the rent would be out of our reach for a one-act play; moreover, you couldn't expect, say, 800 viewers to come to see a one-act play and that too on an odd day. We were frantically looking for a space where we could establish at least a makeshift theatre. Finally Raja Natu's friend, Madhu Lokhande, who was himself a good director, offered us a sizeable space adjacent to his printing press located at Tilak Road, which was considered the heart of the city. The printing press would be closed by five in the evening after which we could enter the campus. We would hang spot lights on the trees and within no time we had an open-air theatre. The campus enabled us to divide the space as we wished. While I preferred a sort of proscenium arrangement for Satish Alekar's *Samna* (Confrontation), for Vrindavan Dandavate's *Khota Natak* (Fake Play), I chose a rectangular space for the acting area, while the audience sat on all four sides of the rectangle.

Some time later, we were asked to shift to a hall on the first floor of a building nearby. I strongly felt that we had lost our freedom! Now most of the one-act plays had to be staged in a proscenium. However, for the play *Sahavaa Ved* (The Sixth Veda), which was mostly improvised, I had the audience standing in a circle and the actors in the centre. Those who arrived late, used a ladder to go to the loft from where they could watch the play. Experimenting with the space gave us a real kick. But we lost that hall soon and Prayog brought down its shutters.

Why am I reminiscing about my days with Kalopasak here? You'll soon find out.

So, when we came to know that a school in Mumbai had allowed Awishkar to establish an experimental theatre on an upper floor, we, the 'refugees' at Kalopasak, felt terribly jealous, my personal friendship with Arvind, Sulabha and Arun (Kakade) notwithstanding! But I couldn't resist the temptation of going to see a play at Chhabildas. I went a few months later. There was no sign at the entrance to suggest where the theatre was. A young boy was sitting on a chair, selling tickets for the performance rather nonchalantly. When I asked him which was the way up, he pointed to a huge staircase. I must have climbed at least sixty stairs up unending flights. Is the audience supposed to do this every time they want to see a play, I wondered. Well, there is a Marathi saying, 'You can't see heaven unless you die!' Along the same lines, one could have said about Chhabildas, 'You can't see a play, unless you kill yourself climbing!'

It took me a few minutes to find the door to the hall, but once in, I was amazed at the size of the hall. A few boys and girls were spreading carpets on the ground. Their friends were busy installing sets and lights at the other end of the hall. None of them took notice of me. I realized that I had arrived too early. That's why nobody was there to check my ticket. The boy on the ground floor too had perhaps taken me to be one of the actors. Who knows? I loitered around for some time there. Arun, who was supposed to manage the Chhabildas theatre, was nowhere to be seen.

A little later, people started trickling in. Among them were several theatre people—Prabhakar Patankar, Dilip Kolhatkar, Nandu Gadgil, Ashok Sathe, Hemu Adhikari, Kamalakar Nadkarni, Vijay Desai and a bunch of friends. We knew each other well, thanks to the State Drama Competitions. I felt a little relieved. However, I held my breath when I saw Madhav Manohar taking his entry. Somebody told me that he came frequently to Chhabildas. Up all those stairs each time! Within no time, the hall was full to capacity. Most of the audience seemed to be in their twenties.

The play was about to begin. The audience took their seats. My friends chose to sit on the small wooden levels placed at one end of the hall. I joined them. I don't quite remember today which play we saw. But I distinctly remember that the audience watched it in utter silence, totally engrossed. But I was terribly distracted by the din in the street. The street vendors shouted and shrieked at the top of their voices. The clatter of dishes, pans and ladles got on my nerves. The young boy sitting next to me was unperturbed. However, he noticed that I was visibly upset. 'You'll get used to it,' he whispered with a smile. He was right. The Chhabildas audience took the hubbub for granted!

After that I went to see plays at Chhabildas quite often. The Deccan Express was a very convenient train. It would reach Dadar early in the evening. I could go straight to the show from the station. After the show, I would join my friends who wanted to conduct a post-mortem on the play there and then. A while later, Arun would ask us to vacate the hall. The whole group would then move to a nearby restaurant and resume its work. My sister lived quite close to Chhabildas. I would go over to her flat after we dispersed. Sometimes I would go with Arun to his flat at Vile Parle and return to Pune the next morning.

On one occasion, the performers appealed to the audience to write down their comments about the play on a wallpaper outside the hall. Everybody rushed to write. I still remember some of the comments: '(Never) see you again', 'Amol nasalaa tari itke pauses!

Astaa tar…?' (Even without Amol you took so many pauses. What if he had been there?), 'Prayogik natak mhantat te hech dhandewaik natak kaa re bhau?' (When they talk of experimental plays, do they mean this kind of commercial theatre, brother?), 'Diwaleela vel aahe babaano! Itke dive kashala re jaaltaa?' (Diwali is still far away. Why burn so many lights now?).

Some of us broke away from Kalopasak in 1977 and formed our own theatre group, Jagar. We performed our play *Abhihat* (Slain) in Chhabildas. Everyone in the group was thrilled with just the idea of performing at Chhabildas. Besides, they wondered if they'd meet Arvind and Sulabha Deshpande there. Madhav Manohar came to see the play and we were transported to seventh heaven. Later, he reviewed the play and praised us in superlatives! A great surprise awaited us after the show. Arvind took centre stage, thanked us all profusely, and handed me an envelope as the director of the play. The envelope contained a few hundred rupees. We felt very embarrassed. They hadn't charged us rent, or any fee for the set material they had provided. And on top of that, they were giving us money! What for? I tried to give it back to Arvind. But guess what he said: 'Look, this is just gate money. You have earned it. So don't feel shy. Accept it and come again!' I was in tears.

Vijayabai seemed to have misunderstood the very premise of Chhabildas. She remarked during an interview that Chhabildas didn't have any quality control. True! Awishkar was simply interested in making a theatre space available to theatre groups from all over the state, the quality of productions notwithstanding. Awishkar was happy with the flurry of theatre activity Chhabildas created. In a way, Chhabildas proclaimed that experimental theatre had every right to fail!

However, Chhabildas saw quite a few pseudo-experimental theatre groups also in its lifespan of eighteen years. Those groups remained faithful to the proscenium. They didn't dare to explore the space that was potentially there in that large hall as Dilip Kolhatkar had done. He disregarded the proscenium and drew a large circle in the middle of the hall for Vrindavan Dadavate's play *Rajacha Khel*. The audience was supposed to form a circle around the acting area. Amol Palekar used the entire hall when he staged Badal Sircar's *Juloos*. Playwrights, directors and actors could have used the Chhabildas space more imaginatively. They could have taken inspiration from the above plays. They didn't. Because they sought success.

Let's go back to where I began. To Kalopasak. That is when we had realized that experimenting with space gave you quite a kick.

Deepa Lagoo

I didn't understand much about theatre. Nor was I connected with politics. So I would rely on Shreeram's (Dr Shreeram Lagoo) judgement of a play. When we did *Uddhwasta Dharmashala*, what I responded to was its form. It was a revelation to me how you could indicate the movement of the mind while sitting in one place. That was a huge education for me. But I could never bring myself to say I had not understood something. I would perform as though I had understood fully. Looking back, I have felt I should have opened myself to discussion. It would have helped me greatly.

Our group Roopvedh was formed at Chhabildas. The play (*Uddhwasta Dharmashala*) was done under its banner. At Chhabildas, you didn't sense any distance between yourself and the audience. The audience would be totally attentive, responding to the smallest nuances. This motivated us to deliver great shows. We had never expected the play to do so well.

Dr Shreeram Lagoo

The first show at Chhabildas was of *Pratima*. I didn't think it was a very good play but it was written entirely in verse and to speak those lines was a challenge. Chhabildas closed for a variety of reasons of which one, definitely, was that theatre people were no longer interested in doing plays there. The younger people were struck by the glamour of larger venues.

Girish Karnad

In Bombay, the space that really mattered a lot to me was Chhabildas. Name any theatre personality of that time and they were at Chhabildas. And it was so conveniently located. You got down at Dadar and simply walked over that bridge to it. That was a real crucible. Because you met outside and you chatted. Seeing a play was only one part of the whole theatre ambience.

Sunil Shanbag

It was Awishkar which got the space at Chhabildas. But what was significant was their decision to open it to other groups. It would be very interesting to know exactly what their reasons were at the time for doing so—what the decision was driven by. But whatever they were, it was a very very important decision. They needn't have shared it. But perhaps they felt they might not be able to use the space entirely on their own at that time. Over the years, Awishkar has grown. It is in a different position today. At that time, it wasn't. Also I guess, things in the seventies were a bit more open in that sense. It wasn't as though the space was being used by other theatre groups every day. They would have barely ten or twelve days in a month for other theatre groups but it was more than adequate at that time.

We were strongly bonded with our respective groups. There was no question of me working with any other group. If I worked with Dubey, then that was it. I worked only with him. My identity was with the group. Every theatre company had a core group of maybe five, eight or ten members, who were completely with that group. The basic identity of the group was drawn from the director. Maybe not in something like Antarnatya which was a younger group, and there were two or three people at its head, but in Theatre Unit, most definitely. Dubey was extremely possessive. There was no way you could work with somebody else. Without his saying 'yes', there was no chance!

There were a lot of people who approached me to work with them, including some of his contemporaries. There was Padatik from Calcutta. That was Shyamanand Jalan's group. But I realized very quickly that these were games between two rajas and I would get screwed in the process. So I just kept away from it all. Anyway, it meant that every play had to be cast from within the same group of actors. Hardly ever did you have somebody coming in because the role suited that person. But it also meant that you developed a style which was very distinct. Everybody worked for two, three or five years at a time. In some ways, I think this repertory system was very nice. Today we work with a motley bunch of actors. Each one comes with a different style, a different experience and a different background. So the first few weeks are spent trying to pull everyone together into some kind of homogeneous style. Also, as a director, you end up having to constantly explain things. If you've been working together over a period of time, there is an automatic understanding.

There was a lot of excitement about Chhabildas as it grew. I think after the first couple of years, it started generating a great deal of activity. Many theatre groups came into being because of the existence of Chhabildas—a lot of the younger people, whether it was Shafaat Khan and his gang, Rajiv Naik and his group Antarnatya, a whole lot of people. A lot of activity started happening because it was possible to perform there. It also started attracting other languages. There was a bit of Malayalam. Hindi, of course. Ketan Mehta, Naseer (Naseeruddin Shah), Om Puri, all of them started working at Chhabildas. Not very often, but they were there. I don't know if IPTA ever came to Chhabildas. I have no memory of that. They may have done the odd show but they never identified with what was going on there.

It was primarily a Marathi theatre movement. Dubey identified very closely with Marathi theatre. He was seen as part of that movement. I think people like Naseer came there because of the excitement of Chhabildas. They had access to it. It was possible for them to perform, to dip into that excitement and that audience pool. A lot of people used to come again and again. It had become like a habit. It was mostly a Marathi audience, but they would come to see

Hindi plays as well. They came from as far away as Thane, because Dadar station was so close by.

Language was not a major issue. I think it was more of a cultural thing than a language thing. Culturally, Dubey was identified very closely with the Marathi theatre scene. Several of the plays he did were originally Marathi plays like *Garbo* or *Baby.* But he also did Shankar Shesh's Hindi plays and Bengali plays. But I think, at that point, Hindi worked as the link language. It was accessible to Marathis as well as non-Marathis.

I saw some very interesting plays at Chhabildas. I remember being very struck by Amol's (Palekar) *Juloos,* as also, Dr Lagoo's *Antigone.* Some of Jaidev Hattangadi's early work—translations of *Irma la Douce* and *Medea*—was very interesting. A little later, Theatre Academy became very popular. I don't think they ever brought *Ghashiram Kotwal* to Chhabildas. The space was too small for that. But they brought other plays. I remember seeing Satish Alekar's *Mahapoor* (The Great Flood) there.

Some of Dubey's own productions were fantastic. His production of (Vijay) Tendulkar's *Baby* was very good. His *Sofa-cum-Bed,* which became a big issue, was a very sophisticated production. In the case of both these productions, Dubey was one of the early pioneers of the use of video, or rather film. We didn't have video in those days so we used to run à film projector. Use of multimedia so to say, which in his later years he completely dismissed as rubbish. But he did try all this stuff and for audiences at that time it was quite an unusual thing. In *Baby,* we used to run a 16 mm film as part of the play. It was silent. We shot the film on 16 mm after borrowing raw stock from various people. Govind Nihalani shot it. We used to have a projector in the back. I used to operate the projector and the music and Harish Patel used to do the lights. We couldn't see each other but our cues were common. So I used to look at the ceiling, and I could tell from the bounce of the light from the ceiling that he was now fading. That was my cue to start the projector. From today's point of view, the technology was extremely primitive, but it didn't seem to hamper people. Some very interesting experiments were done.

But we were very much a bourgeois theatre. Whatever our struggles, they were well within the bourgeois world. The plays didn't reflect the politics of the city or the country very much. The big railway strike, for instance, called by George Fernandes happened in 1974. It impacted everybody. It was a big, big strike and very significant at the time. The textile workers were also very edgy and things were happening there. A few years later, the textile strike took place. The Emergency was also on. A lot of street theatre started happening around these issues. I was at Elphinstone College at the time. It was quite a hotbed of anti-Emergency activity. Whatever protest there was amongst students of Bombay, it was all happening out of Elphinstone College.

I don't think you saw a direct reflection of that in our theatre. A few years later, Dubey did a Polish play called *Vatzlav* by Sławomir Mrożek. In Hindi, it was called *Abe Bewakoof* (Hey Idiot). That was a very political play. In that play, democracy is raped on stage. There is a dictator, there is a slave character who is washed ashore onto this strange land and because nobody knows him, he pretends to be a king. So there was stuff like that but I don't remember that anybody, at least not from the circle of people I was associated with, did anything that directly addressed the question of the Emergency.

However, we did do a play called *Achha Ek Baar Aur*, which was originally a Bengali play called *Raktabeej*, I think. Mohit Chattopadhyay was the writer. It was a typical Bengali political play. It had four characters—a tyrant, the tyrant's chamcha who is a weakling, a young rebel boy and a young rebel girl. They all clash through the play. At that time, it was seen as an important political play. So for instance, the Committee for the Protection of Democratic Rights, which was a civil liberties organization that had just formed post the Emergency, would book forty or fifty tickets for their members and they would come and see the play together. And after the play, there would be a discussion. So you see, that kind of connect was there. You did a show, the next day you were also at a Dalit Panther rally. So I used to see Namdeo Dhasal both as a performer and as a political activist, very dramatic. So a lot of this kind of thing was happening.

The Marathi commercial theatre was different. It was fed largely by the state competitions. They were very big in those days. They used to be *the* showcase of the year. Hundreds of groups would participate. It was incredible organization. So many plays from so many different centres. First you had your regional eliminations. Then the best plays were brought to Bombay—which was a big thing. Then there would be this grand final competition. This happened once every year and it was sponsored completely by the state. Sitting at Ravindra Natya Mandir, you saw plays from Jalna, Kolhapur, Aurangabad, Pune, everywhere, assuming that they made it to that level, of course. The quality too was very interesting. The good plays were really very good. Even the scripts.

If you were a winner in the Marathi state competition, you were picked up by the commercial theatre immediately. It was a time when it seemed important to the state to actually support this kind of thing. Compared to that, today there is virtually no support, although the annual competitions are still being run. But actually, officially, nothing is done. All these years and experimental theatre hasn't been able to find a space for itself! After Chhabildas there has been nothing! Awishkar has that little space in Mahim. We tried to make the Sathaye College space in Vile Parle work, but it was nothing like Chhabildas. Isn't that pathetic, especially in the state of Maharashtra, which prides itself on its theatre?

Actually, I will not blame the state entirely. I think the theatre community in Maharashtra has failed itself. For instance, the big commercial producers have no interest beyond their own. Even though major personalities emerged from the experimental movement, hugely respected personalities like Tendulkar, Damu Kenkre, Arvind Deshpande, yet somehow they just couldn't get their act together and wangle a space. It is mystifying. It wasn't even as if the experimental theatre posed a political threat. At the most, the morality code was being challenged. And anyway, at that time, Maharashtra was much more progressive in its politics. What you see today is a completely reactionary politics that did not exist then.

Within Bombay itself, our experimental theatre was seen as a very important part of a much larger progressive movement which embraced writing, dance, cinema. The new wave cinema had picked up at the time. We used to have a lot of film-makers, political activists coming and seeing our plays. Theatre had a certain cultural status. It was not seen as pure entertainment, but very much as part of this cultural movement. That reflected in the way we were all regarded. I think people thought about theatre much more seriously then than they do now, although there are more people watching theatre today. The media too was supportive, although the critics were often really poor. The reviews we used to look forward to were Vidyadhar Date's. He had a political position. His reviews were not wishy-washy. It was very clear about where he was coming from. He used to write for the evening paper of the *Times of India*, called *The Evening News*. He wrote a Marxist review of *Sambhog Se Sanyas Tak*, translated as *Magic Pill* in English.

There was a lot of translation and adaptation happening during the Chhabildas period. There was recognition of the pan-Indian theatre scene. First of all, the theatre community has to realize that when there is a guy writing in Delhi, there is a guy writing in Manipur, we are all writing for theatre and we need to exchange stuff. Dubey had a big role to play in that because he really encouraged that a lot. There used to be a lot of script readings. I have heard so many first-time plays being read out. I have heard Tendulkar read out his freshly written *Baby* in his inimitable style. Even plays by Mahesh (Elkunchwar). And some of this, we even recorded in those days. The tapes might still exist somewhere. For instance, I remember distinctly that we recorded Mahesh Elkunchwar reading *Party.*

So there used to be a lot of readings. And a lot of people showed up for the readings—theatre people. The space would be thrown open for discussions afterwards. Then Dubey also did his own playwriting workshop. I heard a lot of readings there too. Most of those plays were Marathi. Working with Dubey, I had worked on several translations from Kannada, Bengali, Hindi, Marathi. Also east European plays. We'd get the English version and Dubey would translate. He was a brilliant translator. His translation of *Vatzlav* is brilliant. He'd done an excellent translation of Harold Pinter's *The Caretaker* too. Either he would translate or push other people to translate. Shanta (Gokhale) for one. And I think that kind of had an effect on the other groups. Marathi theatre, even then, tended to be fairly insular. But time forced them to open up and look around. I think Amol's *Juloos*, for instance, was an extremely important production of the time.

The economics at Chhabildas made theatre viable for us. If you added up all the costs, it came to roughly Rs 600 a show. In those days, the *Times of India* had a classified section for theatre ads. You didn't have display ads. Anyway, you couldn't afford them. Everyone just looked in the classified ads for information about shows. So it was, basically, just the title in bold and then text giving you more information. They would be arranged alphabetically. Dubey cracked that system and all his plays at the time started with 'A'! *Aur Ek Garbo*, *Achha Ek Baar Aur*, *Apratyashit* (Unexpected), *Arrey Mayavi Sarovar* (The Illusionary Lake). And when others caught on, he started making it 'Aa'. '*Aah*' was one of those. This was his trick to always stay on top in the classified list. And it cost very little. But when the *Times of India* realized the popularity of these listings, they started to decrease the point size. It became tinier and tinier till you needed a magnifying glass to read the damn thing. By then the time had come when theatre also had slightly more money. But they virtually pushed us into display advertising.

Nobody in the crew got paid for anything. None of the actors, nobody. I never got paid when I was working with Dubey. I began to get paid only later when I started doing Gujarati commercial theatre. I used to act and operate sound. As an actor, I'd get Rs 25 per show. This was around 1976-77. While there was no question of anybody getting paid, Dubey used to make sure that everybody ate well. There was no cribbing about the number of teas anyone drank. He would call a local restaurant to send a bucket full of upma and we'd all have that.

We usually did our own costumes and carried them home with us. It was much later that we started getting specially made costumes. There was no question of a tempo taking your stuff to the theatre. I distinctly remember a huge spurt in our performances once Chhabildas opened. What happened was Chhabildas opened, then after a few years Prithvi opened and then NCPA Experimental opened. And suddenly we were performing in three spaces simultaneously. So the number of performances we started doing was enormous.

Just imagine if there was something like *Shivaji Underground at Bhimnagar Mohalla* playing at Chhabildas, the same slightly 'SoBo-gentry' types who were there at NCPA would turn up to see it. So you would have a Shyam Benegal, you would see a Jennifer Kapoor—who would stick out in that audience—but they would come to see it. That was what it was like when Chhabildas was at its peak. I think to some extent later, the theatre movement ran out of steam a bit. We moved away because Prithvi came up. Though we were performing simultaneously at Prithvi, Chhabildas and NCPA, Prithvi had become the new exciting place. By that time, Antarnatya had become quite an important group. Shafaat and his group had become quite important. There were three or four very important groups performing at Chhabildas even then. But overall, the energy of the movement had started dissipating. Television came in. And that changed things a lot. It was not an overnight change. It was a very gradual process. Over time, audiences stopped coming. I think 'absurdist theatre' had run its course. Suddenly, Chhabildas began to be seen as a very uncomfortable place. But more than anything, I think the time had also changed. Generally, the whole socio-political scenario had changed. Prithvi and NCPA were luxurious spaces for us! Suddenly, you were in well-equipped theatres, wonderful air conditioning, great green rooms.

Then Dubey asked me to direct his play *Aada Chautal*. That was the first play that I directed formally. This was around 1980-81, I think. And it had Soni Razdan, Jayant Kripalani, Sunila Pradhan and a whole lot of others who were hanging around the theatre scene in those days.

After that play, I knew it was time to start doing my own stuff. I had also gotten married at the time. I felt like I had reached a block in theatre. I was not progressing. I was also finding it hard to get a foothold in terms of livelihood. I had just started writing for television. I needed more time to actually do my writing. I had also just started writing for Shyam Benegal and stuff and I needed the time. So for the first couple of years of Arpana, the group that we formed, I used to just light the shows, step in as an actor, etc. The first play was directed by Utkarsh Majumdar, the second by Akash (Khurana). After around 1985-86, I started directing. Initially, we carried on in the same tradition as the poor theatre. We started our theatre group with ten thousand rupees which Shishir Sharma's father gave us. Everything was very tight. But I think we were fairly astute even at that time. The audience too had changed. In the Chhabildas days it was much more discerning. They would come up to you and challenge you and say, 'This is not art!' Today nobody in the audience is going to do that.

Shafaat Khan

At the time when I started writing plays, there were strong influences present in theatre. There was (Vijay) Tendulkar. I had read every one of his plays, including his radio plays. I liked his writing. There was Mahesh Elkunchwar whose one-acts, *Holi* and *Eka Mhataryacha Khoon* (An Old Man's Murder), I had seen and found interestingly different. But when I read Satish Alekar's one-acts, I felt a close affinity with him. I had seen Achyut Vaze's play, *Chal Re Bhoplya Tunuk Tunuk*, directed by Amol Palekar and performed on a terrace with twenty or twenty-five people present. It made me realize that a play could be written even in this form and staged in this intimate fashion. Anyone who aspired to do theatre in those days was fortunate to have such varied and powerful influences to guide him.

Chhabildas was important for a new writer because it put no constraints on how he wrote or presented his plays. The long-established platform for new writing was, of course, the state competitions. But what constrained us there was the fixed running time of plays to make them eligible, and the motivation of winning prizes is what pushed us. For our generation, therefore, Chhabildas provided an important space. Equally important was the fact that the audience came there to see unconventional plays. The new writer had the benefit of this readymade audience.

When I think about why I chose to write plays rather than say, poetry or fiction, I realize it was because plays worked suggestively. One didn't have to spell out things, something I was reluctant to do. At the same time, they had to be so constructed that the audience would understand what one was attempting to do. I loved this entire game. But the question was—who was going to direct my plays? I realized I would have to do it myself. Not just that. I would also have to form a theatre group which would help me stage them. That is how I came to form my own organization, Theatre, and began staging my plays at Chhabildas.

I didn't direct all my plays. For instance, *Mumbaiche Kawale* (The Crows of Mumbai) was directed by Ravindra Divekar for his group Uday Kala Kendra. It was an excellent production. I revived the play for my group, but again it was not I, but Ajit Bhagat who directed it. I did my twin one-acts *K* and *M* also for my group. Then I produced Ratnakar Matkari's *Vitho Rakhmai* (Lord Vitthal and his Consort Rakhumai) also under our banner. It was directed by Vijay Kenkre.

While being able to do plays affordably was the main advantage that Chhabildas gave us, an even greater contribution that it made to theatre was as a cultural hub or adda in which people like me, who were searching for a new kind of theatre, had the opportunity to see and try out experiments. We would watch a show and on the following day, discuss it threadbare, even tear it to shreds in animated discussions. My plays came in for a lot of that. The discussions were always frank, but without malice. In these days when human relationships are handled with care, nobody has the time or inclination to enter into such discussions. I still like to do it. I consider it my responsibility to communicate frankly to the people concerned how I have responded to their play.

Generally speaking, the most crippling limitation on our productions was the lack of money. We were often unable to do things which a production demanded because of this. But perhaps there was an advantage to the situation. Had we had funds, we might not have pushed ourselves to use all our creative resources in quite the same way that we did.

For me, personally, in the absence of formal theatre training, Chhabildas also afforded a springboard to learning. When I saw *Antigone* directed by Dr Lagoo, I felt curious to find out everything about Greek (theatre). That's how I read Western classical drama and tried to understand its principles. When I saw P. L. Deshpande's adaptation of Brecht's *Threepenny Opera* directed by Jabbar Patel, it led me to reading and trying to understand Brechtian theatre. Similarly, I studied Badal Sircar's idea of Third Theatre after watching *Juloos* directed by Amol Palekar. I even got an opportunity to meet Badalda and discuss his ideas with him. That led me to Grotowski. Rekha Sabnis's production of *No Exit* and Meena Deshpande's adaptation of *Bald Prima Donna* as *Takkal Padleli Sundari*, opened up the absurdists to me. I read them and came to grips with their form of theatre.

I vividly remember Amol Palekar presenting two traditional comics from the tamasha in a school in Grant Road. I was so amazed by their skill in repartee and counter-repartee and the effect it had on the audience, that their act strongly influenced the writing of *Mumbaiche Kawale*. These experiences expanded my horizons and the scope of my writing and direction. However, doing plays that did not fall into conventional modes often distanced the audience. When we performed my play *Kisse* (Anecdotes) at the inauguration of Goa's Kala Academy, several members of the audience said, during the discussion that followed, that they had not understood it clearly. I told them they had been looking for a story in the play, and not finding it there had disconcerted them. I urged them to open up to other kinds of plays which went beyond stories and served different aims. They had to cultivate the capacity to respond to such plays too. Our discussion lasted through the night and, by the end of it, I think I had managed to convince them at least to some small extent.

From the time I watched *Pratima*, the inaugural show at Chhabildas and later plays like *Uddhwasta Dharmashala*, I recognized the special quality of the space that altered your experience of plays, bringing them very close to you. This feeling was confirmed when you saw the same productions in other spaces.Their effect there was totally diluted. We also felt a strong emotional bond with the place. In an interview that Dr Lagoo gave when he did Mahesh Elkunchwar's *Atmakatha* (Autobiography) at the NCPA, he said, 'This is a play which demands total concentration from the audience. At Chhabildas, vendors shout on the street which breaks the audience's concentration. So I will never perform this play at Chhabildas.' I remember how hurt we, the faithful, were when we read this—to the extent that I didn't see a single show of the play at NCPA.

The limitations and possibilities at Chhabildas did not affect how I wrote a play. I wrote what I wanted to write, but there were certain plays that could not be staged at Chhabildas because of their requirements which would not be fulfilled in that space. Take my play *Shobhayatra* (Carnival Procession) for example. It was staged in mainstream theatres, not because while writing it I had in mind the aim of reaching a large audience, but because it needed the kind of space and technical support that were not available in informal spaces like Chhabildas. If some of my plays called for the intimacy of Chhabildas, *Shobhayatra* called for the participation of a larger audience but that didn't mean I manipulated it to attract that large audience. It just came.

In those days people had created an unnecessary division between the mainstream and the so-called experimental theatre. The experimenters looked down on the mainstreamers and the latter were indifferent to the former. They characterized them as people who jabbered a lot and thought theatre training was important. Their idea was that theatre was not something that came with teaching. It was a spontaneous art. But those of my generation who were doing experimental work, like Waman Kendre, Prashant Dalvi, Chandrakant Kulkarni and I, ultimately moved to the mainstream. Our presence there did make a difference to the kind of plays the audience enjoyed. As a result, they responded warmly to *Shobhayatra.* They also responded to Ajit Dalvi's *Gandhi Viruddha Gandhi* (Gandhi Versus Gandhi) and Premanand Gajvi's *Gandhi Ambedkar.* I count this as a contribution that Chhabildas made to theatre.

If the movement at Chhabildas petered out, that was a perfectly natural thing to happen. Everything has its own life. When the time comes, a movement has to stop. Around the time this happened at Chhabildas, all socio-political movements in Maharashtra had begun to wind up. People no longer worked together. They worked as individuals. The times had changed and with it the relevance of a space like Chhabildas too had changed.

Prashant Dalvi

Let us not get entangled with what to call Chhabildas. Was it a movement, an activity, a space you had a right to, a platform? Whatever you may call it, Chhabildas was part of something that was happening all over Maharashtra at the time. People were seeking spaces to try to do a theatre that was different from the conventional. In Aurangabad, we had Saraswati Bhuvan, there was something similar in Solapur, something in Nagpur and the Konkan. The interesting thing about these spaces was that you felt at home there and you sensed the force of surging energy there. There was continuous activity happening there—twenty-four hours of the day. You practically lived there. You did theatre, you thought theatre, you were possessed by theatre. I would say Chhabildas was one such centre.

In the days before our group shifted base to Mumbai, we used to invite eminent people as chief guests for our plays. We did it not because we wanted to have big events, but because we wanted to examine our own theatre sensibilities. We were consciously trying to do plays that spoke of our lives and our experiences. In my play *Paugand* (Adolescence), we had explored a phase of life that we had ourselves recently passed through—adolescence. The play was invited to several conferences on psychology. We made trips to Mumbai just to see plays. We held a festival of Theatre Unit plays. There was Dubeyji's *Aada Chautal* directed by Sunil Shanbag; Dilip Chitre's *Mithu Mithu Popat* (Chattering Parrot) directed by Dubeyji; and Shyam Manohar's *Yakrit*, also directed by him (Satyadev Dubey). *Yakrit* blew our minds.

After we moved to Mumbai, I joined *Loksatta*. This was in 1987. I think it was the year after that that *Paugand* was invited to the first Arvind Deshpande Memorial Theatre Festival and we thought something great had happened. Before that in 1985, Theatre Academy, Pune had organized a playwriting workshop where, for the first time, I met playwrights of our generation—Makarand Sathe, Rajiv Naik, Tushar Bhadre. My brother Ajit and I were both there. The play I wrote during that workshop, *Dagad Ka Mati* (Stone or Mud), was the first that we performed at Chhabildas. We felt at home in Chhabildas. With all its inconveniences, people were still doing theatre here. They were possessed by theatre.

Paugand was the only play in which I acted. I used to play the role of Sane Guruji. I vividly recall the show we did at Chhabildas. I was on the stage. The hall was full. The response of the audience to my black comedy made me feel I was among my own people. I felt the joy of a person who meets another speaking his language in a foreign country. Mangesh Kulkarni and a whole lot of others came backstage to talk to every actor individually. They were talking about vocal pitch and light design, and appreciating the black comedy. For us, it was like the culmination of the five years of experimentation we had been doing back in Aurangabad.

My job as *Loksatta*'s drama critic would bring me to Chhabildas frequently. I became closely acquainted with it. I realized that it was an extended activity. It continued downstairs where people drank tea or ate batata-vadas. People came close to each other through these interactions. The atmosphere charged you and, at the same time, made you feel at home. People gave you the courage to try out things. The office was in the wing space. A book on Tendulkar was being planned. So the editors would park themselves there. Someone would ask me for an article. Pradeep Mulye, one of the editors, would show the cover around. A heated argument would be going on, taking off from a big showdown that had happened on the previous evening. All of this amounted to a movement. Sure, it had no ideological underpinning, but it was so powerful as a centre for generating energy that it automatically moulded you.

I saw innumerable plays there, none of which one could claim as being path-breaking. Yet, each contributed something towards one's understanding of theatre. To have an adda like this, to be part of a vibrant atmosphere of this kind, gave your writing a boost. It was important to know that everybody you met was there only for theatre and nothing else. The audience too was a part of this atmosphere. It had grown up watching plays at Chhabildas. Their response when we performed *Dagad Ka Mati* was radically different to the response we received at the NCPA, because the audience there had a different idea of theatre.

Gradually, over the years the energy that had marked Chhabildas dissipated. Discussions and other events where all of us would get together were still being organized. This sense of community was still alive and kept you writing. It was important to have that. But the buzz was over.

Chandrakant Kulkarni

It was a little after 1980 that our group came together. I met Prashant (Dalvi) at college. Within a year or two we realized that doing plays for college days and competitions wasn't what we wanted to do forever. We were all socially conscious. Prashant's father was a socialist, an editor, a leader in the dalit movement. So we were keen to go beyond plays done exclusively to win prizes. We did a play called *Stree* (Woman) for the Stree Mukti Sanghatana and performed over a hundred shows of it. Fourteen to fifteen girls acted in it and soon we had formed a group of about twenty like-minded people of around the same age.

Meanwhile Kamalakar Sontakke (Sir to us), came to Aurangabad as head of the Department of Drama. Many people who had been doing theatre enrolled immnediately. They came from different academic disciplines like science or languages, or they were already lecturers at some college. But they did theatre too and they all joined the drama department. So did we. While continuing to do plays for competitions, we began studying the theory of drama. Soon we formed our own theatre group called Jigisha. Around 1988, the group decided to shift to Mumbai one by one. By 1990, we were all together again.

While we were in Aurangabad, I had read a lot of new plays, among them were *Garbo*, *Party* and Shyam Manohar's plays. Each time, we discovered that the first and best show had been staged at Chhabildas. Sunil Shanbag's sister Sunanda Kango was with us. We used to hear a lot about Chhabildas from her. Ajit, Prashant's older brother, would also talk about Chhabildas. During a workshop we attended, Tushar Bhadre had described his idea of Chhabildas amusingly. He saw Chhabildas as a sethia who sat in Dadar giving everybody money and opportunities to do theatre. This idea approximately matched the image I had of it.

An outsider seeing Chhabildas for the first time would have wondered, can this really be the place where so much theatre activity happens? But Chhabildas wasn't just a space—it was a movement, a force, a cultural environment. Sure, it had serious drawbacks because it was never meant to be a space for theatre. But that itself allowed the creation of off-beat plays. The first play I did in Mumbai was at Ravindra Natya Mandir in the state competition. But I would say my first real play in Mumbai happened at Chhabildas, in the first Arvind Deshpande Memorial festival. This was in January 1988 and the play was *Paugand*. It was a wonderful festival. Groups doing experimental work from all over Maharashtra had been invited. I consider that to be my entry into theatre in Mumbai.

I was working in *Mumbai Sakal* in those days and Prashant was in *Loksatta*. I used to live in Prabhadevi. We would wait all day for the evening when we could go to Chhabildas. We all had jobs. Shafaat Khan was in RCF, Premanand Gajvi somewhere else, many others in banks. But come evening, and everybody would congregate at Chhabildas. I have a vivid memory of two or three plays that I saw at Chhabildas. There was Shanta Gokhale's *Avinash Ek Dhyaas* (Avinash, an Obsession) and G. P. Deshpande's *Andhar Yatra*. I was present for the rehearsals of these plays too. Even when many of the others had scattered, the one man who held my hand all the way through was Dubey. He watched me work at Chhabildas; heard me speak; observed my rehearsals, my workshops. He held a very good playwriting workshop at this house too which Rajiv Naik, Meghna Pethe, Shafaat (Khan), Chetan (Datar) and Sharad Sawant attended. Plays would be read there and discussed threadbare.

Later, I was selected for the Sangeet Natak Akademi's young directors' scheme, under which I did Prashant's play *Dagad Ka Mati*. That and *Paugand* were the only two plays I did at Chhabildas. After Chhabildas closed, I did Shyam Manohar's *Yelkot* (Praise Be to Lord Khandoba) and collaborated with Awishkar on Mahesh Elkunchwar's *Wada* trilogy.

I can't say the limitations of the space at Chhabildas troubled me. It just called for keeping things simple and reducing your needs. It must be admitted, though, that we were constrained technologically, which put limitations on our expression. But I consider the consistency of work that happened at Chhabildas and the fact that plays did not have to submit to commercial pressures there very important.

If we look at Chhabildas as a platform for plays that were contemporary in their thinking, I will call it a movement. The fact is that when crassly commercial plays were happening practically next door, in Shivaji Mandir, totally off-beat, fresh and energetic plays were happening here. A dedicated audience, however small, watched them and discussed them animatedly afterwards. Why should such an activity not be called a movement? When a history of Marathi theatre is written, it is those plays, those writers and directors who will be written about. The concern then will not be how much money they made and how many thousand shows they staged. A thousand shows on the commercial stage are equal, I would think, to fifty shows of an experimental play because they are off-beat, because they are done in rejection of the status quo, including presentation and performance styles. I attach great value to the discussions about theatre that went on downstairs and the stimulation that the plays themselves offered. I will therefore, certainly describe Chhabildas as a movement.

Rajiv Naik

When we speak of Chhabildas, we tend to add the word 'movement' to it. We call it the Chhabildas theatre movement. I think we should get rid of this notion, because Chhabildas was always an activity, never a movement. Take any definition of the word 'movement'—purpose, aim, direction, take-off point, clarity of process—none of these applied to, nor could apply to what happened at Chhabildas. Perhaps this worked to the advantage of theatre. Had it been framed by a programme, theatre would not have grown every which way that it did in that space. All the same, instead of glorifying it as a 'movement', which implies something with a socio-political, cultural political framework, we should call it an intense, abundant or sincere activity. I would say Badal Sircar's theatre was a movement, Vijayabai's theatre was a movement because there was a clear thought behind it, of the kind of theatre both wanted to do. Sahitya Sangh Mandir was also a movement. But not Chhabildas. Whoever came along used the space as s/he liked. It was a very flexible platform. It did not submit to the kind of discipline the word movement suggests. Not that it harmed either theatre or its spectators in any way. I just feel when we use words, we should do so with careful thought and precision.

The plus point of Chhabildas was the large number of plays that were staged there. The large numbers meant that some were good and some bad. The good plays took theatre forward. But was it the quality of the space that did it? I doubt it. As a playwright and member of the theatre group Antarnatya, I will say we performed at Chhabildas when we did because there was no other space where we could. To have the space was very important. But it did not produce in Marathi any writing or directorial experiments that owed their existence to the specific space of Chhabildas as perhaps happened later with Prithvi. This is certainly true of my writing. We needed a space to perform the plays I wrote, and Chhabildas had become ours by right.

Having said that, I would like to mention two set designers who used the Chhabildas space in an extremely effective way. One was Pradeep Mulye for Awishkar's production of *Ek Doha Anolkhi* (Unknown Waters) and the other was Pradeep Sule for our production of *Matichya Gadyache Prakaran* (The Affair of the Clay Cart), our adaptation of *Mricchhakatikam*. Both created spaces for these plays that explored every existing feature of the space—its dimensions, its doors, its windows. Nobody else did this. Most people performed at Chhabildas because it was a readily available, affordable space, located in a convenient place like Dadar, where they could do plays that they could not afford to do in the formal proscenium theatres. A convenient space becomes something you get accustomed to. Then you begin to feel you belong there—not just the actors but the audience too. This allows for indulgence. So we did not mind when we heard noises from outside or if our voices did not reach. The fact that people were there attending to what we were doing gave rise to a feeling of a fraternity or community. In that sense, what Chhabildas did was to create an adda. I wonder now how we used to get together there without the aid of mobiles. We did it through posters that we stuck there. Play-reading on Saturday, they might say, and people would turn up.

Who knows where we would have performed had Chhabildas not been available. And yet, when it shut down, we did continue performing. The plays which we considered significant were all performed at Karnataka Sangh. I consider *Akhercha Parva* (The Final Chapter) and *Apsatlya Goshti* (Our Stories) as two of my most important plays. And both were performed at Karnataka Sangh. Even while Chhabildas was open, we staged *Magova* (Pursuit) at Karnataka Sangh. We did *Sandha* (The Joint) in both places. We did Madhu Rye's *Paan Kaur Nake Jaake* (Hanging Out at the Paan Kaur Corner) and *Purnavatar* (The Full Incarnation) also at Karnataka Sangh. All our big plays too had to be done at Karnataka Sangh. *Anaahat* (Unstruck), *Othello, Macbeth, Galileo*, the translation of *Midsummer Night's Dream*, all of these had to be performed outside Chhabildas. We would have performed *Matichya Gadyache Prakaran* also elsewhere, had we not done it in collaboration with Awishkar. Although it must be admitted that Pradeep Sule created a wonderful set using the limitations of the space. In this context, I would also like to mention three other names—Chander Honaver, Siraj Khan and Rakesh Sarang—because lighting in Chhabildas was an ordeal and yet all three of them produced some amazing light designs.

It is true though that the intimacy Chhabildas allowed, because the distance between actors and audience was reduced to a minimum, made for a heightened experience. No proscenium venue gave us this sense of intimacy. So Chhabildas's contribution to Marathi theatre was intimacy which made us oblivious to all its other drawbacks like terrible acoustics and bad sight lines. Equally importantly, having a space we could call our own encouraged us to write plays. Films were too expensive to make, but plays were fun to write and perform because this space was available. Had it not existed, perhaps some of us would have turned our talents to fiction.

The disadvantage of the Chhabildas space being available was that playwrights wrote with its limitations in mind. Those who wrote for Chhabildas could not write plays with large casts. When Mahesh's (Elkunchwar) *Party* was done there, the space looked cramped. So when Dr Lagoo decided to do his *Atmakatha*, he was very firm on doing it at the NCPA. He said it was a play where every word needed to be heard. We were quite annoyed with him then, because what he implied was that it was all right if our plays couldn't be heard.

There were times when we tried to escape from Chhabildas. My *Mitli Papni* (The Closed Eyelid) was about dreams for which a dream space needed to be created. We looked high and low for a suitable place but couldn't find one. So, willy-nilly, we returned to Chhabildas. When Damu Kaka (Damu Kenkre) directed my *Vandha* (Problem), he too wanted to do it in another space. So often, we did plays at Chhabildas even when they demanded other kinds of spaces only because it was available and nothing else was.

When we saw *Juloos*, the things we had heard about its staging by Badal Sircar didn't happen here. It became ultimately a proscenium play. I must make one thing clear here. I've been giving examples of my own plays for the sake of convenience. But what I'm trying to say goes beyond that. I'm saying that, looking back, people see the Chhabildas years as a golden age during which many important things happened. I am fifty-five today and that's not too bad. But with people who are sixty or sixty-five, this becomes pure nostalgia. That is why an impression is created that whatever mattered happened during those years and theatre kind of collapsed afterwards. Well, that's simply not true. We didn't stop doing theatre. When we did stop, it was because our group members got busy with their professional lives. But this happened much later in 1998. Chhabildas closed down in 1992 after which we did five or six major productions elsewhere.

If we keep our nostalgia under control and look back objectively, we will understand what the plus and minus points of Chhabildas were. For instance, Awishkar held all the strings. Admittedly, they were generous enough to open the space for everybody, but the fact remains that they had a monopoly over the space. Their plays were always well rehearsed. They would occupy the space for months on end, while our plays often did not get dates. We have had fights with (Arun) Kakade Kaka over dates, albeit affectionate ones. Everybody was good to us. We were treated well. But with all that, a sense of ours and theirs did exist, which was inevitable.

I don't think we should pressurize the younger generation by suggesting that they have missed something very important by not being around during the Chhabildas years. Our generation was given a huge complex because we were told we hadn't seen Balgandharva. Logically, then it is possible for the generation before that to say you people didn't see Patthe Bapurao. What does that mean? Nothing. Every generation looks for its adda, its platform. We had Chhabildas and we used it according to our abilities.

There is no such thing as a golden age. It is a myth created by the old. I believe the great is always yet to come. The messiah has never arrived. He is always awaited. We must remember this.

Ajit Bhure

I remember seeing Jaidev Hattangadi's *Poster* at Chhabildas. I used to go there to watch rehearsals of plays, because I was interested in theatre. I watched rehearsals of *Medea* which Jaidev was directing. Rohini Hattangadi had just become a famous star after playing Kasturba in (Richard) Attenborough's *Gandhi*. She was Medea and Ravindra Mankani, another star, was supposed to play her husband. But some problem with his dates cropped up and Jaidev took a big risk and asked me to do the role. The play had a lovely set, tiers of steps made with platforms.

Chhabildas was a lovely space to experiment in. We did *On the Pavements of Life*—an enactment of Narayan Surve's poems. The set gave a sense of the mill area where Surve lived and worked. But there was no line demarcating the audience from the actors. The actors would spring up in different parts of the space to recite the poems. The only other plays I can recall which used the depth of the entire space were Chetan Datar's *Savalya* and Antarnatya's adaptation of *Mricchhakatikam*, done by Rajeev Naik as *Matichya Gadyache Prakaran*.

Although the Chhabildas space wasn't used with much imagination by most people, people were constantly exploring new themes and new forms of presenting them. I would say even a music-and-dance drama like *Durga Jhali Gauri*, although a children's play, was still a huge experiment. After all, it isn't easy to mount a dance drama with 100 to 150 children participating! But Awishkar did it. And not only did it provide beautiful entertainment for the audience, it also gave generations of children who came and went a taste of theatre and a perspective on it.

Our group was merely doing plays as and when we found some we liked. We were not thinking in any focused way about why we should be doing those plays or whether doing them was adding up to anything. This kind of thinking started only when we formed Antarnatya in 1984. Then we did *Macbeth* and *Othello* because we decided it was important to do Shakespeare in the way he demanded to be done. Our set for *Macbeth* was one storey high. By then the wings at Chhabildas had been fixed, turning the acting space into a proscenium stage, albeit an intimate one. There was no way we could perform *Macbeth* there.

We never had money. I remember one show of *Anaahat*. Sitaram (Kumbhar) had erected the set. He had to be paid Rs 60 at the end of the show. We took out a collection and put the amount together. Purushottam Berde, whose play had become a hit on the commercial stage, was watching all this from the wing. He called me and asked, have you distributed all the money you'd collected? I said yes. So he took Rs 1,000 from his pocket and held it out to me. 'What do I do with this?' I asked. 'The show has already been paid for.' He said, 'Keep it for the next show. What I saw just now made no sense to me. This dialogue between Yama-Yami and all that stuff from the *Rig Veda*. But I am struck by your sincerity. This money is for your next production.' That was the spirit in those days. In fact, I remember we would pass a bag around for voluntary donations if we fell short of money to pay for the show. Our ticket rate used to be Rs 7. If fifty people came to see the play, the gate money wouldn't cover our costs. But people readily donated money and that's how we carried on.

Our plays were always experiments. In *Matichya Gadyache Prakaran*, we used dance. Malati Agnishwar choreographed the movements. We also used elements from the *Natya Shastra*. We could do the play at Chhabildas because our set was not realistic but symbolic. Madhu Rye's *Paan Kaur Nake Jaake* was a surrealistic play. Our set consisted of nine blocks with sections of three Dali paintings on their sides. The blocks were put together like a jigsaw puzzle to show one or the other of the paintings as required.

Around the time when we realized we were going to lose Chhabildas, we were wondering where else we could find a similar space. Bhaskar Chandavarkar, who was doing a play based on poems, introduced us to Anmol Vellani who was with Ford Foundation. Bhaskar said if we could find a space, Ford Foundation would help us equip it as a theatre. We formed a group called Samantar Natyamanch that included all the active theatre groups of the time. We looked at a number of spaces, but somehow people were too busy with their own lives to take the idea forward. So nothing came of it.

But even today, when I have turned a commercial-theatre producer, I find support in some of the lessons I learned during my Chhabildas days. For instance, audience numbers don't bother me. I have seen shows at Chhabildas where the cast was fifty strong and the audience was five. But never did we cancel a show on that account.

Whether we could do our plays there or not, Chhabildas was always a meeting point for members of all the groups. It was a space for engaging in discussions, an exchange of views. The bonds created then between us still exist. There was a family feeling amongst us. There was a healthy rivalry among the groups. We criticized each other's work roundly. But we were always there for one another. Even today, if one of us has a play happening anywhere, the others make a point of seeing it. Chhabildas was like that.

Vijay Kenkre

My earliest memories of Chhabildas are of seeing plays like Dubey's *Sambhog Se Sanyas Tak*, which was done without a set, using the whole space freely. Then there was *Uddhwasta Dharmashala*. I vividly recall the entire last scene of Dr Lagoo's. And I can still hear Nana Patekar's voice in Tendulkar's *Pahije Jatiche* (The Right Man for the Right Work). Seeing plays was as much fun as doing plays at Chhabildas.

When I recollect the plays we saw there, I realize more strongly than I did then that what had taken shape there was a movement. It was also a platform for us to understand what theatre was or could be. It motivated people to work and people who were part of that movement went on to do a lot of good work even on the professional stage. I believe Chhabildas has become as historically important a theatre space as Sahitya Sangh Mandir was earlier.

The first play I directed at Chhabildas was Rajiv Naik's *Mitli Papni*. The play was about dreamspace. So we used ultra-violet light and there were things that appeared to float in the air. Raja Natu had planned a festival of one-act plays in Pune and invited us to perform. It wasn't a competition. Just a festival. When we performed at Bharat Natya Mandir, we realized no other space could draw the audience in as Chhabildas did.

My next play there was Ratnakar Matkari's *Vitho Rakhmai*. I had been selected to do a play under the Sangeet Natak Akademi's scheme for young directors. The idea was for directors to do folk plays. When I went to Delhi and saw what others in the scheme had done, I realized I wasn't interested in doing that kind of thing. Those directors actually came from folk theatre, so they had directed folk plays. I was an urban director and my actors were also urban. There was no point in doing a pretend folk play. *Vitho Rakhmai* had a cast of thirty. If they were to be fitted into the Chhabildas space, the set would have to be next to nothing. So we used a single level stretching from wing to wing. That, along with a few blocks, comprised the set. In the play, Vitthal is not shown as a god but as the king of the dhangars—shepherds. Given the place Vitthal has as a god in people's minds, the intimate distance at which they saw him as king created a big impact.

The most irritating thing about Chhabildas was that the person who operated the lights had to sit in a corner to the right of the audience and had to screw his neck around to watch the play and follow cues. The other problem was the negligible wing space available. But there were advantages to the space that outweighed the disadvantages. Dadar station was a short walk away. Across the road was the Ideal Book Store from where we could get stationary, books, whatever we needed. There was a batata-vada stall downstairs and next to it a stall that sold misal. Finally, just round the corner was Powar Dresswala from where costumes could be hired. Most importantly, Chhabildas was an inviting space. It enthused and energized people to come and perform. The same can't be said about the Mahim School Hall which Awishkar now runs as a theatre space. It's not a place that invites you to come and perform. The other thing is that Awishkar had opened the Chhabildas space to all amateur groups. Groups were formed by like-minded people who had a shared vision of what they wanted to do. But if you want to do a play in the Mahim space, it has to be for Awishkar.

What added to the buzz of Chhabildas were theatre journals like *Bhart Shastra* and *Parikshan* in which, mostly, Chhabildas plays were critiqued, discussed and debated. One can say that Chhabildas, being an open space, allowed, even encouraged, different kinds of performance to be conceived. *Mitli Papni* was structured specifically with the Chhabildas space in mind. The same was true of Makarand Sathe's *Charshe Koti Visarbhole* (Four Million Forgetfuls) and Rajiv's *Matichya Gadyache Prakaran.* Because of the varied forms of theatre that could be staged there, one never got the feeling of having to use just one space for everything, although that is what we were doing. Now we have the school hall in Mahim. We have the Sathaye College Auditorium. And yet one feels homeless. Perhaps what one misses is Chhabildas the adda, the meeting place.

Dhananjay Gore

The first play I remember seeing at Chhabildas was Awishkar's children's play, *Ala Adanyacha Gada* (Here Comes the Dunce's

Cart). But the cast was adult. Satish Pulekar, Nana Patekar and Vidya Patwardhan acted in it. I also saw *Pahije Jatiche*, Om Puri's *Satva Sanwar* (Seventh Saturday) and Naseeruddin Shah's *Lesson* by (Eugene) Ionesco. I was part of Shafaat Khan's group in which we did his two one-acts, *K* and *M* and then his long plays, *Mumbaiche Kawale* and *Bhoomiticha Farce* (Geometrical Farce). Earlier, I used to love seeing the professional plays at Shivaji Mandir, with their elaborate sets and glamour. But the first play I saw at Chhabildas simply floored me with its sheer simplicity. In one play, the actors would actually come and sit with the audience when their parts were done. I'm not sure whether this was a theatrical device or whether it was making up for the sparse audience.

There was magic in the absence of distance between actors and audience. The smallest nuance of the voice or the subtlest gesture would get through and create a powerful effect. The first play I directed was for Antarnatya. It was an adaptation of Tom Stoppard's *The Real Inspector Hound*. Vijay Kenkre, Rakesh Sarang, Rajan Bhise, Sunil Tawade, Renuka Shahane, Sumukhi Pendse and Medha Wagle acted in it. The set was done by Rajan. The location of the play is a theatre and I saw it happening in Chhabildas. Even *Ajcha Khel Udya Punha* (Today's Show Tomorrow Again), which I directed for the Goa Hindu Association, was done at Chhabildas. I visualized it in that space. We even built our set there. Sitaram Mama did it. Actually, the place had a lot of depth if you used both the actual stage where the school children performed and the performance area that was created for our plays. We took full advantage of this depth.

It could be my personal bias, but I thought plays had their maximum effect in Chhabildas. I remember seeing a play by the Baroda Amateurs called *Crime of Passion*. In one scene, there used to be a bomb explosion and a window would break and glass shards would scatter over the floor of the acting area. This created a stupendous effect. I also saw Satish Alekar's *Mahanirvan* there. What a show that was! And *Uddhwasta Dharmashala* too. I think stagecraft at Chhabildas became more innovative because the resources were limited. Even the audience was tuned to accepting simpler stage designs and simpler theatrical devices.

We often built our sets on the spot. Pradeep Sule and Pradeep Mulye, who designed our sets, would stay there till the small hours of the morning and flake out there after their work was done. The watchman didn't bother them. His only condition was that the place should be cleaned up before we left, which we happily did. No work was allowed to be done during school hours. That was a strict rule. So during the day, all the stuff we were working on had to be shoved into Awishkar's office room.

The Chhabildas plays added to the prosperity of the batata-vada stall downstairs and the chaiwala at the back. The front wall beside the entrance was used by everybody as a notice board. All kinds of messages would be scribbled on it. You knew who had written a message by its location on the wall and the handwriting. If a message read, 'Gone for tea', you knew who'd gone for tea and where. The place became a meeting point not only because it was near Dadar station, but also because people were simply drawn to it. Why else would Sunil Tawade come there from Borivali and Shafaat (Khan) from Mumbra?

Of course sounds from around the place would filter in. The traffic wasn't as heavy as it is now. We didn't hear too many horns. But the point is, neither the actors nor the audience seemed to notice the noise. It was easy to cut it out once you got into the play. Some people used to close the windows facing the street during a show. But I liked to keep them open, letting in a mild breeze. It also let in the sound of the canteenwala downstairs washing vessels. He would start doing it exactly at the time a show began. Then you shouted down to him, 'Excuse me, but can you wash the dishes more quietly please?'

I think Chhabildas came at the right time and served its purpose.

Pradeep Sule

I joined Antarnatya when they were doing *Othello*. That must have been around 1984-85. I was invited to be a part of the crowd scenes.

I had trained as an architect. An architect's training gives him a sense of space. Around that time, I met Bijon Dasgupta who was doing sets for television and films. He needed someone who would design sets. He asked me if I would. I designed sets for three films for him. Some of my friends used to act in Shafaat Khan's plays. Dhananjay Gore who acted in Chhabildas plays was also a friend. I would go there to watch their plays.

The first set I did for Antarnatya was for *Galileo*. It was a flexible, modular set. We could dismantle and assemble it ourselves. It was a combination of three alumium grids which were placed in different spaces to suggest different locations. Adjusting it for the Chhabildas space was no problem at all. The limitation of the space was that there was no wing space on the left of the audience. Doors on the right opened out into a gallery where the light cabin was. So how we took out and brought in parts of the set had to be adjusted accordingly. You had to change sets mostly through the right-hand wing. That's why we would ensure that there was a minimum changing of sets.

Magova used to open with the maximum width that was available in the space. Then, scene by scene, the acting space was reduced because the play went back in time. The last scene was played in a very narrow space. So pieces of the set had to go out scene by scene. In *Matichya Gadyache Prakaran*, occasionally, two scenes were supposed to happen simultaneously. We couldn't shift sets fast enough from one part of the space to the other which might be quite far away. To overcome this problem, I decided to split the space with four cycloramas and four levels. That created a space for entry centre stage, because you wouldn't see the actor behind the cyclorama. This allowed us to show different spaces and different times at the same time. It also created interesting possibilites for lighting.

Now, the point is that we could use four cycloramas only in Chhabildas because it had depth. We couldn't use that set anywhere else. I learned lighting from Chander Honavar. He was enraged when I used four cycloramas for my set. 'You think you've done something great,' he used to say at every show. 'Try lighting up four cycloramas and you'll know what fun it is.' What he had to guard against when lighting up, was the shadow of one cyclorama falling on another. He would take an hour to adjust the lights just for this to not happen.

Sitaram Kumbhar was a huge help at Chhabildas. If you needed a piece of furniture, he would ferret it out for you. He wouldn't tire of showing you one piece after another till you saw what you wanted. The spirit of cooperation in Chhabildas was terrific. Whether it was Kakade Kaka or Sitaram Mama, their interest was in doing the utmost they could for theatre.

Meena Naik

Around 1985, we formed our own theatre group called Antarnatya. We didn't do our big plays at Chhabildas. The first was *Othello* for which I did the costumes. Then *The Life of Galileo* in which I acted. Then we did *Macbeth* in which I played Lady Macbeth. We did Rajiv's adptation of *Mricchhakatikam—Matichya Gadyache Prakaran*—at Chhabildas. But later, around the time I turned to puppetry as my medium, we performed all our shows for children at Chhabildas. It was perfect for puppet shows which require a small, intimate space. My young audience used to love the intimacy of being able to watch from up close. And we would have very lively interactions with them afterwards. The rent too was affordable. I did two or three children's plays using puppets there. They were all written or adapted by Ratnakar Matkari.

Then I did a serious play using puppets, *Watewarati Kaacha Ga* (Glass Strewn in the Way). It was about child abuse. It was my first serious, issue-based play. I had to handle the theme very delicately to avoid misunderstandings. It was a way of showing how puppets could be used for education. Again, we did all the shows at Chhabildas.

We had no problems doing our shows there. There were enough lights there for our purpose. There was a make-up room at the back; and because our sets were never elaborate, we didn't have much trouble carrying them up and down three flights of stairs. But the stairs were difficult for grandparents who would often accompany children to our shows. One member of our group would sit downstairs to sell tickets which would be available two hours in advance. People didn't mind coming early to buy their tickets. We didn't need an usher because there were no seat numbers. People sat where they liked—on the durries on the floor or the benches on the raised platforms at the back. There was no curtain, so we didn't need extra hands for that. All in all, the place was eminently suitable for our kind of shows. It was a big blow for us when Chhabildas closed down.

PART FOUR

The Later Years

Photo credit: Saattvic

Prithvi Theatre.

Experimental theatre in Mumbai did not come to a sudden halt after Chhabildas School closed its doors on it, although Marathi theatre did feel the loss acutely. For years afterwards, it would set up an intermittent cry of 'Give us a house'. Indeed Antarnatya, the last of the groups to have performed with some consistency at Chhabildas, even applied for and received a grant from the Ford Foundation to retrofit a suitable space for experimental theatre. No such space was found and, over the years, the cry for 'a house' has died down.

That was in Mumbai. Years later, the need for a space for Marathi experimental theatre was fulfilled in Pune with the establishment of Sudarshan Rangamanch by the Maharashtra Cultural Foundation. Its avowed aim was to give young theatre groups an affordable opportunity to do plays that reflected their radically changed times and worldview. This well-equipped black box which can seat 150 people is located in the heart of Pune city and was inaugurated by Satyadev Dubey on March 31, 2003. In Mumbai, Prithvi Theatre was to be the stage where new theatre by a new generation of practitioners was to happen.

The reason why we decided to limit the foregoing oral history to the decades between the late fifties and the mid-eighties was because, after that, what might be called social time as against chronological time, began to change rapidly. The Indian economy was liberalized and, in 1992, a tragic watershed moment in the history and politics of the country was perpetrated. The Babri Masjid was demolished. It was a time when experimental theatre was thrown into a state of creative confusion. While the mainstream writers and directors continued on course—the aim to entertain is never disturbed by political events—it was the fringe groups whose *raison d'être* had been to do meaningful work that reflected social change, who were unable to grasp what had happened. Shafaat Khan, one of the most experimental playwrights of the eighties' generation, simply stopped writing for almost a decade afterwards.

In retrospect, the period we chose for this inquiry struck us as having already become history. This suspicion was confirmed in November 2008 when Prithvi celebrated Satyadev Dubey's contribution to theatre with an exhibition of photographs and text and a theatrical tribute. In the tribute, which I (Shanta Gokhale) scripted and Sunil Shanbag directed, Dubey's old actors reminisced about their work with him. The young theatre people sitting in the audience listened to their stories with something bordering on awe. They could not believe that there had been a time in Mumbai, the commercial hub of the country, when theatre had been done on shoestring budgets with such professionalism, dedication, passion and fun.

Although there were other organizations at the time, like the Bharatiya Vidya Bhavan and the Indian National Theatre, which encouraged new theatre, we chose to confine this history to the Bhulabhai Desai Memorial Institute, Walchand Terrace and Chhabildas School Hall, because these spaces had dovetailed into each other like a relay, each carrying forward the impetus of the work done before. This uninterrupted flow of theatre activity produced a rock-solid tradition of experimental theatre in the city. Further, the emergence of these spaces as addas, where energetic interaction among theatre groups could take place, engendered in them a strong sense of community driven by a common purpose.

My choice of Prithvi Theatre, in the northern suburb of Juhu, to take the story of experimental theatre in Mumbai forward, is not arbitrary. It is the only space in Mumbai that exudes the same warmth and easy informality that suffused the earlier spaces. Geographically, too, it continues the northward graph traced by the Bhulabhai Desai Memorial Institute in south Mumbai, Walchand Terrace in south-central Mumbai and Chhabildas School Hall in north-central Mumbai. One more link—a human link—connects

Prithvi to the earlier spaces: Satyadev Dubey. Although he had done most of his best work by the mid-eighties and did nothing radically new at Prithvi, he was a dynamic presence there; someone who made a point of seeing young people's work and commenting fulsomely on it. His evening adda at one of the stone tables in the cafeteria was the centre of animated discussions and arguments. His demise in December 2011 at the age of seventy-five, after suffering a seizure at Prithvi, ended what had been a magnificent and unique fifty-year journey in theatre.

Prithvi Theatre was founded on the legacy of two repertory theatre companies, Prithviraj Kapoor's Prithvi Theatres and Geoffrey and Laura Kendal's Shakespeareana. When Shashi Kapoor, Prithviraj's youngest son, married Jennifer Kendal, the Kendals' elder daughter, the two companies became a joint inspirational force in their lives. When Prithviraj Kapoor passed away in 1972, Shashi Kapoor bought the leased plot of land on which the Prithvi Theatres' storage shed had stood. He was determined to realize his father's dream of building a permanent brick-and-mortar playhouse in its place. Shashi Kapoor funded the project. Jennifer Kapoor executed it.

Jennifer Kapoor was inspired by what Chhabildas had done for the Marathi experimental theatre. She wished to do the same for Hindi theatre. She chose architect Ved Segan to design and build the theatre that she and her husband had been dreaming of. As an actor, Jennifer knew precisely what facilities and equipment the theatre needed to have. Segan, who shared an excellent rapport with her, put all his experience, expertise and innovative energy to use in executing the design that they had together evolved. What emerged was a 200-seater auditorium with a thrust stage, steeply raked seating on three sides that allowed a perfect view of the action from everywhere, and fine acoustics that enabled even the barest whisper to reach the last row.

Prithvi Theatre was inaugurated on November 5, 1978, with a Hindi production of G. P. Deshpande's *Uddhwasta Dharmashala,* directed by Om Puri. The cast included Naseeruddin Shah, Rohini Hattangadi and Neelam Mansingh Chowdhry—all graduates of the National School of Drama. In the early years, in order to attract theatre groups to perform there and audiences to come, Prithvi charged the ridiculously low rental of Re 1 per ticket sold. Theatre groups were only too happy to come. It was not as if a line-up of other playhouses was inviting them. But audiences were slower in coming. In the early days, the cast often outnumbered the audience and the rent could amount to as little as Rs 5. Gradually, the theatre-going habit formed amongst the Hindi-speaking people of north Mumbai. The worry now was that most of them preferred to see comedies. Jennifer was keen to promote more serious theatre as well. So she put in place a dual-pricing system. In this system, higher ticket rates were charged for popular plays that were staged largely over the weekend and lower subsidized rates for mid-week performances which could be more experimental in nature. This system still continues.

The first generation of theatre groups to perform regularly at Prithvi were Satyadev Dubey's Theatre Unit, IPTA, Dinesh Thakur's Ank, Mahendra Joshi's Avantar (Gujarati), Nadira Zaheer Babbar's Ekjute, Om Katare's Yatri and Om Puri's Majma. In 1983, Jennifer Kapoor held a festival to celebrate five years of Prithvi. This gave it a greater visibility, leading to an increase in audience numbers. A further attraction was the cafeteria that adman Prahlad Kakkar ran on the premises and the small bookshop that artist Tyeb Mehta and his wife Sakina set up in a corner of the compound. Slowly but surely, Prithvi was growing into a cultural hub, the only one of its kind in Mumbai.

Jennifer Kapoor's untimely demise on September 7, 1984 was a big blow to Prithvi. But her elder son Kunal continued her work. Years later, her daughter Sanjna took over the running of Prithvi till 2011, when Kunal returned to Prithvi.

By the mid-eighties, the old Prithvi groups, typically headed by directors born in the late forties and early fifties, had stabilized. Their productions, although well-mounted and professionally performed, were by no means experimental. Many of the plays in Ank's repertoire for example, had once been seen as edgy, but had been comfortably absorbed now into the mainstream. Vijay Tendulkar's 1967 play, *Shantata! Court Chalu Ahe* was a case in point; so was, much later, Motley's riveting production of Samuel Beckett's *Waiting for Godot,* which had once flummoxed even the sharpest of critics and had now become perfectly accessible. In short, the groups were performing good, solid modern classics.

The group that did bring in some fresh writing was Ekjute. Nadira Zaheer Babbar, herself a playwright, wrote and directed two very fine one-actor plays which were replete with sharp, humorous observations of people and life in Mumbai. The first, *Dayashankar Ki Diary* (Dayashankar's Diary) was brilliantly performed by Ashish Vidyarthi; and the second, *Sakkubai,* was equally brilliantly performed by Sarita Joshi, the star of Gujarati theatre. But experimental theatre, in the true sense of the term, came to Prithvi only with the second generation of theatre groups, headed by writers and directors who were born in the late fifties to mid-sixties and were raring to do bold new work.

Before I elaborate on their plays, let me break off briefly here to take in another space where new work was welcome. This was the Experimental Theatre, the black-box theatre located in the National Centre for the Performing Arts complex. It was inaugurated on April 25, 1986, on an initial donation by Tata Steel of five million rupees. It is a 300-seater space which is, supposedly, flexible. However, for various logistical reasons, mostly to do with the corporate rules under which it operates, the moveable seats have rarely been moved and the flexibility of the space rarely exploited. A remarkable instance of this being done was Vikram Kapadia's production of *Romeo and Juliet.* The NCPA complex itself was built on 32,000 square metres of land reclaimed from the sea and leased to the Tatas by the government of Maharashtra for ninety-nine years at Rs 2 per year. Its location and architecture give it a presence that is a trifle forbidding.

Moreover, the Experimental Theatre is not dedicated exclusively to theatre. It is open to events like small-scale dance and music performances, workshops, seminars, and in recent times, to social events like fashion shows. No theatre companies are permanently attached to it. So groups cannot keep their repertoires running there for years as happens at Prithvi. Despite this, some interesting experimental work has been staged there, particularly in the early years.

One of the most memorable was *Zulva* (Courtesan's Live-in Contract), written by Chetan Datar and directed by Waman Kendre, presently Director of the National School of Drama, Delhi. In 1988, when *Zulva* was staged, both Kendre and Datar were working with the eminent musicologist and research scholar, Dr Ashok Da Ranade in the Theatre Development Centre of the NCPA, which was sadly wound up a few years later. *Zulva*, based on Uttam Bandu Tupe's novel of the same name, was a fictionalized account of the oppression and disempowerment suffered by Maharashtra's jogtis and jogtins—boys and girls traditionally dedicated to the gods. Not only was this a new theme, but the form in which the play was cast was also new. Kendre had used live music and, in a departure from the brahminical Marathi of middle-class theatre, he had retained the dialect spoken by the people of southern Maharashtra where the play was located.

To return to Prithvi then, the second generation of theatre groups had arrived and stabilized there by the mid-nineties, and it is their work that we will look at now.

Sunil Shanbag (b. 1956) had worked closely with Dubey, chiefly, on well-crafted, ready-to-stage plays but also on risky new writing. Keen to get out from under Dubey's shadow, he formed his own group, Arpana, in 1985. His initial productions provided an interesting counterpoint to the established aesthetics of Hindi theatre, both in the choice of texts and in performance style. They were doing fresh writing by playwrights like Shafaat Khan, Rajeev Naik and Chandrashekhar Phansalkar, along with plays by senior Indian and

Western playwrights like Mahesh Elkunchwar, Vijay Tendulkar, Harold Pinter, Sławomir Mrożek and Milan Kundera. Arpana's Hindi production of Tendulkar's *Cyclewalla* came before the Marathi.

Shanbag's first move away from readymade playscripts came when he dramatized two short stories—*Do Quame* by Saadat Hasan Manto and *The Hitch-Hiking Game* by Milan Kundera—in 1997. Nine years later, he turned away from fiction drama itself when he directed Ramu Ramanathan's research-based play, *Cotton 56, Polyester 84*, bringing to it his considerable experience in making documentary films. The play used songs and reminiscenses to bring to life the unique culture that had once fired Girangaon—the mill area in central Mumbai. The great textile mills strike of 1982, led by Dr Datta Samant, far from benefitting mill-workers, had triggered the gradual closure of the mills, leaving workers and their families high and dry. Some mill-workers returned to their villages while others eked out a living selling vegetables and other stuff door to door. In many cases, their sons came under the influence of underworld dons and took to crime. This destabilization and dispersal of the community broke its spirit, and Girangaon's vibrant culture of music and theatre died. Although *Cotton 56, Polyester 84* did not criticize the political dispensation of the day overtly, it posed enough of a threat to lead to the closure of one of its shows in Vidarbha, on the borders of Naxal country. The police said they were acting on 'orders from above'.

Shanbag also directed another research-based play, *Sex, Morality and Censorship* which I (Shanta Gokhale) wrote with inputs from Irawati Karnik. It explored the many forms of censorship, institutionalized and otherwise, that theatre had to contend with in Maharashtra. It took, as a central example, Tendulkar's 1972 play, *Sakharam Binder*, in which the Maharashtra Stage Performance Scrutiny Board had asked for over thirty cuts. These cuts, if implemented, would have destroyed the play. The producer took the censor board to court and won his case and the play went on to do more than 500 shows.

After this, Shanbag began to commission text that could be

intertwined with readymade playscripts to produce something that was more complexly layered. *Walking to the Sun* was one such play. Shanbag had been invited by an organization in Kolkata to do a Rabindranath Tagore play. By pure coincidence, he had stumbled on a story about Tagore's 1912 play, *Dak Ghar* (Post Office) that offered an interesting insight into it. The play, which is about a young, terminally ill boy, had been translated into English, French and German and received rave reviews all over Europe. Dr Janusz Korczak, a Polish paediatrician and writer, had translated it into Polish. Years later, when he was looking after orphans in a Warsaw ghetto, it struck him that if the children performed the play, it might help them face their inevitable end with greater equanimity. The children did perform the play and were then taken by train to Treblinka to be gassed. Vivek Narayan wrote the script that meshed *Dak Ghar* with the performance of it by Korczak's orphans, making *Walking to the Sun* a complex and profoundly moving play.

Sunil Shanbag continues to break new ground. In his latest production, *Blank Page*, he abandons prose for poetry, Arpana for his new group Tamasha and formal spaces for intimate spaces. *Blank Page* presents poetry in performance. A group of nine actors in everyday clothes come and go in ones, twos or groups, interpreting seventeen poems in four languages by well-known contemporary poets. The meaning of the recited word is enriched and embellished throughout with music and movement, creating a chiaroscuro of sound and mood.

Chetan Datar (b. 1964 d. 2008) had also been a member of Satyadev Dubey's Theatre Unit. His first full-length play *Savalya* (Shadows), an immaculately crafted realistic play, was directed by Dubey. Like Shanbag, Datar too wanted to escape from linearity and realism. In an informal conversation with this writer, he once confessed that each time he picked up his pen to write, what emerged was a realistic play. Frustrated, he gave up writing and concentrated on direction. Meanwhile, he was still looking for a form of theatre that would not be as totally dominated by a verbal text as the plays he wrote and directed. In the late nineties, he met two dancers—Rajashree Shirke and Vaibhav Arekar—with whom he evolved Ranganritya, a form that combined dance, speech and music, taking us back, in a sense, to the idea of total theatre as described in the *Natya Shastra*.

Of the five Ranganritya productions Datar directed, the most remarkable was *Mata Hidimba* in which Shirke played Hidimba, the single mother struggling against odds; and Arekar played Ghatotkacha who is ultimately sacrificed on the battlefield of Kurukshetra.

Ramu Ramanathan (b. 1967) is arguably Mumbai's only politically driven playwright. He is also a fine director and actor. He has worked closely for many years with Jaimini Pathak's group, Working Title. Ramanathan writes rigorously researched plays, politically weighted towards the left. His most widely seen work is *Mahadevbhai*, which was first performed at Prithvi in 2002 and is still running. It is written in a lively story-telling form. Jaimini Pathak plays an actor who claims a tenuous connection with Mahadev Desai, Mahatma Gandhi's personal secretary from 1917 until his death in 1942. Mahadevbhai kept a diary in which he meticulously recorded every event, exchange of letters, discourse and banter to which he was privy during the twenty-five years that he lived with, and for, Gandhi. Ramanathan bases the events narrated in the play on these diary notings.

Ramanathan's engagement with local history, which produced *Cotton 56, Polyester 84*, also inspired *3, Sakina Manzil.* His protagonists in this two-hander, was a pair of lovers played by Jaimini Pathak and Suruchi Aulakh, whose lives changed irrevocably when the freighter SS Fort Stikine—carrying a cargo of cotton bales, gold, and around 1,400 tons of explosives—blew up in Mumbai's Victoria Dock in 1944, sinking ships, scattering debris, setting fire to the area and killing around 800 people.

Ramanathan wrote *Comrade Kumbhakarna* for well-known Pune-based director Mohit Takalkar who had been invited to direct a play for the National School of Drama repertory in Delhi. The play, at its simplest level, was about the gagging of free speech by the state, of which a recent example was the arrest of political activists Arun Ferreira, Sridhar Srinivasan and Vernon Gonzalves; but there were other layers to the play. The protagonist Kumbhakarna has an ideological affinty with Periyar's Self-Respect Movement of which his father used to be a member. His mother is a folk performer of stories from the *Ramayana*. The family lives a life of deprivation. The mother has named her son Kumbhakarna, in the hope that he will sleep through his life and not ask for food. In this blending of past and present, mythology and contemporary reality, Kumbhakarna is arrested and arraigned before two state officals for a crime he has not committed.

Eight of Ramanathan's plays written between 1993 and 2008 have been published—an acknowledgement of his importance in English-language theatre.

Makarand Deshpande (b. 1966) has authored and directed over forty plays for his group Ansh, formed in 1994. He has also acted in many of them. To say that they are experimental plays is to tell only half the truth. The full truth is that they are experiments from beginning to end in the manner of writing, directing, rehearsing and set design. The outcome of these processes of play-making is never fully known to Deshpande until a play is staged. Even after that, a long run will mean changes that are sometimes pretty radical.

A Deshpande play begins with an idea, an image or a question that has taken hold of his mind. His most natural medium of expression being drama, he begins to directly scribble a play that will help him explore it. His perspective is always a little off-kilter, leaning towards the philosophical. He writes with great intensity and speed. His language is fluent and rich with imagery, metaphor and wit. When rehearsals begin, he gives his actors full freedom to interpret their roles. Since his writing is largely intuitive, the actors' interpretations often reveal his plays to him. Teddy Maurya, who designed his sets initially for many years, worked as intuitively as Deshpande. He too was given a free hand. He was not expected to create illusions of known spaces or to concern himself with logic. As a result, although his sets, which often used vertical space in a striking manner, defied logical interpretation, they looked just right in a Deshpande play. In *Kasturi*, for example, which featured three actors—Sudhir Pandey, Mona Ambegaonkar and Ratna Pathak-Shah—Maurya placed an enormous gong at the supposed entrance to the acting space, which actors would strike to announce their entry.

In 2007, Deshpande broke with surreal theatre—in which he had explored his themes through mythology, fantasy and dreamspace—to embrace human problems. His audience, Naseeruddin Shah amongst them, had often remarked that they did not understand his plays but loved them. He was now keen for people to understand his work and be affected by it. The play that marked this departure, at least temporarily, was *Karodon Mein Ek* (One in a Crore) in which the patriarch of a business family inhabits two worlds as a result of Alzheimer's. One is the real world which his loving family shares with him; and the other is his private world of illusions which the family tries desperately to enter.

The process of playmaking itself, which brings together human beings of diverse temperaments, histories and aspirations, has often been the material from which Deshpande has constructed plays. *Grihalaxmi* (The Goddess of the House) and *Sakharam Binder ki Khoj Mein Havaldar* (A Constable in Search of Sakharam Binder) are cases in point. In the latter play, Champa's husband, from Tendulkar's well-known play *Sakharam Binder*, goes in search of Sakharam who has killed her. He is accompanied by a friend, a police havaldar.

One does not make facile use of the word original in these post-postmodern times; but Makarand Deshpande's work may, without exaggeration, be described as original.

Atul Kumar (b. 1968) came to Mumbai from Delhi where he and Rajat Kapoor had been members of a theatre group called Chingari.

In Mumbai, they formed two companies, Cinematograph and The Company Theatre, respectively. Both young men shared an interest in Buster Keaton, Charlie Chaplin, circus clowns and jesters. These interests inspired three plays—directed by Kapoor and featuring Kumar as the chief protagonist or solo actor—*C for Clown*, *Hamlet the Clown Prince* and *Nothing Like Lear*. Kumar's make-up, costumes and body language had their source in clowning. His verbal language was gibberish, cleverly accented to sound like French or Italian. Interspersed with this nonsense language were key lines from the original texts. The clown's imagined private life was used as a counterpoint to the stories and characters in the original texts, giving rise both to laughter and pathos.

Atul Kumar's other experiment, *The Blue Mug*, had little laughter. It was staged at Prithvi in 2002. The cast comprised Rajat Kapoor, Joy Fernandes, Vinay Pathak, Sheeba Chadha and Ranvir Shorey. This was perhaps one of the first attempts at devised theatre in Mumbai. At the centre of the play was a character modified from a case study described in *The Man Who Mistook His Wife for a Hat* by Oliver Sacks. Shorey played this character who had lost all memory of the past twenty years, leaving him permanently stranded at age twenty. The other actors called up memories of strange, ordinary, embarrassing, tragic events that they had experienced. On the assumption that they, as actors, who normally inhabited the skins of other characters, would have a problem facing the audience as themselves, it was decided that they should place their doubts and self-questioning in this regard directly before the audience. Thus, they would interrupt their recollections to wonder whether the incident they had narrated had happened the way they remembered it or had they unconsciously reconstructed it to fit their present self-image?

Manav Kaul (b. 1976) was born in Baramulla, grew up in Hoshangabad, and started doing theatre in Bhopal. He came to Mumbai in 1998 and formed a group called aRANYA. His first play that stunned the audience was staged at Prithvi in 2004. *Shakkar Ke Paanch Dane* (Five Grains of Sugar), an hour-long monologue, superbly enacted by NSD-trained Kumud Mishra, started with a poem. Kaul is a poet, so poetry often enters his work. *Shakkar Ke Paanch Dane* did not have a conventional beginning, middle and end. What held it together was a visual refrain. Rajkumar, the protagonist of the play who was narrating the story of his life, returned at frequent intervals to the five grains of sugar he had laid out on the floor. They represented the five people who had played unlikely roles in his otherwise unremarkable life.

Kaul's *The Park*, which opened at Prithvi in 2009, is a very different kind of play. Its location is three benches in a park habitually occupied by three men. When somebody disturbs this distribution of space, arguments follow. They begin light-heartedly enough, but soon escalate into a vicious battle bristling with jibes over religion, caste and community. The benches now expand to become symbols of territory, including everything from the sons-of-the-soil politics played by chauvinistic parties like the Shiv Sena and the Maharashtra Navnirman Sena to the festering problems of Kashmir and Palestine.

Colour Blind was Kaul's attempt at a totally different form of theatre from his previous work. It was devised in response to an invitation from an organization in Kolkata to do a play based on Rabindranath Tagore's life or work. What he produced was a research-based fictionalized account of Tagore's relationship with Victoria Ocampo, the Argentine writer and intellectual, whom he considered his muse. Kalki Koechlin, who also part-wrote the play, played Ocampo. Lyricist-singer-actor, Swanand Kirkire played Death. The play suggested that it was through Tagore's relationship with the concrete Ocampo and the abstract Death that he discovered himself.

Quasar Padamsee (b. 1978) came into full-time theatre after a stint in advertising. His group, Q Theatre Productions, formed in collaboration with members of his batch from college, did a few conventional plays in their initial years, like Arthur Miller's *All My*

Sons. Their *Khatijabai of Karmali Terrace* was an adaptation of Stella Kon's popular *Emily of Emerald Hill*. However, the group broke out of readymade plays in 2009, when it devised *Project S.T.R.I.P*, scripted from actors' inputs by Bangalore-based award-winning playwright Ram Ganesh Kamatham. The play addressed issues of environmental destruction and erasure of peoples and cultures by corporate greed.

Mumbai's experimentalists, always starved for space, have been on a constant look-out for new venues to perform in. In 2013, Quasar Padamsee discovered the Cama Institute in the Fort area of south Mumbai for his off-beat staging of *So Many Socks*. Written by Annie Zaidi, this play, dealing with loss of home and the politics attending it, was based on *Kora*—a collection of poems by Tibetan exile-activist Tenzing Tsundue.

The Industrial Theatre Company formed in the early nineties by Karan Makhija, Nadir Khan, Pushan Kripalani and Rehaan Engineer, had once vowed never to use formal auditoria for their work because they were over-used and contributed no character of their own to plays. They believed that the ideal thing would be to rehearse in the very space in which the play was to be performed. They did their first play, *Macbeth* on the fourth floor of an old run-down textile mill. *Agamemnon* was also performed in a mill that had been refitted as an art gallery. They did Girish Karnad's *Hayavadana* in the round at Cama Institute. But perhaps the most experimental of their work was a piece called *8*, comprising eight monologues written by Seagull publisher Naveen Kishore. They were presented eight times to a limited audience of eighteen each time. The monologues had been pruned, re-sequenced and licked into shape (with the author's permission) to form a roughly coherent narrative about three characters—the man (Rehaan Engineer), the girl he dreams about (Mahrangiz Acharia) and his ex-wife (Shanaya Rafaat).

The performance was held on the mezzanine floor of a restaurant in Colaba with the audience of eighteen and the three actors seated around a long rectangular table covered in red. The whole space was uniformly lit, making the audience unwitting participants in the play. The actors spoke across the table to each other and occasionally directly to their neighbours—the audience. The monologues were dark and full of sexual violence, nightmarish imagination and scatology. The audience was under direct attack and was denied escape. Their unrehearsed expressions in response to what they were hearing contributed to the drama.

Jyoti Dogra has been performing highly evocative solo pieces in informal and formal spaces. She performed her first piece, *The Doorway*, at Gallery Beyond in south Mumbai in 2011. It was a collection of imagined and real stories woven together and performed through body images, gestures, postures and chanting. There was very little verbal text. Some of the narrative material was autobiographical, but much of it was drawn from fairy tales, folk tales and imagined experience. Together, it explored the idea of closed and open spaces and how we inhabit them.

Dogra's latest performance piece, *Notes on Chai*, is a collection of snippets of everyday conversations interwoven with abstract sounds, inspired by Tibetan chanting, Western harmonics and other vocal techniques. Her attempt here is to engage with the inner and outer landscape of our individual lives. The piece has the immediacy, humour and pathos of the everyday, evoked through metaphors created with the body, voice and text. Dogra has performed this piece at the NCPA's Experimental Theatre and also in the more informal space of Keya Rangamanch, Rangakarmee's studio theatre in Kolkata.

Some of the experiments mentioned above have not been totally successful. But the risk of failure is a vital part of experiment. Perhaps the most fitting way to end this rapid review of contemporary experimental theatre in Mumbai, would be to cite Edward Albee's defence of his 'bad' plays. 'If you write plays because you just want them to be liked, you have to lie too much. People like theatre that is safe, generally speaking—things that are easy, that are not too deeply troubling. In other words, people want to go to the theatre and waste their time. You can't let anything get in the way of letting what wants to happen happen, on its own terms. If I started saying to myself, "Oh, this is going to be too difficult for the audience," I'd be destroying my talent.'

In Mumbai, talent is alive and well exactly because experimental writers and directors haven't said, 'Oh this is going to be too difficult for the audience.' They have assumed that the audience will be with them if the performance is truthful. The winding queues at Prithvi, when their plays are staged, is a continuous confirmation of this belief.

Shanta Gokhale

Acknowledgements

This book has been five years in the making. It began with an idea that Ashok Kulkarni and Sunil Shanbag had of documenting, in some way, the five decades of experimental work that had been happening without a break on the Mumbai stage. Gradually, the idea grew into this oral history project. A list of forty-two possible interviewees was first drawn up, of playwrights, directors, actors and set designers, who would have interesting stories to tell about the theatre they had done. Some had to be dropped from the list for logistical reasons. But thirty-two remained.

The next step was to identify writers who had sufficient interest in and knowledge of theatre to conduct the interviews. Sucharita Apte, Pronoti Datta, Madhav Vaze, Mukta Rajyadhyaksha, Vikram Phukan, Sunil Shanbag, Shanta Gokhale, Devina Dutt and Alka Sahani readily came on board. We acknowledge with deep gratitude the expertise, sensitivity, precision, care and professionalism they brought to the work. Sunil Shanbag co-ordinated the videographing of the interviews.

We cannot thank the interviewees themselves enough for giving so unstintingly of their time and allowing our interviewers to press them doggedly for details of past times, people, places and events which had all but faded into history. These stalwarts of theatre obliged by digging deep into their memories to come up with the lively narratives that make this book what it is. Sadly three of the interviewees have since passed away—Satyadev Dubey on December 25, 2011, G. P. Deshpande on October 16, 2013 and Prafulla Dahanukar on March 1, 2014.

Working indefatigably in Pune, Mrs Vandana Bokil-Kulkarni transcribed the interviews with remarkable accuracy for which we are extremely grateful. We are also grateful to Hemant Hazare for so ably shouldering the responsibility of reasearching for the photo archive and to Vinesh Gandhi for taking the non-archival photographs.

Lastly, we thank Nilesh Kulkarni for generously letting us use his lovely home for our innumerable and never-ending meetings.

ALSO IN SPEAKING TIGER

THE ENGAGED OBSERVER

The Selected Writings of

SHANTA GOKHALE

and with an Introduction by Jerry Pinto

[illegible]

Candid, intense and often humorous, *The Engaged Observer* is an invaluable record of the social, political and cultural changes that have taken place in Bombay, Mumbai and beyond.

ALSO IN SPEAKING TIGER

THE ENGAGED OBSERVER

The Selected Writings of

SHANTA GOKHALE

Edited and with an Introduction by ***Jerry Pinto***

A collection of writings by an incandescent and gloriously eclectic intellectual of contemporary India. For over four decades, Shanta Gokhale has entertained, informed and challenged us with her insightful, witty and forthright writing in both English and Marathi. With rare objectivity and consistency, Gokhale has tried to decode our unique social etiquette while subtly exposing our hypocrisies, and celebrated tradition-defying women while forcefully criticizing the patriarchal and misogynistic structures of society. Her essays on theatre not only illustrate its evolution in India, but also provide arresting portraits of theatre personalities such as Satyadev Dubey, Vijay Tendulkar and Veenapani Chawla. And her detailed yet accessible articles on Indian classical music are a delight to read. In her short stories, she shapeshifts effortlessly from old men to teenage boys and college students. And finally, her two takes on Shakespeare show us how the Bard's ideas continue to remain relevant and, more importantly, how little attention he paid to his women characters.

Candid, intense and often humorous, *The Engaged Observer* is also an invaluable record of the social, political and cultural changes that have taken place in Bombay, Mumbai and beyond.

